China Unveiled

Insights into Chinese Strategic Thinking

China Unveiled

Insights into Chinese Strategic Thinking

Jayadeva Ranade

Introduction by
Air Commodore **Jasjit Singh** AVSM, VrC, VM (Retd)

KW Publishers Pvt Ltd
New Delhi

in association with

Centre for Air Power Studies
New Delhi

2011 FPBA BEST PUBLISHERS AWARD (ENGLISH)

Eighth Reprint September 2023

The Centre for Air Power Studies is an independent, non-profit, academic research institution established in 2002 under a registered Trust to undertake and promote policy-related research, study and discussion on the trends and developments in defence and military issues, especially air power and the aerospace arena, for civil and military purposes. Its publications seek to expand and deepen the understanding of defence, military power, air power and aerospace issues without necessarily reflecting the views of any institution or individuals except those of the authors.

Jasjit Singh
Director General
Centre for Air Power Studies
P-284, Arjan Path
Subroto Park
New Delhi 110010

Tele: (91-11) 25699131
E-mail: diroffice@aerospaceindia.org

Published in India by
Kalpana Shukla
KW Publishers Pvt Ltd
4676/21, First Floor, Ansari Road, Daryaganj, New Delhi 110002
Tele: +91.11.43528107 E-mail: kw@kwpub.in • www.kwpub.in

ISBN 978-93-81904-43-5

Printed and Bound in India

CONTENTS

Abbreviations

CCP	Chinese Communist Party
PBSC	Politburo Standing Committee
PB	Politburo
CC	Central Committee
CYL	Communist Youth League
PLA	People's Liberation Army
PLAAF	People's Liberation Army Air Force
PLAN	People's Liberation Army Navy
Second Artillery	China's strategic missile force
MR	Military Region
MSD	Military Sub District
TAR	Tibet Autonomous Region

PREFACE

It was a chance meeting over tea with – whom I could now with some immodesty call a perceptive – journalist friend soon after my retirement from the Service, that led to my putting quill to paper! The advice was to utilise the direct and unique knowledge and experience regarding China and East Asia that I had acquired over more than a quarter of a century. This led to the decision to now inform a wider audience through articles in mainstream national newspapers and magazines.

The Centre for Air Power Studies (CAPS), which I later joined, offered me the luxury of being able to think, read and write without being bound by the constraints of time, topic or location!

The idea for this book surfaced a couple of months ago when Air Commodore (Retd) Jasjit Singh, AVSM, VrC, VM, the Director General of CAPS and among India's pre-eminent strategic analysts, suggested that my articles which had been disseminated as Issue Briefs be compiled as a book. It was only when his staff began trying to arrange the articles, however, that I was stirred into action! We agreed that the book should be released to coincide with China's Eighteenth Party Congress. I must in all honesty, therefore, acknowledge that credit for the appearance of this book is due largely to Air Commodore (Retd) Jasjit Singh's initiative and unflagging interest.

Since the Issue Briefs cover a range of topics of a generally enduring nature, I chose not to re-write them but compile them as a book. Two lengthier and, hitherto unpublished, essays are included. For a smooth flow and ease of the reader, the articles have been arranged in the specific order in which they appear. The various chapters can be categorised into five specific sections dealing with important aspects of China's national strategic policies. Each subject covered in the book is of strategic significance and impinges directly on India's security and territorial integrity.

China's internal political scene, the two centre-pieces of its military strategy namely the Navy and Cyber Warfare, the India-China relationship, and Sino-US relations – described by Beijing as its single most important bilateral relationship – have all been examined. The competition among cadres for elevation to the Chinese Communist Party's highest echelons, suggestive of a new trend in domestic politics with potential to fracture the Party, has attracted specific attention. Sino-US relations, which will impact on the foreign and strategic policies evolved by other nations especially those in the Asia-Pacific region, have been focused upon. This book additionally examines a subject not usually touched upon, but which India is uniquely positioned to observe. This is China's strategy towards Tibet, Tibetan Buddhists and the Dalai Lama.

Admittedly, the articles are crisp, but the words have been carefully chosen. The book has no pretensions to being an academic dissertation or reference work and, therefore, contains no citations, footnotes or references. Its strength is its analysis, which is backed by decades of experience. In most cases the source of information is revealed in the body of the article. All the information in the book has, however, been vetted as best I could and is based primarily on official Chinese media reports, Chinese websites, Hong Kong media reports, and foreign media reports including of foreign journalists reputed for their insights or access to Chinese sources. This information has been supplemented by useful inputs from friends in different places who shall remain unnamed. Ultimately, the aim is to inform and enhance understanding of China's policies, strategies and actions, in an objective manner and without being needlessly critical, but certainly in the expectation that India's policy makers remain forewarned and prepared.

Libraries are invaluable repositories of information moreso when they obtain voluminous quantities on demand each day. Grateful acknowledgement is, therefore, due to the Librarian at CAPS, Ms Sushma Zutshi and her assistant, Ms Surbhi Sareen, who cheerfully coped with my demands.

Thanks are due to the publishers, KW Publishers, for ensuring that this book is ready in time while not compromising on the high standards expected. The role of Mr Jose Mathew, in quietly ensuring this high quality production, needs special commendation.

Finally, as with all who undertake perilous ventures like writing a book, I must commend my wife, Vinita's patience and tolerance at the truly odd hours that I observed. My sons, Pratap and Vikram, extended invaluable and unwavering support while located at a safe distance!

October 2012 **Jayadeva Ranade**
New Delhi

INTRODUCTION

Jasjit Singh

China remains a complex and paradoxical country and people to understand; even in the age of globalisation and information-communication revolution. Perhaps it had much to do with its inward-looking isolation from the rest of the world except in the trade over long and difficult routes. Or it has been due to its long periods under different types of regimes. But what most people tend to forget is the parallelism that exists between China and India. Both have been subject to outsiders ruling the country during their earlier history. Both have a historical record of being defensive: one built the 7,000-km Great Wall in what in those periods would have been a Herculean effort to help keep the foreigners out; and the other, India, fortified every city, the capital of the state, and even every village to keep the intruders and raiders out.

Both rely on the writing of their wise old strategists to lay down the role of force in the management of the state; and the answers are quite different from those of the Western civilisations of a corresponding era. Whether it is Sun Zi, using metaphors, or is it Chanakya in the Arthashastra using more indirect language, both specify the same thing: use of force only in the last resort. Hence other tools available to the King and state must be used first to subdue the potential threatening state or target, though after three millennia one may find nuances that differ in each case. There is also an apparent duality of aims, means and goals in both cases. But the central point that we are

Air Commodore **Jasjit Singh**, AVSM VrC VM, IAF (retd) awarded the Padma Bhushan in 2006 by the President of India is currently the Director General, Centre for Air Power Studies, New Delhi.

concerned is that while we can seek answers to many questions in the beliefs and expressions in the hoary past, we have to deal with each other in a modern world leaning heavily toward consumerism and the impatience that goes with it.

Here perhaps we can conclude that the average person in China believes in stability and hence conformity more than other values; and the average Indian is far more individualistic and the freedom of the individual. But the real question that we must seek answer to is: are there any serious conflicts of interests among the two nations? Are the oft repeated statements of "rivalry" which might lead to conflict have any real basis? There is no doubt that both countries have been rising in the scale of power in the power equations of the world, so much so that the shift of global power from West to East is ascribed to the rise of these two giants. But didn't the then Prime Minister of India, Jawaharlal Nehru state as far back as 1949 while addressing officers at Srinagar that "Chinese revolution has upset the balance of power and the centre of gravity has shifted from Europe to Asia thereby directly affecting India." If that was so in 1949, then it has been with us for more than six decades. Conceded that the two countries fought a war --- brief and bitter --- in 1962; but that itself was half a century ago, and the frontier has been far more peaceful than, say India-Pakistan which composed a single nation state a little earlier.

Theory assumes that rising powers would almost inevitably get into convenient alliances and hegemonic wars with or without clash of arms. But if we accept that the past half century has been generally peaceful, especially since 1967 when the troops of either side exchanged fire, then there is sufficient cause for optimism that Asia can show a different way of peaceful co-existence even among the giants who would inevitably have different, and even conflicting, interests. Actually, in the world that is emerging countries like China and India can ill afford any armed conflict. In this context it will be useful to recall the bilateral agreements of early 1990s, when the world had gone through tectonic changes, China and India signed formal agreements to maintain peace and tranquility based on the principle of "mutual and equal security."

On the other hand, it would be prudent to keep one's guard up, especially as the country moves along the vector of increasing capabilities and hence also of increasing and expanding interests in space and importance. What both countries would inevitably do is to study each other more closely and pre-empt any growth in conflict of interests. In other words, this means continuing objective studies and exchange of dialogue at various levels to ensure misperceptions do not derail what could be the 21st century greatest development: the rise to prosperity of 2.5 billion people.

It is from the above perspective that we, at the Centre for Air Power, have been carrying out objective studies to remain abreast of developments in China and their trends. We have been extremely fortunate to have had an outstanding scholar-expert, Shri Jayadeva Ranade, to lead from the front these studies. A prolific writer and an eloquent speaker and a virtual fount of knowledge about China, Jayadeva has been writing for various publications over the past nearly three years or more. I felt we should put all those together in a single volume to make their access easier for those interested in development in the People's Republic of China.

This book is a compilation of 31 essays/chapters on developments and strategies relating to contemporary China. Except for two hitherto unpublished essays, all have been issued by the CAPS as *Issue Briefs*. They have been selected for their enduring yet topical interest. Written over a period of over three years (2010-2012) the essays remain current and are of topical value.

The essays/chapters cover five different aspects viz. leadership and domestic politics; two areas of emphasis for China's military i.e. Navy and Cyber power; the India and China relationship; the China-

US relationship; and China-Tibet and China's policy towards Tibetan Buddhism and the Dalai Lama.

The first two chapters give an insight into the two leaders whose influence will shape China's policies for the next few years. These are Hu Jintao, who relinquishes power at the upcoming 18th Congress and his successor Xi Jinping. The sketch of Hu Jintao brings out, contrary to the popular image of his not being an adequately strong leader, that he is astute, shrewd, built up strong support and has exercised full power. The article on Xi Jinping shows his penchant for holding cards close to his chest while yet being clear as to the policies he should follow. He is not averse to business or entrepreneurs but his experience in the remote poorer areas would have influenced him. He has close relatives abroad and that would expose him to foreign ideas. At the same time, the article brings out the fact that he has links in the PLA and is committed to the Chinese Communist Party.

Five chapters discuss the changing political scenario in China and how politics in the CCP are undergoing a change. Cadres' ambitions are pushing them to attract favourable attention by different methods and, without the restraining hand of a veteran cadre, at times this pushes the limits of what the Party will accept. An example is the case of Bo Xilai.

China's decision making process is examined briefly in the two chapters on the deliberations of sessions of the National People's Congress—China's version of a parliament. These also indicate the changes that are taking place in the composition of the CCP and other institutions of government. The two main areas of strategic interest and emphasis of China's leadership are its cyber capability and the Navy. Both these are discussed.

China's foreign policy with specific reference to India's interest are covered in some detail. These cover China-US relations as also the India-China relationship. China's ambitions and the obstacles to improved relations are highlighted. Of special interest and a topic which receives little coverage normally is that of China's policy towards Tibet, the Dalai Lama and Tibetan Buddhists, particularly how this affects India. Seven chapters discuss this in fair detail. The chapters contain a lot of facts and data and cover the politics and strategy of contemporary China. At the same time they would be of enduring interest for individuals studying China.

Finally, while the essays present a candid view, from the Indian perspective, of China's policies and actions they are not alarmist. As the author quite correctly says: the aim is to inform and enhance understanding of China's policies, strategies and actions, in an objective manner and without being needlessly critical, but certainly in the expectation that India's policy makers remain forewarned and prepared.

I am delighted and feel honoured to write this introduction to the vast knowledge and wisdom of the author. I am confident that diplomats, military men, academic experts and the laymen interested in India's future would benefit greatly from the study of this volume which will also perform the role of being a reference volume for the events as they happening. I would also like to express my gratitude to the Government of India for their moral and material support in this endeavour. I also must record my gratitude to Dr. Ms Shalini Chawla, who did an excellent job of handling the Issue Briefs. More often than not, she had to ensure that each and every Issue Brief written by Jayadeva goes out on time against all odds to the couple of hundred recipients. Hopefully, this volume will reach out to a much larger interested audience.

1. Hu's in Charge?

China's President Hu Jintao will hand over at least two of his positions, namely those of Party General Secretary and President of China to Xi Jinping at the 18th Party Congress scheduled to be held in early November 2012. Though Hu's tenure has been dogged by comments that he is not as powerful as his predecessors, his career path shows otherwise. It is likely that Hu Jintao's influence will, in fact, continue to linger well after he steps down from office.

By the end of 2004, Hu Jintao became the most powerful individual in China, combining the posts of General Secretary of the Chinese Communist Party (CCP) Central Committee (CC) (November 2002), President of the People's Republic of China (March 2003) and Chairman of the Military Commission (September 2004). His elevation to this unrivalled position provided a substantive boost to China's ongoing military modernization effort. Hu Jintao's re-election as Party Chief in October 2007 and as China's President and Chairman of the Military Commission in March 2008, ensured continuation of the military's modernization and refinement of its operational capabilities in accordance with its evolving doctrine. It also allowed Hu Jintao, as head of the country's foreign policy formulation establishment and armed forces, to combine the strengths of both and craft a foreign policy designed to advance China's national interests. In a bold initiative reflecting China's confidence in its economic strength and armed forces, Hu Jintao in late 2008 deliberately discarded Deng Xiaoping's advice of 'taoguang yanghui', or 'lie low, conceal capabilities and bide time', and steered an assertive China on to the world stage.

Hu Jintao, a quintessential Party apparatchik and technocrat, was earmarked for rapid elevation fairly early in his career. While

Party elders generally assessed him as politically correct, intelligent, dynamic, loyal and articulate, Hu Jintao actually received crucial breaks because of the support of his mentor Song Ping, a veteran cadre associated with the Ya'nan Central Party School, who steered career-building opportunities his way. Hu Jintao's close association with Song Ping and possible association with Chen Yun, together with exposure to China's poorer provinces, impressed on him the positive aspects of central planning and inclusive economic reforms, which he applied later. Hu Jintao's family background – he was the son of an educated tea merchant of Shanghai – would have given him access as a youth to the fringes of the city's elite.

Hu Jintao's mentor, Song Ping, ensured that Hu Jintao switched to the fast-track and, in a far-sighted move, arranged for him when he was Deputy Director of the Gansu Ministry of Construction, to go to Beijing in 1981 along with Deng Xiaoping's daughter, Deng Nan, for training at the Central Party School. Later, in 1982 he manoeuvred to have Hu Jintao elected as alternate member of the Party's 12th Central Committee. Hu, at 39 years of age, became the youngest member of the Central Committee and that too when he was only a Deputy Head of a provincial organization, namely the Gansu Provincial Communist Youth League. This major break would certainly have fuelled Hu Jintao's aspirations and, as he moved up the central Party hierarchy he would have become increasingly aware that he lacked a military background or strong linkages to the People's Liberation Army (PLA). Hu Jintao's opportunity to address this lacunae came very soon with his transfer to Beijing and appointment in 1984 as Head of China's Communist Youth League (CYL), the country's largest youth organization which continues to be the crucible for potential members and cadres of the Chinese Communist Party. During this tenure he had a minor run in with two 'princelings', Chen Haosu, son of PLA Marshal Chen Yi and He Jiawei, son of General He Changgong, both of whom complained against him to their 'elders' who conveyed their complaint to CCP CC General Secretary Hu Yaobang. The incident served to remind Hu Jintao of the influence wielded by the Army in China's power structure. More importantly, it highlighted to him that though he belonged to an educated and relatively well off family and was an alumnus of the prestigious and well-networked Tsinghua University, he was not a 'princeling' and needed to cultivate this influential and powerful grouping of China's power elite.

Hu Jintao's big opportunity to remedy his lack of influence with the PLA came in December 1988 when he was appointed Party Secretary for the Tibet Autonomous Region (TAR). Already a key assignment, it came in to greater prominence as major riots erupted across Tibet in February 1989, very shortly after Hu Jintao's appointment. Hu Jintao had moved fast after his appointment to develop ties with the PLA. As the situation became increasingly tense and he apprehended more serious rioting during the anniversary of the Lhasa Uprising in March, Hu Jintao coordinated with the Chengdu Military Region Commander and had almost 17 divisions, or 170,000 PLA troops, deployed in Tibet prior to obtaining approval from the Party Centre. In fact, he had been advised by Party General Secretary Zhao Ziyang to try and avoid using force. When serious rioting erupted on March 3-4, the PLA troops quickly locked down the city and fanned out across Tibet preventing further rioting. By the 10th March, Hu Jintao had the situation in Tibet under control. His bold action in deploying PLA troops without approval of the Party Centre, in reality very unusual for Party apparatchiks who normally prefer to unwaveringly adhere to the line laid down by the Party Centre, was noticed by Deng Xiaoping who promptly earmarked Hu Jintao for important higher appointments.

By the 14th Party Congress in 1992, Hu Jintao had been elevated to the 7-member Politburo Standing Committee, the highest decision and policy making body of the CCP, ignoring the claims of many others senior to him. More significantly, Hu Jintao was given charge of the all-important personnel and propaganda portfolios which ensured that he was privy to the records of all senior officials of the Party, Government and PLA and had a major input in their career progression. This helped Hu Jintao cultivate PLA officers with promise and, probably, do a select few some favours. From 1993-2002, Hu Jintao was Head of the Central Party School, which is the training base for all Party cadres in the Party, Government and Army, who have been earmarked for further promotions. This appointment broadened his opportunities for contact with upward mobile Party and military cadres.

Once Hu Jintao took over as General Secretary of the Party in 2002, he began expanding his influence in the Army through the Party and began inducting his supporters into the Party Central Committee. In a departure from past practice, Hu Jintao ensured the election of a large number of persons – 94 percent – among the 65 PLA representatives in the CCP CC. Of them around 60 percent were later elevated to higher military rank between 2005 and 2007 when Hu Jintao was Military Commission Chairman, thus confirming patronage links.

His position was strengthened once he was appointed Vice Chairman of the Central and Party Military Commissions (both have identical membership and are generally referred to as Central Military Commission) in September 1999. Unlike previous civilian appointees to the position of Central Military Commission Vice Chairman, Hu Jintao took active interest in the PLA and the military reforms initiated by Jiang Zemin to divest the Army of its business ventures. Hu Jintao continued to expand his influence in the PLA and soon demonstrated this in September 2004 when the time came for Jiang Zemin to retire from the post of Chairman of the Central Military Commission. Informed speculation was rife in the months preceding the 4th plenary session of the 16th Central Committee of the CCP (16-19 September 2004) that Jiang Zemin was reluctant to step down. However, Hu Jintao had adequate support in the Politburo and among the Party 'elders' who strongly suggested to Jiang Zemin that he retire fully. An important demonstration of Hu Jintao's confidence were his remarks at the centenary birth anniversary celebrations of Deng Xiaoping. On this occasion Hu Jintao pointed out in his speech that Deng Xiaoping had stepped down from his posts two years before he had to, thereby indicating that he reposed confidence in the successor. Meanwhile, in a clear demonstration of Hu Jintao's influence in the PLA, PLA Commanders separately complained of confusion in the PLA's chain of command because of the existence of two centres of power. Jiang Zemin was left with little alternative but to step down and Hu Jintao took over as Chairman of the Central Military Commission. Hu Jintao's victory was complete, in that Vice Premier Zeng Qinghong, who was Jiang Zemin's favourite, was not appointed to the Central Military Commission as Vice Chairman. Promptly on taking over as Chairman of the Central Military Commission, Hu Jintao reiterated his interest in the PLA's modernization programme and particularly its doctrine of Integrated Joint Operations. He expanded the Central Military Commission and, for the first time ever, included the Commanders of the PLA Air Force (PLAAF), PLA Navy (PLAN) and Second Artillery as members.

Hu Jintao accorded priority to ensuring the PLA's 'absolute loyalty' and 'absolute obedience' to the CCP at a time when economic reform policies were causing instability in Chinese society. This was important for him to personally tighten his grip on the PLA. He also had a long-range objective since the succeeding generations of leaders would increasingly be CCP cadres with no experience of the Army or, in many cases, with few linkages. He initiated a series of measures to ensure the PLA's 'absolute' loyalty. Successive 'study sessions' and 'education' campaigns were launched throughout the PLA emphasizing that the CCP led the PLA and that the PLA must always be 'absolutely obedient' to the Party Centre. Distinction was made between the PLA and armies of other countries by pointing out that the PLA was the guarantor of 'socialism with Chinese characteristics' and was a 'people's army' unlike those of other nations. The Communist Youth League (CYL) and Chinese Communist Party (CCP) were directed to launch recruitment drives throughout the PLA to increase membership in the PLA. The PLA's General Political Department was strengthened and Political Commissars were given a greater say in the promotion of officers. Political Commissars also began being rotated within the PLA, PLAAF, PLAN and Second Artillery and posted to different operational commands to provide them all-round experience.

Hu Jintao has contributed a lot to the modernization of the PLA and initiated concrete measures to ensure that the PLA develops its capability to fight modern wars as per its revised doctrine. He reinforced Jiang Zemin's policy of placing Defence on the same footing as the other Modernisations and ensured double-digit budget hikes for defence. He took forward the doctrine of fighting hi-intensity, hi-tech local wars envisaging integrated joint operations. To facilitate the latter, Hu Jintao expanded the Central Military Commission, the country's highest military policy decision making body, in September 2004 when he for the first time ever included the Commanders of the PLAAF, PLAN and Second Artillery as members. The following year he effected a restructuring of the Military Regions, including protocol-wise. They were listed as: Shenyang, Beijing, Lanzhou, Jinan, Nanjing, Guangzhou and Chengdu. More importantly and again in a significant departure from traditionally past practice, Hu Jintao for the first time in 2006 inducted an officer each from the PLAAF and PLAN as Deputy Chief and Assistant Chief respectively of the PLA General Staff. A PLAAF Major General has, at least since 2006, been appointed Deputy Director in the PLA General Staff Department's First Directorate (Operations).

Integrated joint operations are clearly a high priority with Hu Jintao viewing them as a follow-up to the creation of high-mobility Rapid Reaction Forces in the PLA. Hu Jintao enunciated his policy on national defence on 15 October 2007, when he declared: 'To strengthen national defence and the armed forces occupies an important place in overall arrangements for the cause of socialism with Chinese characteristics. Bearing in mind the overall strategic interests of national security and development, we must take both economic and national defence development into consideration and make our country prosperous and our armed forces powerful while building a moderately prosperous society in all respects'. The number of integrated joint service exercises conducted by the PLA in the past few years has shown a steady increase. These now involve Group Armies and formations from different Military Regions and services. The exercises envisage complex electromagnetic environments and others include satellite overflights and UAV reccee activities. The exercises reflect the PLA's effort to develop counter-attack capabilities under these conditions.

Hu Jintao effected a major innovation at the 17th Party Congress (2007) in the Central Military Commission Secretariat. For the first time the Secretariat of the Central Military Commission included no PLA officer. The Secretariat, which is responsible for the agenda, daily roster of events etc. exercises influence on the decisions of the Central Military Commission. By this singular move, Hu Jintao ensured total control over the PLA, the control of the Party over the Army and distanced the PLA from politico-military affairs. No other civilian sits on the Central Military Commission either. The severe earthquake in 2008 that caused devastation in Sichuan demonstrated the extent of Hu Jintao's grip and control over the PLA. The PLA and People's Armed Police divisions did not initially fully respond to Premier Wen Jiabao's presence in Sichuan where he was directing relief operations, but the forces got deployed only once instructions by Hu Jintao were issued. Analysts have seen a parallel in Hu Jintao's decision to return hastily to Beijing from the G-8 Summit in Italy in July '09, prompted by the outbreak of rioting by the Uyghurs, with the need for him to personally direct military operations in Xinjiang.

Analysis of the composition of the 17th CC (2007) reveals that Hu Jintao, while moving to induct individuals loyal to him into the CCP CC, did not lose sight of his larger objective of pushing rapidly ahead with modernization of the People's Liberation Army with the emphasis on fighting and winning a high intensity local war and Integrated Joint Operations. The PLA representatives to the 17th CC included 37 of the most important military leaders including members of the Central Military Commission, the senior leadership in the four General Departments, the four services and the three top military academic institutes. Of these PLA representatives 60 percent were promoted to their current military posts since 2005 and the remaining 40 percent in 2007, in other words during Hu Jintao's tenure. The Commanders and Political Commissars of all 7 Military Regions were made full members of the 17th CC with 12 of them being appointed to the CC for the first time. Of the 35 top military officers in the 17th CC, 21 entered this body for the first time and of them 20 received their military promotions after 2007, or during Hu Jintao's tenure as Chairman of the Central Military Commission. Of the 19 officers of the rank of General/ Admiral, 10 were granted this rank after Hu Jintao took over from Jiang Zemin as Military Commission Chairman in 2004. Hu Jintao was hampered in his effort to induct loyalists into the CCP CC by the more or less fixed number of PLA representatives in this high-level political body. He, therefore, reshuffled the membership and inducted more representatives from the other services. This move had the effect of giving the PLAAF and PLAN greater exposure to the country's higher political decision-making bodies. The combined percentage of PLAAF and PLAN officers in the CC doubled from 14 percent in 1992 to 25 percent in 2007. Broken down further, the PLAAF representation increased 200 percent and the PLAN's 133 percent over the 15-year period ending 2007.

This change in composition of the 17th CC from those earlier was of major consequence because it reflected the change in the doctrine of war of the PLA and shift from a defensive posture to a more outward looking posture focused on projecting power offshore. The representation of the PLA ground forces, however, continues to be dominant in the CC though it declined in percentage terms from 83 percent in 1992 to 69 percent in 2007.

The PLA has since the early 1990s followed rigid regulations regarding promotions of officers, which includes the need for them to complete a specified tenure in a rank before promotion to the next. This was a limitation on Hu Jintao's effort to build a base of loyalists in the PLA. He got around this by elevating his candidates to higher posts without conferring on them the attendant higher rank. In many cases the PLA officers, who were younger than their seniors and had little opportunity of holding important higher level assignments for many years, suddenly found themselves appointed to these posts. Except for the formal military rank, which followed in due course in accordance with military regulations, the newly elevated officers enjoyed all the attendant perquisites and authority of the senior assignment. A number of officers in the PLA were beneficiaries of Hu Jintao's policy. Examples include the Beijing Military Region (MR) Commander Fang Fenghui, Lanzhou MR Commander Wang Guosheng and Nanjing MR Commander Zhao Keshi. Each of them was a Chief of Staff when promoted and not a Deputy Military Region Commander as they should correctly have been. Similarly, Wang Xibin and Tong Shiping, the new Commandant and Political Commissar respectively of the National Defence University were, prior to their promotion, Chief of Staff of a MR and Assistant Director of the PLA's General Political Department. The 17th CC also saw the induction of younger officers and 11 of the 65 PLA representatives held the rank of Major General or lower. These were: Cai Yinting, Chief-of-Staff of Nanjing MR; Ai Husheng, Chief-of-

Staff of Chengdu MR; Xu Fenlin, Chief-of-Staff of Guangzhou MR and Liu Yuejun, Lanzhou MR Chief-of-Staff. All these officers were Major Generals at the time of their promotion and were in their mid-50s. Other similar elevations/appointments occurred recently in the PLA's four General Departments. In the General Staff Department the Chief-of-Staff of the Shenyang MR Lt General Hou Shusen was promoted Deputy Chief of General Staff in PLA Headquarters, possibly vice Deputy Chief of the PLA General Staff Department and Commander of the Guangzhou MR General Liu Zhenwu; and Maj General Chen Yong was shifted from the post of Dean of the Nanjing Army Command College and promoted to Assistant Chief-of-Staff for the PLA Headquarters of the General Staff, in place of Maj General Yang Zhiqi who retired. In the General Armaments Department, Maj General Niu Hongguang was elevated as Deputy Director of the General Armaments Department vice Lt General Zhang Jianqi, who was due to retire.

Hu Jintao has carefully nurtured those loyal to him and, conscious of their influence in the Party and Army, began building a support base among the 'princelings' ('taizi'). In late July 2009 he promoted 3 more officers to the rank of General. Included in these were the Deputy Chief of the PLA General Staff and PLA Air Force Major General Ma Xiaotian, who has been in charge of Intelligence in the PLA and been outspoken in his comments regarding the US' designs in the Asia-Pacific and its defence relationship with Taiwan. He is a 'princeling' and assessed to be a loyalist of Hu Jintao. Significantly, the other two promoted to the rank of General are also 'princelings'. They are Zhang Haiyang, son of a former Vice Chairman of the Central Military Commission and Politburo Member, General Zhang Zhen, and Liu Yuan, son of the late Liu Shaoqi at one time Mao Zedong's designated successor as President of China but who was purged during the Cultural Revolution. Like Ma Xiaotian, Liu Yuan is reputed to be a hardliner on Taiwan. He is credited with replying, to a remark about a possible strike on the Three Gorges Dam by Taiwan, that it would provoke a retaliation that would 'blot out the sky and cover up the earth'. The remark generated considerable negative comment in the US.

Other 'princelings' promoted to the top echelons of the PLA in Hu Jintao's tenure are Li Jinai, Wu Shengli and Xu Qiliang. All are in the Central Military Commission. There are at least a dozen 'princelings' at senior levels in the PLA. Their details are given below.

Name	DoB	Post	Relationship
Li Jinai	1942	Dir,GPD-CMC Member	Nephew of Li Jin Former PLA Dy CGS
Wu Shengli	1945	PLAN Cdr-CMC Member	Son of former Governor of Zhejiang
Xu Qiliang	1950	PLAAF Cdr-CMC Member	Son of former Dy Cdr PLAAF
Peng Xiaofeng	1945	Pol Com Second Arty	Son of Peng Xuefang revolutionary veteran
Liu Yuan	1951	Pol Com Academy of Military Sciences	Son of Liu Shaoqi
Zhang Youxia	1950	Cdr Shenyang MR	Son of Zhang Zhongxun former Dir GLD
Zhang Haiyang	1949	Pol Com Chengdu MR	Son of Zhang Zhen former Vice Chmn CMC
Ma Xiaotian	1949	Dy CGS, GSD	Son of Ma Zaiyac former Dean PLA Pol Academy
Liu Xiaojiang	1949	Dy Pol Com PLAN	Son-in-law of Hu Yaobang
Liu Yuejun	1954	Chief of Staff Lanzhou MR	Son-in-law of Liu Zhimin former Pol Com GLD of Guangzhou MR
Ding Yiping	1951	Chief of Staff, PLAN	Son of Ding Qiushang former Pol Com PLAN North Sea Fleet
Ai Huisheng	1951	Chief of Staff Chengdu MR	Son of Ai Fulin former Dy Cdr Arty Corps Shenyang M

The other privileged category of individuals in the Chinese Communist Party and PLA are the 'mishu', or those who have served as personal assistants to senior PLA or Communist Party cadres. The 'mishu', by virtue of their appointment, develop close ties to other senior leaders which helps them in their career progression. Among the current PLA elite at least 8 belong to this category. They include Jia Ting'an, Director of the CMC General Office who was Jiang Zemin's 'mishu' at one time, Cai Yingting, Nanjing MR Chief of Staff who was CMC Vice Chairman Zhang Wannian's 'mishu', and Cao Qing, who used to be Defence Minister Ye Jianying's bodyguard. The majority of these beneficiaries, all of whom received out-of-turn elevation or promotion during Hu Jintao's tenure, would owe their loyalty to him while they would, of course, contribute to the PLA with their youth and better education.

The most important and prominent 'princeling' who also served for a while as 'mishu' is the current Politburo Standing Committee member, Xi Jinping, who is widely regarded as Hu Jintao's successor. A substantive indication was his appointment as Vice Chairman of the Central Military Commission – usually leaders designated to succeed the incumbent Party General Secretary and Chairman of the Central Military Commission are appointed Vice Chairman of the CMC at least a year before the current incumbent is scheduled to retire. Xi Jinping is also the only 'fifth generation' leader who has links with the PLA. He acquired these when he served as 'mishu', from 1979-82, to General Geng Biao who was Secretary General and Standing Committee Member of the CMC in January 1979 and became Defence Minister in 1981. Geng Biao was a loyal subordinate of General Xi Zhongxun. Xi Jinping's father, General Xi Zhongxun, was a prominent Long March veteran and associate of Mao Zedong, though he criticized Mao and was purged during the Cultural Revolution. Hu Jintao and Wen Jiabao also had a close association with Xi Zhongxun. The other 'princelings' elevated to senior positions in the PLA have close ties to Xi Jinping.

Hu Jintao has been deft in his maneuvering for power and consolidation of his position. In his journey to becoming the most powerful man in China, he demonstrated a few characteristics unusual in the normal Party apparatchik earmarked for higher office. He quickly learnt the importance of building and consolidating a loyal support base in key areas and though this could have had inherent the risk of arousing the unwanted – and often undesirable – interest of his senior, he worked to bring it about. He also displayed, from fairly early on in his political career at the Centre, an unusual boldness in action. His action in co-opting the Army's support to quell the trouble in Tibet was an indicator. Soon after being elected General Secretary of the Chinese Communist Party (CCP) Central Committee (CC), Hu Jintao began inducting loyalists into the Party Central Committee to consolidate and solidify his position. After identifying the PLA as an enduring important pillar of China's power structure and one whose support was essential, Hu Jintao built and expanded his influence in that organisation. In a series of nimble, multi-pronged moves he ensured that he exercises unchallenged authority over the PLA. He is the only civilian in the highest decision-making body of the Chinese armed forces namely, the Central Military Commission, and replaced members of the influential Secretariat of the Central Military Commission with civilians hand-picked by him. There are today no military personnel in this Secretariat. At the same time Hu Jintao took care to push ahead with the military modernization programme so that the younger and professional officers would feel a greater loyalty towards him.

As military modernization began to show results and China's military doctrine reflected its new strategic orientation, China's leadership became more confident. Hu Jintao now commenced knitting together military and strategic objectives and using diplomacy to push his agenda. At the same time he encouraged Chinese military and civilian strategists to redefine the country's strategic frontiers more boldly. Chinese military and civilian strategists have begun describing it as: 'China's entire continental shelf, the north Pacific contiguous to Russia and Japan, the Bohai Gulf, the Taiwan Strait, the East China Sea and even west-ward through the Malacca Strait into the Indian Ocean'. Some Chinese strategic analysts stretched the definition to include the Persian Gulf. Huang Kunlun, a commentator in the Liberation Army Daily, expanded this further by articulating the 'theory of boundless national interests'. He wrote: 'wherever our national interests have extended, so will the mission of our armed forces'. A strategist at the Chinese Institute for Contemporary International Relations (CICIR), a think-tank affiliated to China's Ministry of State Security, Chen Xiangyang, said 'Beijing wants to occupy the vantage point' and 'seize the initiative in global geopolitical contention'. He added that 'we want to articulate China's voice, safeguard China's image and expand China's national interests'. The remark in May 2009 by a senior PLA Navy officer to US Admiral Keating suggesting that: 'as we develop our aircraft carriers why don't we reach an agreement, you and I. You take Hawaii East, we'll take Hawaii West and the Indian Ocean. We'll share information and we'll save you all the trouble of developing your naval forces west of Hawaii', confirms that the Chinese armed forces feel they already have such a capability, or are close to acquiring it. Chinese maps depicting their so-called traditional sphere of influence remain in circulation and include areas well beyond the newly defined strategic frontiers.

Since fairly early on in his political career at the centre, Hu Jintao has displayed an unusual sensitivity to ways of furthering national interest in foreign policy. The first publicized test was the EP-3 spy plane incident involving an US Air Force aircraft in 2001. Jiang Zemin, then President of China and Chairman of the Central Military Commission, had just completed a tour of USA and was visiting Latin America. Hu Jintao was in charge in Beijing and he allowed the rhetoric surrounding the incident to escalate to rather high levels before defusing it in time to avoid damage to China-US relations. His action combined self-confidence, calibrated boldness and an understanding of the importance of China-US relations. At the same time his action sought to signal the preparedness of the Chinese armed forces to confront US forces. Subsequent and more recent actions by the Chinese Navy in confronting US survey, or spy, vessels in the South China and Yellow Seas have been more obviously confrontational and intended to convey a message. Similar confrontations, at times accompanied by clashes, have occurred with Vietnam and the Philippines. The PLA has, under Hu Jintao's chairmanship of the Central Military Commission, in recent years begun to conduct major military exercises whose scope has increased steadily each year. Other non-military demonstrations of China's assertiveness in foreign policy are its hardened unyielding posture regarding the Dalai Lama – examples are that of France, Germany and Norway – and its toughened diplomatic and military stance on border disputes with India and other countries with competing claims in the South China and Yellow Seas and the Sea of Japan.

As Head of the Party's all-powerful Leading Group on Foreign Affairs, Hu Jintao crafted a policy which combines China's military, economic and diplomatic strengths to further its goals. Hu Jintao has used this policy to signal that China will no longer adopt a low profile, but is ready to assume its self-perceived rightful role in international and regional affairs. At the second Summit between Obama and Hu Jintao on 22 September 2009, little noticed in the coverage of statements on climate change and later, China's 60th anniversary celebrations, were the proposals put forward by Hu Jintao. China's official news agency, Xinhua, reported that the Chinese President had put forward four proposals on international issues in the context of the bilateral relationship. Hu Jintao urged greater coordination and cooperation on 'major regional and international issues' including that 'the two countries should push for a proper resolution to the regional issues relating to the Korean Peninsula, Iran and South Asia'. He added that the 'US should take real action to support the peaceful development of relations across the Taiwan Straits'. He appreciated US recognition of Tibet as part of China and for opposing 'Tibet independence' and, after referring to the recent riots in Xinjiang, called on the US to 'prevent the conducting of separatist activities against China in US territory'. US President Obama repeated the US official stance on both the latter issues, but refrained from responding on South Asia. Hu Jintao's proposals, roughly indicate China's areas of interest, and have been made at the highest level suggesting that China is becoming pro-active. Hu Jintao's statements were preceded by remarks by others, which outline the area perceived by China as within its sphere of strategic interest. Hu Jintao's strategy is clearly to try and occupy the vacuum in global influence created by the US' distraction during this interregnum, occasioned by its involvement in Afghanistan and Iraq and the global economic crisis. He will seek to test the limits of China's influence and advance its territorial ambitions and strategic frontiers.

Under Hu Jintao's leadership China has ushered in this year with a revised muscular foreign policy reinforced by a visibly robust military. Hu Jintao's focus on modernization of the military and especially readjustment of the strategy and tactics of the People's Liberation Army (PLA) has contributed considerably to the success of the new policy. Its objective is the consolidation of China's influence in international affairs and the securing of an arrangement by which its national interests are recognised by other major world powers. As part of this policy, China is asserting its role in the region and seeking to define its presumed sphere of influence. The global economic downturn and China's economic strength, which together make Beijing's cooperation essential to the developed nations, has added considerable heft to China's foreign policy initiatives. The latter has been particularly noticeable in areas where China's territorial and national interests are perceived by Beijing as being affected. This interregnum, when the world powers are preoccupied with their domestic economic crises, has been assessed by the Chinese leadership as opportune for China to test and expand the limits of its influence and territorial ambitions. The extravagant and largest ever military parade in the world on 1st October 2009, was designed to project China's might and convey that it henceforth intends to play the role of a major world power and certainly that of the dominant power in the Asia-Pacific and South Asia. By appearing in a Mao suit, not publicly worn at such functions by Chinese leaders for many years, Hu Jintao simultaneously signalled that the Chinese Communist Party remains unchallenged and that China stays committed to communist values.

This essay, while not published earlier, was written in January 2011.

2. China's Next Chairman: Xi Jinping

Tucked away virtually at the end of the communiqué issued on October 17th after the Fifth plenary session of the Seventeenth Central Committee in Beijing, was a one-line paragraph announcing that China's Vice President, Xi Jinping, had been appointed Vice Chairman of China's Military Commission. The announcement confirms that Xi Jinping, viewed since 2007 as Hu Jintao's putative successor, is firmly on the path to taking over the three all important posts of General Secretary of the Chinese Communist Party (CCP), President of China and Chairman of the Central Military Commission (CMC), after the Eighteenth Party Congress scheduled to be held in Beijing around October 2012, unless some drastic unforeseen event occurs. It simultaneously negates all speculative reports of factional infighting surrounding Xi Jinping's elevation to the top jobs.

Xi Jinping's appointment was widely anticipated at the last Central Committee plenary session. His appointment now, however, indicates that he will have an apprenticeship of almost two years before he assumes supreme command of the People's Liberation Army (PLA).

The decision to combine the powers of the Party and Military was taken by Deng Xiaoping in 1987 when he anticipated that future generations of Party leaders would not possess military credentials and also not have the support of veteran cadres wielding sufficient authority over the military. These future leaders would, therefore, require greater authority to effectively command and control the PLA. Party General Secretary Zhao Ziyang was to be the first such leader, but that did not materialize because of the 'Tiananmen Incident' one and a half years later. Jiang Zemin took over in November 1989 as Chairman of the Central Military Commission (CMC) without any preparatory period as the first Vice Chairman because of Deng Xiaoping's insistence that, during that troubled period, the Party must demonstrate its effective and visible command over the PLA. Deng Xiaoping was, however, present and able to intercede when necessary to support Jiang Zemin. The system of phased transfer of power was resumed with Hu Jintao's appointment as first Vice Chairman of the CMC in 1999 and later as Chairman of the CMC, replacing Jiang Zemin, in 2004. Hu Jintao became the first civilian Party leader to take over the reins of the CMC from a civilian predecessor without the benefit of a supportive veteran cadre present on the sidelines. Though Hu Jintao's appointment as CMC Chairman was delayed because of Jiang Zemin's reluctance to relinquish the post, Hu Jintao, in effect took over as CMC Chairman two years after he had become the General Secretary of the Party.

In contrast to Jiang Zemin and Hu Jintao, neither of whom had any military credentials, Xi Jinping does have some experience in the PLA. After his graduation in Chemical Engineering from Qinghua University, Xi Jinping began work in 1969. He joined the Communist Youth League in 1971 and the CCP in 1974. Because of his father's position in the Party and PLA, Xi Jinping worked in the General Office of the State Council and CMC for almost three years from April 1979 till 1982 when he served as personal secretary to Geng Biao (1909-2000), Politburo member and China's Defence Minister and Secretary General of the CMC. Interestingly, during this period Xi Jinping was an officer in 'active' service. Xi Jinping's military connections were sought to be buttressed in the official account of his career, released by Xinhua on the occasion of the announcement of his recent appointment. This stated that Xi Jinping had almost always been a member of the National Defence Mobilisation committees in the various provinces to which he was posted. In that capacity he would have attended meetings convened by the concerned Military Region and interacted with senior PLA officers. These periods of service together with his father's military associations have consolidated Xi Jinping's entrée into China's senior military hierarchy. Coincidentally, Xi Jinping's second wife, 47-year old Peng Liyuan, is an accomplished Chinese folk singer who graduated from the Beijing Conservatory of Music and holds the rank of Major General in the PLA!

Xi Jinping, born on June 1, 1953, is the third child of Xi Zhongxun (1913-2002) and his wife Qi Xin. He has two elder sisters and a younger brother. Xi Zhongxun was a veteran Party cadre and one of the founders of a communist guerrilla army of north China and, during the epochal Long March in the mid-1930s, gave Mao Zedong and his troops shelter in the Ya'nan area. Xi Zhongxun was accused of plotting against Mao in 1962 and purged for the second time. He was later rehabilitated, but again purged during the Cultural Revolution and this time exiled to the countryside. Xi Jinping's life was scarred by the Cultural Revolution when, following his father's purge, he was sent to the countryside to be re-educated as a peasant and kept away from his family for several years. According to Xinhua, from 1969 to 1975, Xi worked as an "educated youth" sent to the countryside at Liangjiahe Brigade in his home province of Shaanxi where he served as party branch secretary. Xi Zhongxun, who was highly respected in the Party, was a friend and comrade of Deng Xiaoping's who rehabilitated him and appointed him Vice Premier. Xi Zhongxun, was the architect of the Special Economic Zones.

Significantly, Xi Zhongxun opposed the crackdown by the People's Liberation Army at Tiananmen in June 1989. Also, among the websites shut down by the authorities in late 2009, when the conservative viewpoint on handling minorities began to gain ascendance, were some operated by NGOs and cadres with more liberal viewpoints associated with the late Party General Secretary Hu Yaobang and Vice Premier Xi Zhongxun, father of current Chinese Vice President Xi Jinping.

As the son of a senior Party cadre, Xi Jinping is a 'princeling'. The 'princelings' constitute a fairly powerful grouping in the Party and military apparatus in China. They have also been assiduously cultivated and promoted by Hu Jintao especially in the PLA. Xi Jinping can currently bank on the support of a number of senior military cadres who are also 'princelings'. These include: Ma Xiaotian, Deputy Chief of General Staff of the PLA; Li Jinai, Director of the PLA's powerful General Political Department; Wu Shengli, Commander of the PLA Navy and CMC member; Xu Qiliang, Commander of the PLA Air Force and CMC member; Peng Xiaofeng, Political Commissar of the Second Artillery; Liu Yuan, Political Commissar of the Academy of Military Sciences; Zhang Youxia, Commander of the Shenyang Military Region; and Zhang Haiyang, Political Commissar of Chengdu Military Region. Xi Jinping will additionally benefit from the Party's strengthened grip over the PLA brought about by Hu Jintao. Hu Jintao launched successive and thorough year-long 'education' campaigns throughout the PLA for three consecutive years to instill the concept that the Party exercises 'absolute' control over the army. He also augmented the powers of the General Political Department and political commissars by giving them veto authority over PLA officers' promotions. Hu Jintao has simultaneously, since his term as Vice Chairman of the CMC, built up a core of loyalists in the senior echelons of the PLA. He is thus far estimated to have promoted over 50 officers to the rank of General and a number of others in grade promotions to senior appointments while awaiting rank promotions that come in routine course. This consolidation of civilian political control over the PLA will help Xi Jinping too.

Additionally, Xi Jinping has supporters in the top echelons of the CCP which include Song Ping, Zhu Rongji, Li Peng, Hu Jintao, Zhou Yongkang and the former Head of the CCP CC's Organisation Departmment, He Guojiang. Other supporters include some of the 'princelings' in the Party.

Whether Xi Jinping's elevation finally to the top posts will signal a change in China's domestic and foreign policies is debatable. Prior to this appointment and in an indication that he is being groomed for the top jobs, Xi Jinping had visited countries viewed by China as important including Japan, Australia, Mongolia, Myanmar and Bangladesh as well as countries in Latin America and Europe. The communiqué mentioning Xi Jinping's appointment particularly dwelt on the international political situation and the challenges that are likely to confront China. It contained a suggestion that the review of China's Asia policy that had begun late last year had either been finalized or was nearing finalization. Xi Jinping's military affiliations and pronounced linkages with senior PLA officers suggest that the military will continue to receive high budgetary allocations. The emphasis on modernization of the PLA will remain and the focus on 'Integrated Joint Operations' and fighting 'short duration regional wars under hi-tech informatised conditions' will continue. Xi Jinping's tenure will, therefore, probably see continuation of the present policy which combines diplomacy with a strong suggestion of military muscle.

While Xi Jinping has not yet visited India, he has met Indian officials and leaders in Beijing. For example, on August 8, 2008 Xi Jinping met Congress President Ms Sonia Gandhi and her son, Rahul, in Beijing when they had gone to see the Summer Olympics. He had then thanked India for taking "effective" steps to ensure smooth passage of the Olympic torch relay in New Delhi and for backing Beijing's efforts to stage a "unique and well-run" Games. Xi Jinping said India had ensured the success of the Indian leg of the Olympic torch relay in New Delhi and "for that, we express our deep gratitude". The reference was to the threats by pro-Dalai Lama Tibetan protesters to sabotage the torch relay in New Delhi on April 17. The following month, on September 8, he met M.K.Narayanan, then India's National Security Advisor and Special Representative, who was in Beijing to attend the 12th Sino-Indian meeting on the boundary issue. During the meeting, Xi Jinping appreciated the all-round development of China-India relations. He pledged that China was committed to developing the strategic and cooperative partnership of peace and prosperity with India, adding that friendly Sino-Indian relations would benefit both, Asia and the world as a whole. "The two sides should view the bilateral ties from a strategic and long-term perspective, and expand the common ground and properly handle the differences so as to push forward the long-term and stable relations," he added. On the boundary issue, Xi Jinping hoped that under the guidance of the leaders of both countries, a fair and reasonable framework acceptable to both sides would be worked out at an early date through equal consultation and friendly dialogue. He concluded with the remark that "both should maintain peace and tranquility in the border area before the boundary issue is resolved". More recently on May 28, 2010, Xi Jinping met visiting Indian President Ms Pratibha Patil and Foreign Secretary Ms Nirupama Rao at a reception in Beijing to mark the 60th anniversary of establishment of ties.

Xi Jinping is well versed with Taiwan issues and developed connections with numerous Taiwanese businessmen during his almost seventeen years in Fujian province. He has also headed the Leading Group on Hongkong and Macau. His wife visited Taiwan for eight days as part of a cultural delegation in 1997 and his brother-in-law has been living for some years in Taiwan's southern Chiayi county.

Xi Jinping met North Korean 'leader' Kim Jong Il during the latter's visits to Beijing in 2008 and subsequently. An oblique suggestion of North Korea's desire to continue the present level of bilateral relations during Xi Jinping's upcoming term was contained in a congratulatory message. The official North Korean newspaper Rodong Sinmun published the message issued on the occasion of Xi Jinping's appointment to "the important post".

In domestic matters pertaining to the minorities, though Xi Jinping has experience of remote and poor provinces and can be expected to encourage their development, he is unlikely to introduce relaxation in national policies and programmes. Xi Jinping's presence at both the national work conferences held in the first half of this year, on Tibet and Xinjiang where certain tough measures were approved, were in fact specifically pointed out in official 'Xinhua' newsagency despatches. It is nevertheless interesting that Xi Jinping's father, Xi Zhongxun, was an interlocutor for the Dalai Lama's Special Envoy Lodi Gyari in the 1980s and apparently carried a photo of the Dalai Lama. Prior to that he had some association with the 10th Panchen Lama, Tibet's second most important religious leader. Such links, however, are unlikely to influence Xi Jinping's stance on Tibet as that will have wider implications for the six million Tibetans and also for the peace and stability of China and the border region.

On domestic political issues as on most others, Xi Jinping has been very circumspect. He has not commented on issues like political reform. However, his father's 'liberal' thinking and viewpoints could have left an imprint. At the same time, Xi Jinping is a Party apparatchik who has been a beneficiary of the system. Xi Jinping is very unlikely to do anything that could weaken the Party or its monopoly on power, though he might tinker on the edges of limited and gradual political reform. Xi Jinping is credited with pushing economic reforms and has earned a reputation for 'getting things done'. His management of the prestigious Summer Olympics was appreciated. These views could be reflected in the ensuing economic reform policies.

This was published as an Issue Brief by the Centre for Air Power Studies on October 25, 2010.

3. China: Signs of Nervousness?

Leadership transition is a sensitive phase for all governments. This is especially the case with dictatorships and authoritarian regimes. China is in the penultimate stages of leadership transition at the highest echelons of the Chinese Communist Party (CCP), which is expected to culminate in October 2012 and its authorities are, therefore, presently at a high state of vigilance. The winds of change blowing relentlessly across the Middle East and, which have already seen the downfall of some long-entrenched regimes, provide cold comfort.

Certain developments of the past few months have given cause for added and serious concern to China's leadership. Uppermost are the rising prices of food and essential items, the steadily increasing consumer price index and, growing inflation. Cereal prices increased 14.7 percent by end November while China's consumer price index (CPI) rose to 4.6 percent in December, down from 5.1 percent in November, but still in the entire year the CPI touched 3.3 percent or .3 percent more than the official target. The severe drought this year, the worst in sixty years, that has affected large swathes of northern China has added to the leadership's woes. An officially estimated 5.16 million acres of crops have been adversely affected till now and 2.57 million people are suffering from drinking water shortages. Beijing has taken steps to ease the suffering of the people and allocated US$ 334 million as drought relief aid and an additional US$ 2 billion to combat drought. If the drought continues till March/April this year, almost 10 million tonnes of crops will be lost. This has generated fears of a rise in global food prices, though these have been dismissed as unfounded by official Chinese spokesmen who assure that China has abundant reserves of grain to meet the nation's needs. Inflation is having an impact on the common people too and immediate relief is not yet in sight. Zhou Xiaochun, President of the People's Bank of China, recently warned that inflation is higher than expected and could still go up a little. Beijing has initiated a series of monetary tightening measures to rein in consumer prices and tame runaway house prices, but it will take a while before these begin to show results.

The leadership's concern at the popular dissatisfaction caused by inflation, unemployment etc was manifest in the Twelfth Five Year Plan targets outlined at the Fourth session of the Eleventh National People's Congress (NPC) in Beijing on March 5, 2011. The session was attended by almost 3,000 NPC Deputies and 2,000 members of the National Committee of the Chinese People's Political Consultative Conference (CPPCC). The Plan proposal said that the growth rate of GDP would be sought to be kept at 8 percent and the target for economic growth would be 7 percent over the next five years. The Consumer Price Index would not be allowed to exceed 4 percent with top priority given to stabilising prices. Efforts will be made to create at least 9 million jobs a year and keep urban unemployment at 4.6 percent or lower. Reports in the official media similarly emphasized that stabilizing of commodity prices and grain prices would be the focal points for 2011.

These factors have all contributed to the growing popular discontent reflected in the escalating incidence of public protests across China. A survey conducted by the Public Opinion Research Laboratory of Shanghai's Jiao Tong University disclosed that "public crises" occurred every five days in China in 2010. The report conceded that the number of events had decreased in 2010, but were still numerous. Of the seventy two "relatively influential" public crises examined by the laboratory, 18 percent related to the judicial system and law enforcement while 15 percent had to do with diseases and accidents. Other official reports attributed the causes for protests to delayed payments, land expropriation, building demolition and labour disputes. Corruption is another major cause.

The visit on January 24, by Chinese Premier Wen Jiabao to the State Bureau for Letters and Calls in Beijing was widely reported by the official Chinese media. Offices of the State Bureau for Letters and Calls, popularly referred to in China as 'petitioners offices', are located throughout the country and people frequent these to present their problems and seek redress. Described as a "rare" visit, some newspapers pointed out that it was the first time since 1949 that a Chinese Premier had a face-to-face communication with the people. The visit was in contrast to media reports of petitioners being forcibly dispersed by the police prior to sensitive anniversaries, festivals or a visit by a senior cadre to the county or provincial headquarters. This New Year's Eve, for example, seven hundred petitioners were rounded up and sent to the Xu Jiujingzhuang detention centre, or 'black jail'. Later, on February 2 and 3, enthused by the Premier's apparent show of empathy hundreds of petitioners tried to approach Premier Wen Jiabao's residence, but were detained by police.

Reports in the official Chinese media have also mentioned a number of instances of public protests throughout 2010 and the current year. These have included protests by workers, 'ultra-Left' political activists, farmers etc. On January 16, 2011, five persons were shot when the police opened fire in Wuzhou City, capital of Guangxi Zhuang Autonomous Region, when workers were demonstrating to demand payment of salary arrears. Five hundred workers struck work in Shenzhen, Guangdong, on January 18 to protest the non-payment of bonus for three years by a Japanese-invested plastics firm. 'Left' political activism also causes some concern, but is dealt with differently. The Maoist website 'Utopia' publicized that on January 27, 2011, Zhao Dongmin, a Maoist activist and leader of the 'Xi'an City Mao Zedong Thought Study Group', was sentenced to three years imprisonment with three years reprieve and released. He was arrested in August 2009 for organizing a hundred retired workers to petition officials of the Trade Union office of Shaanxi province.

Significantly, the Jiao Tong University's survey report also touched on the role of the 'new media' and highlighted that it is becoming increasingly prominent in such crises. It noted that 67 percent of the cases recorded by the survey were publicized by 'new media'. This represented a 14 percent increase over the previous year. A commentary in the Party mouthpiece 'People's Daily' more bluntly warned of the threat of internet manipulation which 'spreads viruses of public opinion to stir up public sentiment'.

Aware of the dangers of exposing the Chinese people to reports of the popular disturbances in the Middle East, the Chinese authorities had promptly imposed strict controls on the Chinese media. Reporters and Editors of major newspapers in Beijing, Shanghai and elsewhere were instructed to use only reports disseminated by the official news agency, Xinhua, and the internet was strictly policed. Pictures of bloody street protests and army tanks in Cairo's Tahir Square were banned. Microblogs are being heavily censored while access to Facebook, Twitter, Youtube and Linkedin have been blocked.

Dissident Chinese elements have nevertheless been able to bypass intense censorship and send out seemingly innocuous messages – avoiding the use of words like jasmine, demonstration or protests – to citizens in Beijing and 26 other cities to stage protests on two consecutive Sundays so far. The messages have been intercepted by the authorities who have deployed numerous plainclothes policemen to successfully disperse and round up the activists. The authorities have additionally quietly picked up and detained the more prominent dissidents. Separately, the Beijing, Shanghai and other dailies have front-paged commentaries criticizing calls for protests like those in the Middle East as calculated to bring about chaos. These have bluntly accused "...people inside and outside the country with ulterior motives..." of wanting to create instability and chaos. Later, in mid-February, the People's Daily and its English-language subsidiary Global Times, said instability was caused by wanting to profit from social allocation of benefits, exploitation of others, social injustice etc.

Notwithstanding the stringent security precautions taken by the Chinese Communist leadership, dissident elements have succeeded in registering their unhappiness. On February 12, a group of dissidents in Hangzhou, capital of Zhejiang province, gathered to celebrate the 'success' of the Egyptian revolution. A group of civil rights activists in Guiyang, capital of Guizhou province, similarly displayed materials about Tunisia and Egypt. In both cases the demonstrators clashed with the police and were arrested. On Valentine's Day on February 14, scores of people in Beijing tried to send flowers to the Egyptian Embassy to 'congratulate the Egyptian people', but were prevented by the police. In what would have been an unpleasantly sharp reminder to the authorities, a photograph showing the Chinese characters "6" and "4" written in snow covering the ground of Tiananmen Square in Beijing was recently widely circulated on the internet. The figures "6" and "4" represent the bloody crackdown on students in Beijing on June 4.

The restive autonomous regions of Tibet and Xinjiang continue to be a cause for serious concern. Earlier in 2010, the Chinese Communist Party (CCP) leadership for the first time in many years convened a work forum each for Tibet and Xinjiang. The main theme of the forums was the maintenance of stability and ethnic unity. Large sums of money were set aside for development plans for both regions in a bid to improve the peoples' living conditions.

In moves suggestive of some relaxation, the authorities replaced Wang Lequan, who had been Party Secretary for fifteen years, with Zhang Chunxian, who was moved from Hunan province. Internet services in the Xinjiang-Uyghur Autonomous Region were also restored after almost 312 days in May 2010. Simultaneously the public security apparatus in both the autonomous regions was strengthened. Funding for public security in the Xinjiang-Uyghur Autonomous

Region was doubled in 2010 with RMB 2.89 billion (US$ 423 million) being allocated. The Xinjiang People's Armed Police (PAP) Corps was also expanded. In addition to the couple of hundred thousand closed-circuit security cameras already installed in trouble-prone cities and areas across the Autonomous Region, additional cameras are planned to be installed. The Municipal Government of Urumuqi has decided to bring the entire city under camera surveillance by augmenting the 17,000 cameras already installed in 2010 with tens of thousands more by the end of this year. Instances of violent protest against the Beijing regime, however, continue to occur. In Aksu city on 19 August there was an explosion in a market place when seven people were believed killed and 14 injured. Official reports stated that in 2010, Xinjiang tried 376 crimes of "endangering national security", including those related to the 'July 5' violence in Urumuqi and Kashi.

Tibet has been similarly restive with intermittent reports of sporadic violence. On May 21, 2010 in the Kham region's Pelyul County, some Tibetans from Sokchen Village in Namling County of Shigatse Region went to the village government to protest against a mining company from Weifang, Shandong province. They protested that mining causes ecological damage, drinking water pollution and problems for cattle etc. The local authorities reportedly deployed a thousand People's Armed Police personnel who arrested a number of protesters including some Tibetans. Later last year at least two incidents occurred. In one incident, fifteen Tibetans including five monks were arrested by police in a crackdown against protesters in Tamo township in Shigatse. Earlier on November 22, hundreds of Tibetans had tried to disrupt mining activity near Linka monastery in Tamo. A report of an official study group sent to examine implementation of the recommendations of the Fifth Tibet Work Forum, and presented to the Central Discipline Inspection Commission (CDIC), indicated that Tibet continued to be a disturbed region. The report stressed the need to 'further strengthen' rapid development and 'long-term stability in Tibetan areas' and called for a 'high degree of strict political discipline' where 'Party members and cadres maintain a high degree of consistency with the Party Central Committee with firm belief and faith'. It asserted that it was 'important to discover and severely punish various violations of political discipline in a timely manner'. It warned that there cannot be 'fuzzy understanding or the slightest wavering attitude' in safeguarding national unification or ethnic unity and recommended intensification of education and publicity among the masses. The Tibet Autonomous Region Party Secretary, Zhang Qingli, on the sidelines of the ongoing NPC session on March 5, said that Tibet is still facing "very grave challenges" in the fight against separatist activities this year, when the region will mark the 60th anniversary of its 'peaceful liberation'. Meeting the delegation from Tibet attending the NPC session, PRC President Hu Jintao reinforced this message.

In this backdrop the Chinese Communist Party leadership has accorded high priority to internal security. The focus, as discernible from Premier Wen Jiabao's work report, will be on cyber security and internet policing, monitoring of wireless communication platforms, the public security apparatus and its capacity for responding to emergencies and, the hardening of public safety infrastructure. The current top Party leadership as well as the emerging leaders are firmly wedded to the preservation and continuance of the CCP's pre-eminent position in China. They will reinforce efforts to strengthen the internal public security apparatus. It is not surprising, therefore, that the budget presented on March 5, at the ongoing Fourth session of the Eleventh National People's Congress, or China's parliament, proposed an allocation of US $ 95 billion for the internal security apparatus – even higher than this year's considerably boosted defence budget!

This was published as an Issue Brief by the Centre for Air Power Studies on March 15, 2011.

4. Chinese Communist Party Celebrates 90th Founding Anniversary, But Faces Decade of Uncertainty

As China's communist party celebrated its 90th founding anniversary on July 1, 2011 – the fifth and tenth years in each decade being of particular importance in Chinese tradition – it reviewed the past decades with legitimate satisfaction. With the Chinese Communist Party (CCP) standing poised at the start of its centennial decade, however, its leadership is acutely concerned that this will be a tough and uncertain ten years. The Party's hitherto unrivalled leadership role could come in for serious questioning. Additionally, the unanticipated global economic crisis accelerated China's unprecedented rise in international influence and economic clout, placing it at the high table with the world's major powers possibly ten years ahead of time. China's emerging top leadership will now be challenged to find ways to avoid conflict while realizing China's ambitions of 'reclaiming' territorial sovereignty without diminishing this new-found influence. Some major challenges threatening the primacy of the Party are discernible.

In his speech, CCP Central Committee (CC) General Secretary and China's President Hu Jintao rightly recalled that throughout the past ninety years the CCP has effectively influenced China's politics and, for over sixty of these it reigned over China shaping its destiny and that of the country's over one billion people. Consolidation of the Party's ruling position was followed by the attempt to cater to the people's basic needs in consonance with the principles of Marxism-Leninism-Mao Zedong Thought. This thirty year period was interrupted by the

Great Leap Forward and Great Proletarian Cultural Revolution, both later acknowledged as experiments with disastrous consequences. His speech, though, avoided all reference to these movements, which the Party took decades to remedy and after years of protracted introspection assess Mao Zedong as only 'seventy percent good'!

Deng Xiaoping was credited with initiating the 'Four Modernisations' and the rapid progress made by China to become the major power it is today. The Party began adapting to the new situation and, despite opposition from equally respected veteran Party cadres, Deng allowed 'some to get rich first'. He relaxed policies observing that the 'colour of the cat doesn't matter as long as it catches the mice'! Agricultural production increased with the introduction of 'private plots' and per capita incomes grew. GDP rose from approximately RMB (Yuan) 460,906 million (US$ 1= RMB 6.5) in 1980, to RMB 9,921,500 million in 2000 and still further to RMB 25,506,956 million in 2010. There was a surge in growth of GDP and per capita incomes in the last ten years. A middle and upper class emerged in China which today has 120,000 millionaires and 106 billionaires. Private businessmen are Party members and even Deputies to the National People's Congress (NPC) – China's version of a Parliament. A couple of months ago China emerged as the world's second largest economy next only to the US.

China simultaneously focussed on science and technology and began investing 1.3 percent of the GDP in R&D from 1995. China today boasts the world's fastest indigenously developed super computer located at Tianjin. It will have its own 35-satellite GPS navigation system called the 'Beidou' by 2020. Its defence industry has indigenously developed, among other technologies, an Anti-Satellite weapon capability, Anti-Ship Ballistic Missiles, the J-20 Stealth fighter aircraft, and will soon launch an aircraft carrier. Military exports are part of China's military diplomacy.

CCP Central Committee (CC) General Secretary Hu Jintao's

9,797-word carefully scripted speech recounted all these successes achieved under the leadership of the Party, but also offered glimpses of potential future political tensions. With the grand 90th anniversary celebrations orchestrated by the Party at the Great Hall of the People as the backdrop, Hu Jintao spoke for over 72 minutes harping extensively on China's colonial past, humiliations and poverty, and the CCP's role in eliminating these. He dwelt on the need for enhancing 'socialist values' and the 'socialist spirit' among Party cadres to bring them closer to the people. He warned that the challenges ahead are "more strenuous and pressing than at any point in the past."

Unlike on past occasions this time Hu Jintao invoked Mao's legacy. He referred oftener to Mao Zedong and his contributions and to a lesser extent to Deng Xiaoping. Mao was mentioned five times while Deng merited only three mentions and Jiang Zemin and Hu Jintao's 'scientific development concept' even fewer. Hu Jintao pointedly referred to the 'Four Cardinal Principles', which though enunciated by Deng Xiaoping later became a buzzword of the 'Left'. Hu's speech paid unmistakable obeisance to Mao's legacy and Mao Zedong Thought.

The surprising presence of conservative, 94-year old veteran Party leader, Song Ping, on the rostrum at these official celebrations in the Great Hall of the People reinforced this impression. This, along with Jiang Zemin's absence, prompted analysts to speculate that a pronounced pro-Mao tilt is becoming evident and that Jiang Zemin's absence either signalled loss of influence or his demise. It is important to note, though, that Song Ping has been Hu Jintao's mentor and first brought him to Deng Xiaoping's notice thus ensuring his rise to power.

In his speech Hu Jintao stressed progress and continuation of reforms, implying that there would be no relaxing of momentum, but the dominant theme in Hu Jintao's speech was stability. This underscored the leadership's awareness of, and preparedness to tackle, growing popular discontent caused by the reforms. He referred to the need for stability ten times in this speech in contrast to six references in his speech at the 85th anniversary (2006), four during the 80th anniversary (2001) and five at the 70th (1991). In fact Hu Jintao for the first time declared that: "development is the fundamental principle, stability is the fundamental task; without stability, nothing can be accomplished, and the gains we have already made will also be lost. This principle is something not only comrades throughout the Party must bear firmly in mind, but that the whole people must be induced to bear firmly in mind." A confidential Tsinghua University survey had recently disclosed that 180,000 protests occurred across the country in 2010. The budget for security was earlier enhanced to US$ 95 billion, exceeding the defence budget.

Predictably the armed forces merited a separate paragraph. Hu Jintao emphasised: 'we must adhere to the fundamental principle of the Party exercising absolute leadership over the army and the fundamental purpose of the army as a people's army and cultivate core values for contemporary revolutionary military personnel. It is important to expand and intensify military preparedness and conduct military exercises with IT applications and raise independent defense and weaponry-related R&D capabilities.' Foreign policy figured in proforma fashion towards the end of Hu Jintao's 17-section speech. 'Continuing the policy of peaceful development of relations with Taiwan' found mention, but the routine assertion that China needs a peaceful neighbourhood environment for its development was omitted.

It is the domestic political landscape that will throw up most of the major challenges for the Party in the coming decade. The emergence of different trends in political thinking is a cause for concern.

Neo-Maoist sentiment, or 'Red Revival' as it is called, has quietly gained strength in recent years and elicited the tacit support of many 'princelings'. Some top echelon cadres have tapped in to this popular sentiment to shore personal credentials and possibly garner support of the Party's 'Cultural Revolution-era' cadres who number over 30 million. Contents of the twenty seven identified 'neo-Maoist' websites reflect that this nostalgia for Mao has been fuelled by diverse factors including rampant corruption, unchecked inflation, efforts by liberal economists to dismantle State owned Enterprises (SOEs), grabbing of arable lands of farmers by rural cadres, and perceived dilution of purist communist principles. Prior to the National People's Congress (NPC) session this March these websites severely criticised some liberal personages, including a couple of 'princelings', but were pointedly not shut down.

Politburo Standing Committee (PBSC) member Li Changchun and Director of the CCP CC's Propaganda Department, 1947-born Liu Yunshan keep a tight grip on the Party's propaganda apparatus. They have not fought shy of subjecting even Premier Wen Jiabao and President Hu Jintao's public utterances, made while travelling abroad, to censorship. Liu Yunshan, is a candidate for elevation at the next Congress. Chen Kuiyuan, who is associated with the hardline 'Left' and is Vice Chairman of the Chinese People's Political Conference (CPPCC) and President of the Chinese Academy of Social Sciences (CASS), was photographed by the official media attending an important Propaganda Department conference in January 2011. Li Changchun and Chen Kuiyuan joined the Party in 1965 and Liu Yunshan in 1971 – all during the Cultural Revolution and the upward progression in their careers was uninterrupted throughout that tumultuous decade.

In the forefront of this 'Red' movement is veteran Party leader Bo Yibo's son, Bo Xilai, who is a 'princeling' and Party Secretary of Chongqing Municipality. He is an aspirant for the Politburo Standing Committee (PBSC) at the Party Congress in 2012. Other senior Party leaders have exhibited support. Vice President Xi Jinping, who is tipped to succeed Hu Jintao at the next Party Congress in 2012 and joined the Party during the Cultural Revolution, visited Mao's birthplace in Shao Shan at least thrice in the past six months and visited Chongqing. Others like PBSC member and Security Czar, Zhao Yongkang and PBSC member in charge of Propaganda, Li Changchun, both due to retire at the next Congress, have visited Chongqing and expressed support for Bo Yibo's 'Red' movement. The Director of the powerful General Political Department (GPD) of the People's Liberation Army (PLA), Li Jinai, recently visited Chongqing.

Hinting at the strength of these 'neo-Maoist' sentiments some reports claimed that all but three of the seven Politburo Standing Committee members attended the lavish 90th anniversary celebrations organized by Bo Xilai at Chongqing. Hu Jintao, Wen Jiabao and Li Keqiang stayed in Beijing along with the Director of the Party's all-powerful Organisation Department, Li Yuanchao. The tenor of Hu Jintao's speech at the Party's 90th founding anniversary appears to reflect the popularity of these sentiments. They would be acknowledgement of the influence of the over thirty million members who joined the Party during the Cultural Revolution and Party entrants born between 1960-70, or the *hong er'dai.*

Interesting is the emergence of political thinking encapsuled in the comments of General Liu Yuan, Political Commissar of the PLA's General Logistics Department and tipped to soon enter the Central Military Commission. Liu Yuan was appointed full General in 2009. He is the son of former President Liu Shaoqi. At a conference in Beijing this May, attended by at least six other PLA Generals, he presented an essay calling on China to rediscover its 'military culture' and asserted that 'the Party has been repeatedly betrayed by General Secretaries, both in and outside the country, recently and in the past.' The essay was a preface to "Changing Our View of Culture and History," a book-length collection of political tracts by Zhang Musheng, also son of a Chinese official. The book advocated a 'New

Left' to save China and the CCP. Liu Yuan is close to Vice President Xi Jinping, another 'princeling'.

How long these differing thoughts would be tolerated by senior Party echelons is uncertain. Many emerging leaders are 'princelings' and have personally suffered, or witnessed the tragic suffering of their families, during the Cultural Revolution. Many remain unwavering in their loyalty to the Party, which they joined during the Cultural Revolution and see as vital for China's rise, and a few venerate Mao's legacy. They are unlikely to allow neo-Maoist or other sentiments to become disruptive or derail reforms. Additionally, many of the Cultural Revolution entrants to the Party would be nearing retirement when their influence would diminish.

The other major challenge threatening the Party's legitimacy as the sole ruling party is the increasing popular discontent and protests triggered by the reform process. The authorities deployed almost half the country's armed police force to tackle domestic unrest, which spread across the country and peaked last year to 180,000 protests. The Party apprehends that the nearly 200 million illegal migrant workers, who are denied any benefits by the state, could stage violent protests. Resentment among factory workers caused by non-payment of back wages and factory lock outs is also growing and China's media has demanded that trade unions become active, particularly in factories of foreign enterprises. The All China Federation of Trade Unions (ACFTU), however, is weakened. Widening income disparities accentuate the problem. If these elements combine they will endanger urban social order.

The planned shift in economic development from an export and investment-led model to one driven by Chinese consumers could cause severe disruption. Low incomes combined with traditional thrift will additionally be hampered by growing inflation and unemployment estimated presently at between 12-14 percent. A volatile element is the unavailability of jobs for fresh graduates. It is essential to create 8-9 million jobs annually, control prices and maintain economic growth at least at 7 percent. As people's incomes increase they are demanding greater accountability from Party and government cadres from the village level up. Mobile phones and the internet have facilitated prompt communication and coordination of protests. The number of 'religious believers' is growing and people's fear of authority has reduced. These economic contradictions, which have the potential to trigger violent country-wide protests, could hobble the Party.

Restiveness among ethnic minorities is assuming serious proportions. Tibet and Tibetan areas are already tense and prone to sporadic outbursts of violence despite stringent security. Depending on how the leadership handles the Tibet issue and deals with the Dalai Lama and Tibetans abroad will determine whether tensions escalate. The present juncture is critical. Violence in Xinjiang is now home-grown and not perpetrated only by activists from across the borders. Indigenous Uyghur groups, however, continue to receive financial, propaganda and other support from abroad, but have local grievances too. They are unwilling to accept Han domination or marginalisation of their language and culture. A new feature is the intensity of anger among ethnic Mongolians evidenced by the recent wide-spread violence in the Nei Mongol Autonomous Region. The sentiments of minority nationalities are ready for exploitation by indigenous elements and 'hostile foreign forces'.

Finally, international and sovereignty issues will come to the forefront this decade. China's unrelenting bid to establish itself as the dominant power in Asia-Pacific and claim its 'territorial sovereignty' has contributed to current tensions in the South China Sea and elsewhere. Beijing has not relented, but now seeks to assuage declared US concerns regarding neutrality and freedom of international passage-ways while separately urging Vietnam and the Philippines to negotiate bilaterally. China's Navy remains deployed in the area. The

US, increasingly wary of China's rise, demonstrated its intention of remaining in the region and, for the first time ever, recently carried out a naval exercise in the South China Sea. Maritime territorial tensions with Japan have temporarily receded, but are likely to resurface. The unsettled border issue with India, which has been complicated by the introduction of fresh territorial claims in Jammu & Kashmir and Sikkim, has a real potential to get out of hand. China's domestic developmental programmes, like diversion of the Brahmaputra river, could heighten existing suspicion of China's intentions making India-China relations more fragile. Whether Beijing's newfound global influence and status prompts it to appropriately mould its behaviour will determine whether these territorial issues erupt into conflict and derail China's modernizations, possibly irreparably crippling the Party.

It is the emerging generation of new Chinese leaders who will steer the Party and China through this decade. How they tackle these issues is crucial and will determine whether China's modernization gets derailed and the Party loses its status as the solitary ruling party. The leaders appear doctrinaire, unwilling to brook relaxation of political controls, and approve Beijing's policies towards the minority ethnic nationalities. Some have exhibited a partiality for tough measures. The linkages, especially of 'princelings' in the Party with those in the PLA, implies they are unlikely to compromise on issues of territorial or national sovereignty. Nevertheless, they are well-educated and firmly believe that the primacy and sole ruling status of the CCP is essential for China's stability and progress.

This was published as an Issue Brief by the Centre for Air Power Studies on July 12, 2011.

5. China: Differences in Political Thought and Styles Manifested in Run up to 18th Congress

As Chinese prepare to usher in the New Year of the Dragon – regarded as a symbol of good fortune and sign of intense power – on 23rd January this year, China will usher in major leadership changes at the Eighteenth Party Congress scheduled for this October. The leadership also confronts critical domestic issues that could threaten social stability. In fact, a postage stamp depicting a dragon issued earlier this month itself attracted criticism that the picture was needlessly fierce. Additionally, China's seventh Five Year Plan (2011-2015), which initiates a bold far-reaching attempt to slow down the economy and convert the country's export-led economy to one that promotes domestic consumption, is entering its second year.

Leadership transition is a particularly sensitive phase for all governments and, especially for dictatorships and authoritarian regimes. The winds of change in the form of *'jasmine revolutions'* blowing relentlessly across the Middle East, which have already seen the downfall of some long-entrenched regimes, provide cold comfort to the Chinese Communist Party (CCP). This is accentuated by the magnitude of the imminent changes. In the CCP's three most powerful bodies, almost 60 percent of the Central Committee will be replaced, 14 of 25 Politburo (PB) members will relinquish office and 7 out of 9 members of the all-powerful Politburo Standing Committee (PBSC) will retire. The new leadership that emerges will steer China through this decade.

Growing societal restiveness makes the situation more sensitive. A Blue Paper issued by the prestigious Beijing-based Chinese Academy of Social Sciences (CASS) cautioned that people are losing confidence in the 'government's capabilities and integrity'. It added: 'masses in urban areas believe real estate is a racket overseen by governments in collusion with real estate developers. People also have no trust in food and medicine safety'. Volatility is added by the rise in public discontent. There has been a steady rise in the number of mass protests and demonstrations since 2003. A confidential Tsinghua University survey estimated that last year 180,000 disturbances occurred across China, a sharp escalation from the 120,000 protests in 2008 and 60,000 in 2006. Suggestive of their serious concern, the CCP leadership and Public Security authorities enhanced this year's public security budget to over US $ 95 billion, more than the national defence budget!

It is, however, the domestic political landscape that will present most of the major challenges for the Party in the coming decade. Different trends in political thinking have emerged and, over the past eighteen months, a degree of political ferment is discernible in the ideological straight-jacket that regulates present day China. While the more extreme views, widely criticized domestically as reflecting Western thinking, remain on the ineffectual outer fringes of Chinese society, other strains that deviate somewhat from the current mainstream of political thought are beginning to find resonance. The latter do not strike a discordant note with the majority of Chinese who, having grown up in the People's Republic of China and known only CCP rule, have a deep seated fear of *dongluan*, or chaos. For this overwhelming majority, as instilled by the Chinese Communist Party, the latter remains the guarantor of stability and, in the three recent decades, also of economic prosperity.

The Chinese Communist Party has itself changed in the decades since Deng Xiaoping initiated the 'Four Modernisations' and drifted away from purist communist ideology. A middle and upper class has emerged in China which today boasts 120,000 millionaires and 106 billionaires. Private businessmen are Party members and even

Deputies to the National People's Congress (NPC). 70 of the Deputies to the Eleventh NPC session held in March 2011, actually accounted for a total wealth of US$ 70 billion!

Veteran cadres will gather this summer at the seaside resort of Beidaihe to decide most top appointments, but the tradition of them deciding all Politburo (PB) and Politburo Standing Committee (PBSC) appointments without wider discussion has got diluted after 'Long March' veterans disappeared from the scene. Most impacted are the Party *apparatchiks,* who traditionally attracted the notice of leaders either through work association, social interaction because of family connections, or during inspection visits. The Party *apparatchik* has, for the most part, risen to higher positions by sacrificing initiative and avoiding taking any action without prior approval of the higher Party authority. Persons aspiring for elevation to higher echelon bodies, however, now require support from the Party Central Committee. This has led to those aspiring for top positions adopting new methods of promoting themselves, or new styles of 'campaigning'. Most significantly, this time the 'princelings', who zealously guard their privacy and whose families wield immense political influence, have chosen to become politically active.

A few illustrative examples of differences in thought and styles of self advancement are highlighted.

Neo-Maoist sentiment, or 'Red Revival' as it is called, has quietly gained strength in recent years and elicited the tacit support of many 'princelings'. On Mao Zedong's 118th birth anniversary on December 26, 2011, for example, an estimated 17.5 million people visited his birthplace and crowds at his mausoleum in Beijing were double the usual. Some top echelon cadres have tapped in to this popular sentiment to shore personal credentials and garner support of the Party's 'Cultural Revolution-era' cadres who number over 30 million. Prior to the National People's Congress (NPC) session in March 2011, these 'neo-Maoist' websites severely criticised some liberal personages, including a couple of 'princelings', but were pointedly not shut down. An analysis of the content of twenty seven such identified websites reflects that this nostalgia for Mao has been fuelled by diverse factors including rampant corruption, unchecked inflation, efforts by liberal economists to dismantle State owned Enterprises (SOEs), grabbing of arable lands of farmers by rural cadres, and perceived dilution of purist communist principles. There is a strong sense that the Party 'has lost its way' and been weakened.

1949-born Bo Xilai, veteran Party leader Bo Yibo's son who is a 'princeling' and Party Secretary of Chongqing Municipality, has positioned himself in the forefront of this 'Red' movement and initiated campaigns to popularize Mao-era revolutionary songs and sayings. He fortified his popular credentials by successfully unleashing 'strike hard' campaigns to eliminate triads and cleanse Chongqing Municipality. He is an aspirant for a position in the Politburo Standing Committee (PBSC) at the Party Congress in 2012.

Vice President Xi Jinping, who is tipped to succeed Hu Jintao at the next Party Congress in 2012, visited Mao's birthplace in Shao Shan at least thrice in the past eight months and visited Chongqing. Expressing support for Bo Xilai and the 'Red' movement, PBSC member and Security Czar, Zhao Yongkang and PBSC member in charge of Propaganda, Li Changchun, both due to retire at the next Congress, visited Chongqing as did the Director of the powerful General Political Department (GPD) of the People's Liberation Army (PLA), Li Jinai. Hinting at the strength of these 'neo-Maoist' sentiments, reports claimed that all but three of the nine Politburo Standing Committee members attended the lavish 90th anniversary celebrations organized by Bo Xilai at Chongqing. Chinese President Hu Jintao's speech at the Party's 90th founding anniversary also acknowledged the influence of the over thirty million members who joined the Party during the Cultural Revolution and Party entrants, or the *hong er'dai,* born between 1960-70.

Wang Yang, a Communist Youth League (CYL) cadre who is 56 years old and Party Secretary of Guangdong province, opted for a different method of attracting favourable attention. In contrast to Bo Xilai, he has sought to project a more 'open' style of governance and urged the media to play a watchdog role. The 'peaceful resolution' of the four month-long (Sept-Dec, 2011) stand-off between authorities and peasants in Wukan village netted him a lot of praise and was lauded as an 'act of political courage in a tense situation' by the authoritative Party paper 'People's Daily'. Critics, however, allege that it was the presence of foreign journalists that prompted him to act in this manner. Whether Wang Yang will be able to maintain this 'style' of governance will be tested as protests spread through Guangdong province. If his conciliatory approach leads to more and bolder protests, he could be accused of soft-heartedness and strategic miscalculation endangering the Party's grip. The tough handling recently of a few demonstrations indicates there might be limits to 'gentle' handling. He also allowed Guangzhou, the provincial capital, in October 2009 to publish its budget for the first time. In contrast, Shanghai Party Chief Yu Zhengsheng, a 'princeling' and member of the PB who is also in line for promotion to the PBSC, at the same time preferred the orthodox style of administration and prohibited publication of Shanghai's provincial budget. Wang Yang is close to China's President Hu Jintao with whom he worked in Anhui and the former Vice Premier and veteran cadre, Wan Li, was his mentor.

A notable intervention in the emerging debate on the CCP's rights and prerogatives has been that by Hu Deping, a former Vice Minister of the CCP CC's United Front Work Department and son of former popular reformist CCP CC General Secretary Hu Yaobang. Hu Deping, a 'princeling' who at 69 years is out of the reckoning for any position, commented publicly on the contentious issue of land property rights in the context of the incident in Wukan village. He supported Guangdong Party Secretary Wang Yang's stance. He criticised as erroneous the thinking of many cadres on local property rights issues, which he described as among the most pressing issues since the period of opening up and reform. Asserting that the sale price of rural land should have the same value as state-owned land, he regretted this was not the case because many cadres believe that all rural land belongs to the state. These cadres, commenting on land belonging to the rural collective, say the collective belongs to the state and that land occupied by individual peasants also belongs to the collective, and the collective belongs to the state, which in turn belongs to the Communist Party. He attributed the forced demolition of rural housing to this distorted thinking. Hu Deping emphasised that the rural land collective system does not suggest that land cannot be transferred, nor that it cannot follow a business model, adding that this is integral to agricultural modernization. He felt that Guangdong would evolve a good resolution to these problems. This issue is, incidentally, being separately addressed by Hu Jintao and Wen Jiabao and a pilot programme was initiated a few years ago in Chengdu, capital of Sichuan province.

Separately, Liu Yunshan, Director of the CCP CC's powerful Propaganda Department and Politburo member, has attracted favourable notice in the run up to the Party Congress because of the initiatives he took at work. Liu Yunshan's achievements include overseeing the dramatic rejuvenation of the Party's propaganda from a failing policy of control to an energetic policy aimed at actively shaping public discourse. He pro-actively managed the propaganda apparatus during the 2008 riots in Lhasa and successfully drove a wedge between the majority Han population and Tibetans. The CCP CC's decision to adopt culture and propaganda as the sole item for its agenda at its sixth plenary session (October 18-24, 2011) was a singular success for Liu Yunshan. It demonstrated the support for him within the Party's incumbent top leadership. This was reinforced by Chinese President Hu Jintao's declaration, in a signed essay in the

Jan 2012 issue of the Communist Party policy magazine 'Seeking Truth', that: "we must clearly see that international hostile forces are intensifying the strategic plot of westernizing and dividing China, and ideological and cultural fields are the focal areas of their long-term infiltration". His assertion that "we should deeply understand the seriousness and complexity of the ideological struggle, always sound the alarms and remain vigilant, and take forceful measures to be on guard and respond", not only indicated that the major policy initiatives announced at the October plenum would continue through 2012, but that the tough measures introduced by the CCP CC Propaganda Department in the past months had Hu Jintao's approval. Vice President Xi Jinping reinforced this on January 4, 2012, by observing that ideological control and political education in universities needs to be strengthened. Liu Yunshan is a Communist Youth League (CYL) cadre reputedly close to Hu Jintao.

Quite unusually, General Liu Yuan, Political Commissar of the People's Liberation Army (PLA) General Logistics Department, espoused a sentiment which related not to the military but the Party's politics. Liu Yuan, appointed full General in 2009, is the son of former President Liu Shaoqi and a 'princeling'. He is tipped for elevation to the Central Military Commission this October and is close to Vice President Xi Jinping. His essay in a book launched last May, asserted: 'the Party has been repeatedly betrayed by General Secretaries, both in and outside the country, recently and in the past.' The book advocated a 'New Left' to save China and the CCP.

Significant in the run up to the leadership changes imminent at the Eighteenth Party Congress is the initiative taken by the normally reclusive and publicity-shy 'princelings'. Their activism, though low-key, is reminiscent of the move by Chen Yuan, a 'princeling' and son of Chen Yun who was one of the 'Eight Immortals', to safeguard the state's assets (State-owned Enterprises) at a time when after the 1989 'Tiananmen event' the Party was perceived to be under threat.

On the present occasion a group of 'princelings', of impeccable revolutionary pedigree and immense influence, reportedly gathered on October 6, 2011 at the China World Trade Centre in Beijing to pay tribute to those who ousted the infamous 'Gang of Four'.

The gathering pointedly expressed concern that the 'Party had lost its way'. Ye Xiangzhen, daughter of Marshal Ye Jianying who along with Deng Xiaoping ousted and incarcerated the 'Gang of Four', said "in today's China we are facing tremendous challenges that range from the rapid decline of moral standards, to poisonous and genetically modified food, to rampant official corruption". Lu De, son of Lu Dingyi the former Director of the CCP CC Propaganda Department and close associate of Deng Xiaoping, regretted that party and government officials spent a third of all government revenue on their own luxury cars, travel, healthcare, banquets and other perks. He added: "and yet we still call it the Communist Party and socialism." Recently leaked reports claim that the central government's expenditure on luxury automobiles is estimated at US$ 15 billion! Ma Xiaoli, daughter of a veteran communist revolutionary and Head of the Party School Ma Wenrui, observed that "in the '80s when the Party faced criticism we defended it and explained its actions, in the '90s we sympathised with the critics, but today we almost want to join them." Denigrating efforts to use "methods from the Cultural Revolution to solve the problems of contemporary China", these 'princelings' nevertheless felt that the younger generation "need another force to fight back and balance (those) voices".

Those present at the gathering hosted by Ye Xuanji, Marshal Ye Jianying's nephew described as a 'princeling' in his own right, included Ma Xiaoli, daughter of veteran communist revolutionary and Head of the Party School, Ma Wenrui; Ye Xiangzhen, daughter of Marshal Ye Jianying; Hu Deping, eldest son of late CCP CC General Secretary Hu Yaobang; Lu De son of former Director of the CCP CC Propaganda Department Lu Dingyi; and Xi Oianping, elder sister of Vice President Xi Jinping. The children of former Party Chief Hua Guofeng, Mao's chief bodyguard Wang Dongxing and former Chinese President, CPPCC Chairman and one of the 'Eight Immortals', Li Xiannian, were also present. Many of them called for democracy, the rule of law and bringing the Party under supervision. Their assembly and views would appear to reflect the sentiments of many other 'princelings' and their elders. An interesting aspect of those assembled at the event is that all of them have close family ties to Vice President Xi Jinping.

A sizeable number of 'princelings' are expected to enter the PB and PBSC when these sentiments will probably find expression in official policy. Some of the other new entrants, having broken out of the mould of *apparatchiks*, will also be cadres with distinct views. It is anticipated that the new leadership is likely to be more uncompromising on matters relating to Party discipline, political education, the Party's grip over the PLA and minority nationalities issues. They will also be less flexible on issues of sovereignty and territorial integrity.

This was published as an Issue Brief by the Centre for Air Power Studies on January 13, 2012

6. Leadership Struggle Highlights China's Fragile Power Structure

The severe in-fighting in the upper echelons of the Chinese Communist Party (CCP) for top posts, spilled out of the Party's strictly defined bounds of discipline and into adverse public glare in early February 2012. Deng Xiaoping's script for leadership succession had ended with Hu Jintao, and the absence of pre-eminent veteran leaders with adequate stature and unchallenged authority got clearly accentuated. More significantly, the events provide a glimpse of the tense, vicious struggles underway and highlight the fragility of China's power structure.

Bloodlines of candidates, patron-protégé linkages, mentor-*mishu* connections and rancorous relationships that had lain apparently dormant for decades, are all at play. The main issues are not ideology or pace of reform, but the ambition of the large numbers of cadres aspiring for the unusually numerous vacancies that are to become available at the 18th Party Congress in October this year. So many openings have not become available at one time for decades, thus increasing the number of hopefuls. The new entrants will lead China through this decade. For some aspirants this Congress is the last chance for promotion before the age criteria, announced at the 17th Party Congress, compels them to retire at 67 years.

62-year old Bo Xilai was a candidate who stood out. He came of 'red' lineage and was the son of Bo Yibo, one of the so-called 'Eight Immortals'. He had independent patronage linkages and built an independent support base. He had a proven track record of competence at the Centre as Commerce Minister when he impressed foreigners – especially Americans – during negotiations with his memory, grasp of the subject and fluency in English. He had done well in the provinces and was popular in Dalian and Chongqing. In the centrally-administered Municipality of Chongqing, he smashed the underground triads and mafia, boosted economic growth to 16.4 percent, reduced income disparities and eased the restrictive *hukou* system to allow for freer movement of rural folk to urban areas. Even China's 'liberal economists', like Sun Liping, this March lauded his performance. Bo Xilai, cleverly, additionally tapped in to the reservoir of pro-Mao sentiment to enhance his appeal. He was conscious that he had missed elevation to the PBSC at the last Congress by a very slender margin.

Bo Xilai demonstrated his influence by organising lavish celebrations for the Party's 90th founding anniversary in Chongqing, which were attended by many senior Party cadres including at least 6 members of the PBSC. Regardless of whether they all supported him or were hedging their bets, it was clear that Bo Xilai was rising and widely considered as having a very good chance to enter the PBSC. Cadres would have recalled that at an 'internal' conference of the CCP CC's Organisation Department in January 2011, Vice President Xi Jinping had identified Bo Xilai as one of the upward mobile cadres.

Prominent supporters of Bo Xilai in the Party include China's powerful Security Czar Zhou Yongkang, PBSC member in charge of Propaganda, Li Changchun, and China's former President Jiang Zemin. This support became evident in the decision to take Wang Lijun away to Beijing under the escort of Vice Minister Qiu Jin of the Ministry of State Security instead of keeping him in the jurisdiction of the Party's Central Discipline Inspection Commission (CDIC). It was followed by Chongqing Mayor Huang Qifan's public statement during the NPC plenum on March 5, 2012, recounting that Wang Lijun had sought sanctuary in the US Consulate in Chengdu and had to be talked into leaving peacefully by the Mayor and other colleagues. The Mayor's statement seemed to suggest that he was taking responsibility for the actions of his direct subordinate and deflecting responsibility away from Bo Xilai.

In the PLA, the Director of the PLA's powerful General Political Department (GPD), General Li Jinai has been a supporter of Bo Xilai and attended the Party's 90th founding anniversary celebrations in Chongqing. The Political Commissar of the Second Artillery Zhang Haiyang is a childhood friend. Bo Xilai had nurtured relations with the 14th Army, founded by his father, and visited them in Yunnan in late February this year, after the Wang Lijun incident became public. He cultivated relations with the Chengdu Military Region by making substantial contributions to personnel welfare. Demonstrating his close relationship with the PLA, when Hu Jintao was in Hawaii on November 10, 2011, to attend the APEC Summit, Bo Xilai staged a large "defense mobilization" military exercise in Chongqing where he invited Defense Minister Liang Guanglie and other southwestern Party and military leaders.

Bo Xilai's policies paid off and he succeeded in building a wide popular support base. However, his brash style, in violation of the low-key norm approved by the CCP, attracted adverse attention. His success in building an independent base was viewed by the Party Centre as a potential alternate power centre, which could threaten the Party's cohesion and unity. An alternate power centre would be a source of serious discomfiture to Party General Secretary and China's President Hu Jintao and Vice President Xi Jinping, and had to be neutralised.

As the dust settles it is becoming clearer that the move to prevent Bo Xilai's entry to the PBSC was premeditated and carefully planned. Bo Xilai's aide and Vice Mayor in charge of Public Security, Wang Lijun, was manipulated to investigate Bo Xilai so that he could be embarrassed into giving up the race. In case he resisted, Bo Xilai would be threatened with disciplinary action on charges of corruption. But Wang Lijun, either because he exceeded his brief or feared for his life or some other reason, strayed from the script and made an abortive attempt to defect to the US. This action immediately sealed Wang Lijun's fate and stunned the Party.

Within a week of being divested of the public security portfolio by Bo Xilai, on February 6, 2012, Wang Lijun drove to the US Consulate at Chengdu and sought political asylum. For the CCP, which goes to great lengths to conceal the true crimes of those who defect or are guilty of espionage, Wang Lijun's action was unforgivable. His timing was also drastically wrong. Granting Wang Lijun political asylum on the eve of Xi Jinping's visit to the US would have jeopardized US' relations with China. This the US does not want and Wang Lijun's request was turned down. That Wang Lijun had backers in Beijing is indicated by the initial reports claiming he had suffered a nervous breakdown and was being given "vacation-style treatment". But confirmation that Wang Lijun's supporters were not sufficiently strong and that the Party Centre was unwilling to condone such a serious breach of discipline came from China's President Hu Jintao. In an 'internal' briefing on March 3, to CCP cadres who were delegates to the CPPCC conference, Hu Jintao labeled Wang Lijun a 'traitor'.

Though a serious tussle was underway in the Party's top echelons, including retired veteran cadres, on what was to be done with Bo Xilai, it was evident that all were unanimous in the view that Party unity was paramount. The Party's core united around the Party Centre. This facilitated Hu Jintao and Wen Jiabao's efforts to muster support to remove Bo Xilai from Chongqing, dismiss him from the PB and CC and punish him.

Around this time Vice President Xi Jinping, publicly revealed the gravity of the situation for the CCP and his support to Hu Jintao, and cautioned Party cadres against taking sides. In a lengthy article in the Party's theoretical journal *Seeking Truth* on March 16, 2012, Vice President Xi Jinping urged cadres to "safeguard the purity of the party." He insisted that "we must resolutely stop and combat any wrong political tendencies that veer from the party's basic lines" and asserted that "leading cadres must resolutely uphold the Party's principles, charter, goals and policies." The article was publicised by the official newsagency Xinhua the following day. Ultimately Hu Jintao, Wen Jiabao, Xi Jinping and Li Keqiang secured a decision to remove Bo Xilai. After weeks of further wrangling and negotiation, Hu Jintao, Wen Jiabao and Xi Jinping scored a signal success and initiated proceedings to dismiss Bo Xilai from the CCP's CC which was announced on the evening of April 10, 2012. The following day an unsigned, front-page editorial in the authoritative Party paper 'People's Daily', asserted that "China is a socialist country under the rule of law. The dignity of its laws and authority cannot be damaged." It added "Regardless of an individual's stature, anyone who breaks the law will be punished. There is no preferential treatment in the eyes of the law." All of China's official media front-paged the article the next day. This could be the prelude to Bo Xilai being put on trial and punished, though the severity of the punishment is probably yet being negotiated. The blunt message that has been sent out by the Party is that no threat to the CCP's cohesion, unity and primacy would be tolerated.

Old loyalties undoubtedly played an important part and old scores were settled. Hu Jintao and Wen Jiabao are both proteges of Hu Yaobang and Xi Jinping also had family ties to him. While Wen Jiabao was the more overt supporter of Hu Yaobang, all three had mantained links with Hu Yaobang's family and annually visited their residence. Some reports claim Qiao Shi played an important role in ensuring the decision against Bo Xilai. The warnings issued by Hu Deping, Hu Yaobang's son, during at least three public gatherings of 'princelings' and liberal economists in Beijing since last year, had relevance. It was Wen Jiabao too who fired the first public salvo against Bo Xilai at the press conference on the last day of the NPC plenum in mid-March when he cautioned Chongqing's leadership to "learn lessons" from the Wang Lijun incident and mentioned the possibility of another Cultural Revolution. The irony of Bo Xilai's father, Bo Yibo, having been among Hu Yaobang's harshest critics during a five-day criticism session at the time of the 'Anti-Bourgeois Liberalization Campaign' in 1987, just two years before Hu Yaobang's death, cannot be missed.

Once the decision was taken, the Party moved swiftly to contain damage and diminish Bo Xilai's popularity by putting out a steady stream of stories about his and his wife's corruption. A People's Daily article of April 12, hinted at serious politcal implications by suggesting that Bo Xilai's wife, Gu Kailai, may be holding a foreign passport. It referred to corrupt officials who "commit crime abroad or transfer dirty assets abroad, and some even secretly acquire foreign citizenship or dual citizenship." A former Ming Pao journalist has alleged that Gu Kailai holds a Hong Kong ID and Singapore Green Card. She is presently under detention pending investigations into the death of British national, Niel Heywood who, according to unconfirmed reports, had intimate relations with her of which Bo Xilai was aware.

Functionaries of the CCP CC's Propaganda Department, who had stayed inactive for a few weeks waiting to see which leadership group got the upper hand, swung into action after Xi Jinping's article of March 16. Chongqing Radio and TV were directed to curtail the 'red' programmes started by Bo Xilai in February 2011. On April 12, Xinhua disclosed that between mid-March and early April, China had shut down 42 websites and deleted more than 210,000 on-line posts in a crackdown on "internet-based rumours", A few better known neo-Maoist websites and portals began to feel the effect and *Utopia* and *maoflag.com* websites were shut for 'maintenance'. Chongqing Satellite Television station resumed its broadcasting of popular drama series and news programs during prime time on March 26, as publicised by the state-run newspaper *China Daily*. Many policies associated with Bo Xilai, like the revolutionary themes from the Mao Zedong era, were suppressed and the Chongqing television singing program that featured Maoist anthems, called *Daily Red Songs*, were reduced to a weekly show. *Chongqing Daily* on March 28, publicized City Propaganda Chief, He Shizhong's call to municipal propaganda workers to "firmly avoid movement-style (propaganda) methods" and "resolutely maintain a high degree of uniformity" with the CCP's Central Committee.

There was, however, some opposition. Within a week of its activities being suspended the neo-Maoist website *Utopia* demonstrated unusual pugnacity and, on April 12, posted a banner which read: "However you shut us down or censor us, we *Utopia* will always support Bo Xilai!". Popular resentment at the action against Bo Xilai, though quickly quelled, surfaced when protests occurred in Chongqing on April 10-11 and banners eulogizing Bo Xilai and demanding his return to Chongqing were unfurled on April 12.

The Party Centre did not lose sight either of Bo Xilai's fairly wide support in the PLA, implying that his links in the PLA were being investigated and negotiations over his future must have been tough. At least four leading articles and editorials were published in the Liberation Army Daily and People's Daily between February and April 12, exhorting the PLA to unite "more closely around the Party centre with comrade Hu Jintao as General Secretary" of the Party. The PLA was urged to adhere to the principle of "absolute loyalty" to the Party. On March 25, hours before Hu Jintao departed for Seoul, the Global Times website headlined an article urging all PLA troops to be "more tightly united around the Party Center, the CMC and Chairman Hu (of the CMC)." On March 27, a Liberation Army Daily article candidly declared: "new developments have arisen as profound changes have taken place in the world, nation, and the Party. … We should ensure that all troops resolutely follow the command of the Party Central, Central Military Commission, and Chairman Hu."

Separately, inspecting troops in late March in the Lanzhou Military Region and Shaanxi Military District, Guo Boxiang, CMC Vice Chairman, asked for "greater stress on building the forces ideologically and politically" and greater emphasis on "maintaining the security and stability of the military forces." Controls on the Party's and national security apparatus were simultaneously sought to be tightened. Reports in this period revealed that 3000 public security cadres had been sent for "political re-education". Early this April, a national conference of heads of county public security organisations was convened in Beijing.

It is now virtually certain that top Party leaders and influential veteran retired cadres will converge on the seaside resort of Beidaihe this summer for intense negotiations and bargaining to select candidates for the PBSC, PB and many for the Central Committee (CC). Bo Xilai's removal from the race has created an opportunity for other aspirants. Those closely associated with him, however, will come in for special scrutiny and might see their chances blighted. This would be equally applicable to those in line for promotions in the PLA and to the Central Military Commission. Influencing negotiations will be veterans like Song Ping, Qiao Shi, Li Ruihuan, Jiang Zemin and Li Peng. Chances of the emergence of compromise choices is high because it would allow for greater consensus among top leaders. Xi Jinping will also prefer to back individuals who have only one term so that he could more easily elevate his supporters at the next Congress.

A tussle is simultaneously underway between Hu Jintao and Xi Jinping for installation of their respective loyalists and supporters in the PBSC, PB and CC. Hu Jintao is keen to ensure his legacy and retain some influence, while Xi Jinping wants to strengthen his hand and authority and minimise Hu Jintao's influence by inducting more supporters into the higher echelons. Xi Jinping, however, has to tread cautiously as he cannot afford to be deprived of Hu Jintao's crucial support. The manner in which he chose to side with Hu Jintao against Bo Xilai, though he had earlier indicated support to Bo Xilai and also tried to co-opt Maoist sentiment, shows that Hu Jintao wields a lot of influence. Xi Jinping would have also decided to oust Bo Xilai to pre-empt having to contend with a potential alternate centre of power that could impose curbs on his authority.

The months leading up to the 18th Party Congress this October, will be sensitive and crucial for China's leaders. Many of the personnel selections for senior positions in the Party and military will now be subject to review. There is increased probability of Hu Jintao retaining the position of Military Commission Chairman for another year. Recent events have dented the CCP's image and China's leadership will be vigilant for signs of dissidence, including in ethnic minority-dominated regions. Strict inner-Party discipline and stringent security precautions will be enforced in the coming months, accompanied by a tougher posture on issues of sovereignty. Recent events nonetheless confirm that serious tensions exist within the Party and that reining in ambitions of senior Party cadres will become increasingly difficult.

This was published as an Issue Brief by the Centre for Air Power Studies on April 15, 2012.

7. China's Internal Policy: Iron Fist in a Velvet Glove

Having recalibrated China's foreign policy, to reflect Beijing's perception of its enhanced international standing, by ushering in a muscular approach, Chinese President Hu Jintao has now turned his attention to domestic issues. The focus is on the two restive, sensitive border provinces of Tibet and Xinjiang. Strong suspicion has occasionally been officially voiced that the US and US Congress-funded National Endowment for Democracy (NED) have been supporting Tibetan and Uyghur separatist groups in both Autonomous Regions. The Chinese Communist Party (CCP) leadership, which earlier this year finalized its policy for Tibetans and the Tibet Autonomous Region (TAR), is now hammering out a long term policy for the Xinjiang-Uyghur Autonomous Region (XUAR). This will be promulgated by mid-2010. Tibetan 'separatism' and Uyghur 'terrorism', both listed as China's highest priority internal security issues, are now at centre stage. The violent disturbances, which erupted across Tibet and Tibetan dominated areas in March 2008 and the fresh outbreak of violence in the Xinjiang-Uyghur Autonomous Region last September, were the catalysts. Both caught the authorities unawares. The policy is being formulated at the highest levels of the Party under the personal direction of China's President Hu Jintao and the nine-member CCP Central Committee (CC) Politburo Standing Committee. 'Nei jun, wei sung', or as the Chinese translate it: 'Iron fist in a velvet glove', aptly describes these policies which combine development and suppression. There is now, however, going to be more iron in these fists.

After the March 2008 riots the Chinese authorities intensified armed patrolling in the Tibet Autonomous Region (TAR) and Tibetan majority areas and redoubled domestic propaganda efforts. Re-education was stepped up and stiff punishments were meted out to those found guilty of abetting or participating in violence. Units of the People's Armed Police (PAP) and PLA were deployed in areas considered sensitive throughout TAR. Negotiations with the Dalai Lama's envoys, intended mainly to assuage international concern about human rights and contain restiveness among Tibetans inside China, continued however and the invitation extended for the next round of talks in early 2010, set the time table for finalization of policies relating to Tibet.

Policies have now been put on a long term basis and an enlarged meeting of the CCP CC Politburo, the first such held in nine years, was convened in Beijing on January 8, 2010 under the chairmanship of Hu Jintao to discuss Tibet. This was the first meeting of the Politburo since the riots in Tibet in March 2008. The presence throughout the meeting of Hu Jintao, who combines the posts of CCP CC General Secretary, Chairman of the Central Military Commission and China's President, Premier Wen Jiabao, Vice President Xi Jinping, widely tipped to be Hu Jintao's successor, and Li Keqiang, tipped to take over as the next Premier, underscored its importance. The policies and decisions regarding personnel appointments adopted at this meeting, therefore, have the endorsement of the successor leadership.

The tone for this high-level meeting was set by Hu Jintao, who launched a rare personal attack on the 74-year old Dalai Lama. He accused the exiled Tibetan leader of engaging in 'Tibetan independence' activities and 'sabotaging' social stability in the Tibetan region. He warned that his government would take 'substantial measures' to ensure 'normal order' of Tibetan Buddhism in Tibet. Hu Jintao, unusually candidly, admitted the existence of discontent in Tibet and influence exerted by the Dalai Lama by stating that Tibet faced 'special contradictions between people of all ethnic groups and separatist forces led by the Dalai clique'. Hinting at future policies, he exhorted the TAR Government to prevent and strike at 'penetration and sabotage' by 'Tibetan independence' separatists to 'safeguard social stability, the socialist legal system, national unity and ethnic solidarity'.

This Politburo meeting was followed by the TAR People's Congress from January 10-15, 2010, which unveiled tougher policies and more stringent controls over Tibet and Tibetans. Most obvious was the appointment of Padma Choling as Governor of TAR. 58-year old Padma Choling, who served seventeen years in the People's Liberation Army (PLA) from 1969-86 in the Tibet and Qinghai provinces and was TAR Deputy Governor since 2003, is reputed to be a tough enforcer of Beijing's uncompromising policy against the 'three evil forces', namely separatism, terrorism and religious extremism. He served as Secretary of the Party cell in the important TAR Party General Office when Hu Jintao was TAR Party Secretary from 1988-92 and has easy access to the Chinese President. Padma Choling's appointment will reinforce the policies being pursued by Zhang Qingli, the powerful TAR Party Secretary. Zhang Qingli, who also has a PLA background and is a hardliner, had described the Dalai Lama as 'a wolf in monk's clothes' and 'a devil with a human face, but the heart of a beast' after the March 2008 riots.

The immediate riposte from TAR authorities to the Dalai Lama's 10th March 2010 statement confirm that a tough policy for dealing with the Dalai Lama is in place. Padma Choling described it as 'divisive' and asked him to stop 'splittist' activities, while Lhasa Vice Mayor Jigme Namgyal described the Dalai Lama as 'a separatist who uses religion as a cloak'. He dismissed the Dalai Lama's claim of 'annihilation of Buddhism' as an 'audacious lie'. All official Chinese reactions noted the Dalai Lama's use of the term 'East Turkestan' to refer to Xinjiang as evidence of his explicit support to Uyghur separatists and China's official media reacted sharply. Days earlier the Chinese-selected Panchen Lama had, for the first time, been elevated to an official position and appointed Vice President of the Chinese Buddhist Association.

The high-level Tibet Planning Forum held in Beijing from January 18-20, 2010 which followed these meetings, was the fifth such meeting ever held. In a departure from past practice, delegates from all Tibetan areas in China participated. The Forum, which had development and stability as its themes, approved a massive package for TAR as well as Tibetan areas in the adjoining provinces of Sichuan, Yunnan, Gansu and Qinghai – the first time that the scope of developmental assistance was expanded to these Tibetan areas outside TAR. The decision confirmed that in addition to developing Tibet and improving the peoples' living standards, enhanced and stringent controls on the populace will be enforced. Hu Jintao described the slogan for the conference as 'Chinese characteristics, Tibetan flavour' (zhongguo tese, xizang tedian). He promised an influx of investment, technology and experts and fixed the target for growth of TAR's GDP at 12 percent. It is estimated that Tibet's GDP in 2009 would touch US$ 6.4 billion. Another brief report which has attracted little comment was that PLA personnel would receive a bonus of approximately US$ 24,000 as incentive for serving in Tibet. The terms governing grant of this bonus are yet unknown, but it could be a precursor to creation of a Corps similar to the Xinjiang Production and Construction Corps.

Long term policies are now being formulated for the restive, violence prone Xinjiang-Uyghur Autonomous Region (XUAR) and likely to be promulgated in the coming months. These will be discussed and approved at the highest level by the nine-member CCP CC Politburo Standing Committee, also in a 'Forum on Xinjiang'. Security and stability along with development will be the main items on the agenda. After the recurrence of severe rioting in the Xinjiang-Uyghur Autonomous Region (XUAR) last year, officially labelled as the 'March 14th' and July 5th' incidents, hard-liner XUAR Party Secretary Wang Lequan declared that it had been a 'profound lesson learned in blood'. He asserted that the authorities would take 'most resolute and strongest measures to deal with the enemies' latest attempt at sabotage'. China promptly launched a 'strike hard' campaign in Xinjiang resulting in the arrests of thousands of individuals, and Uyghurs throughout China were singled out for checks.

Since the beginning of this year a series of measures have been taken to further augment the security infrastructure in XUAR. In addition to intensified re-education and propaganda campaigns, China additionally unleashed a propaganda offensive against the US-based World Uyghur Conference and Uyghur leader Ms Rebiya Kadeer. It was decided that funding for public security would be doubled in 2010. A proposal in the current budget has accordingly been made for RMB 2.89 billion (US$ 423 million) in contrast to the RMB 1.54 billion allocated in 2009. A new set of 'Regulations on the Comprehensive Management of Social Security in the Xinjiang-Uyghur Autonomous Region' have been drafted and began to be enforced from February 1, 2010. The Xinjiang People's Armed Police (PAP) Corps set up its brigade-strength Sixth Detachment on February 8, 2010 in Urumqi. The PAP Deputy Chief of Staff Pan Changjie and XUAR Vice Chairman Jappa Abibulla described it as the 'Fist to maintain Stability'. PAP units, totalling 30,000 troops, are already spread across XUAR and deployed in Urumqi, Kashgar, Ili, Hotan and Bayingolin.

Paving the way for the Forum on Xinjiang and on the occasion of the 10th anniversary of the 'Western Region Development', XUAR Chairman, Nur Bekri recently enumerated the Autonomous Region's achievements over the past decade and indicated the areas of focus for future development. He noted the rapid increase in people's incomes and the accelerated development of transportation infrastructure. He added that XUAR will have 3 more airports by 2010 raising the total to 17. Crude oil output and natural gas production, in which the XUAR is already ranked second and first in the country respectively, is set to rise. The number of state-owned enterprises is expected to increase from the present 89. In conclusion, Nur Bekri asserted that though last year's 'July 5th incident' had caused 'huge damage' to the enterprises in XUAR, 'no force can destroy' the unity of the people or alter the development trends.

The emphasis on security is evident in the appointment of Zhou Yongkang, Politburo Standing Committee member and Head of the CCP CC Central Commission of Political Science and Law – the country's highest body overseeing the security apparatus – as Head of the 'Leading Group for the Preparation for the Central Work Conference on Xinjiang'. In his address to the plenary meeting of the Leading Group, Zhou Yongkang stressed the need to promote ethnic equality and unity. He said that harmony and stability were essential to national unification and security for maintaining lasting stability and peace in Xinjiang. Over a hundred reports have been prepared by the Research Office of the State Nationalities Affairs Commission on 'new problems' in the relationship between ethnic nationalities. Like the Forum on Tibet, this proposed Forum also has 'leapfrogging development' high on the agenda.

Extensive preparatory work has been done for this first ever Forum on Xinjiang. According to reports over 500 cadres from 64 departments travelled to villages and towns in different parts of Xinjiang. Special attention was paid to the Xinjiang Production and Construction Corps. A number of central departments despatched study groups to examine their respective areas and these included the: CCP CC Organisation Dept; CCP CC Propaganda Dept; CCP CC United Front Work Dept; Ministry of Foreign Affairs; the Ministry of Public Security; and the Chinese Academy of Social Sciences (CASS). A number of central enterprises like the China National Petroleum Corporation (CNPC), PRC National Energy Adminstration etc are involved. The Forum will issue documents clarifying regulations for the proper development of Xinjiang's oil, gas and other 'superior resources'. It will try to resolve the uneven development between North and South Xinjiang and issue guidelines for the protection of Xinjiang's ecology and environment. Importantly, the Xinjiang Production and Construction Corps is to be reorganized and transformed to fight against 'Xinjiang independence' and 'splittist forces'.

So as to ensure proper implementation over the longer term, the Forum on Xinjiang will also decide on large-scale reshuffles of Ministry and Commission-level officials and PLA Generals. A number of new officials will be drafted in.

The policies finalized by the Forums on Tibet and Xinjiang will be long term and intended to quell resistance by China's largest ethnic minorities. In addition to neutralizing the Dalai Lama's influence among Tibetans inside China, another publicly undeclared objective is to neutralize US support to the separatists in Tibet and Xinjiang. A likely side effect of the prospective massive development plans will be to reorient China's economy inwards and boost domestic consumption. The Forums will boost exploitation of the mineral and other natural resources in both provinces, thus enhancing China's energy security and facilitating it's modernization effort. Additionally, the problem of uneven economic growth between coastal and hinterland provinces will be somewhat ameliorated. Finally, after reorienting China's foreign policy, Hu Jintao would have left a lasting imprimateur on the country's domestic policy concerning minorities.

This was published as an Issue Brief by the Centre for Air Power Studies on February 15, 2010.

8. Highlights of Recent Session of China's National People's Congress

The 10-day Fourth Plenary Session of China's National People's Congress (NPC), which convened in Beijing on March 5, 2011, launched China on an entirely new development path. Attended by 2,987 Deputies, it revealed some interesting facets with potentially long term implications. The nomination of former Chinese Foreign Minister Li Zhaoxing as official spokesman for the session indicated the Chinese leadership's sensitivity to the international audience.

Reminiscent of 2005, when Hu Jintao and Wen Jiabao successfully effected a major policy shift away from Deng Xiaoping's philosophy of 'allowing some to get rich first' to that of 'common prosperity', Chinese President Hu Jintao and Premier Wen Jiabao again boldly discarded the economic model followed by China for the past three decades. They have sought to anticipate the requirements of the current decade and balance the nationwide upgrading of human resource skills with pronounced emphasis on science and technology, along with the compulsions of retaining the Chinese Communist Party's (CCP) popularity and support among the masses.

Three reports presented to the NPC, all of which had been discussed by the Politburo over six months, signal that China will switch to a development path which gives greater emphasis to: scientific and technological innovation; upgrading of peoples' skills and education; boosting domestic consumption; and expansion of social insurance and health benefits to the majority of people in the rural and urban areas.

Wen Jiabao's work-report particularly appreciated the "major breakthroughs" in "cutting-edge science and technology such as the manned space mission, the lunar exploration programme and supercomputers". He said GDP will grow by 8 percent this year – the minimum to stave off social unrest – and the Consumer Price Index (CPI) will be kept around 4 percent. Over 9 million jobs will be created for urban residents and efforts made to reduce income disparities and raise earnings of low-income groups. Special reference was made to ameliorating conditions of the 200 million rural migrant population. The need to allow people who have left agriculture for other work and meet the conditions for settling in cities to become urban residents would be addressed. Focus was maintained on the agriculture sector, irrigation works and enhancing foodgrain production. China will extend the experiment for new type of old age insurance for rural residents to 40 percent of the counties and expand medical insurance subsidies for rural and urban residents. Premier Wen Jiabao specifically mentioned expanding use of the RMB in cross-border trade and investment and making it convertible under capital accounts.

"Great progress" in "modernization of national defence and the army" was acknowledged as was the need to strengthen the security apparatus, especially information security and secrecy, and maintain social stability. The defence budget was raised by 12.7 percent to 601.1 billion yuan (US$ 91.7 billion).

Highlights of the Twelfth Five Year Plan are: population will be controlled below 1.39 billion, or natural growth rate will be kept under 6.5 percent; the average economic growth rate is targeted at 7 percent and GDP should exceed 55 trillion yuan (RMB), up from the 39.8 trillion yuan in 2010; rate of urbanization will be 51.5 percent; value added output of emerging strategic industries will account for 8 percent of GDP; coastal regions will transform from being the "world's factory" to the hub of R&D, high-end manufacturing and service sector; spending on R&D will rise to 2.2 percent of GDP; foreign investment will be welcomed in agriculture, high-tech and environment protection industries and nuclear power will be developed more efficiently with preconditions of ensuring safety; construction of large scale hydropower plants will gain momentum in south west China; the country's optical cables will extend to 10.95 million kms and number of internet access ports will rise to 223 million, an increase of 1 million and 35 million respectively; length of high speed railway will increase by 13,000 kms to reach 45,000 kms, totaling 99,000 kms; length of highway network will reach 83,000 kms; China will open six new airports to air traffic, including an airport being built at Beijing, bringing the total to 181; and China will build 36 million affordable apartments for low-income people.

The economic development path now outlined moves China away from the export and investment-led model to one that is driven by Chinese consumers. The Twelfth Five Year Plan (2011-2015) envisages three major shifts. The manufacturing model that has promoted exports and investment-led growth is to be replaced by a labour-intensive services model. This will include wholesale and retail trade, domestic transport and supply-chain logistics, health care, leisure and hospitality. This is expected to boost job creation and yield the benefits of cleaner and greener growth. The second feature will be enhancement of especially rural-sector wages, which are planned to increase annually at 7 percent in real terms. Wages in the rural sector are currently 30 percent less than in urban areas. Reforms and tax policies that will increase rural purchasing power, broaden rural land ownership, and use technology to raise agricultural production, will be introduced. Shrinkage of cultivable land will not be allowed and foodgrain production will not only be maintained at 500 million tons but be enhanced by 50 million tons. There will be need to revise the '*hukou*' system, which restricts movement of people away from their birth-place, to address the problems of the 15-20 million annual rural-to-urban migrants. The third aspect of the Plan is intended to promote domestic consumption by accelerating building of the social safety net to reduce fear-driven high savings. This includes policies and subsidies to encourage rural residents to purchase home appliances. Social security, pensions, medical and unemployment insurance schemes are to be expanded substantially, with basic pension insurance and medical insurance systems covering the entire population by the end of the Plan period. Last year basic medical insurance covered 432.06 million urban residents, an increase of 30.59 percent over last year, and 835 million rural residents or 96.3 percent of the population. The government also decided not to allow the Consumer Price Index (CPI) to rise above 4 percent and will ensure availability of grain and essential food items in rural and urban areas. The increase in CPI this year has been attributed to international market pressures.

There is pronounced focus on the upgradation of science and technology and scientific innovation. The NDRC report stresses that the government will promote projects in the National Broadband Internet Agenda, cloud computing, the Internet of Things, integrated circuits, flat panel displays, space infrastructure, regional aircraft and industrialization of general aviation aircraft as well as health and internet application. Education plays a major role in this effort to transform China's economic profile from being a mere manufacturer to an innovator and producer of high-technology goods for export. Accordingly in 2011, spending on education is planned to reach 4 percent of GDP and gross enrollment ratio in secondary education is expected to reach 84 percent. Plans call for enrolling 6.75 million undergraduate students and 560,000 graduate students (against the 6.618 million undergraduate and 538,000 graduate students in 2010) in regular institutions of higher learning. China's taxation, fiscal and insurance policies will be appropriately amended to facilitate Chinese companies to 'go global'. China will continue to 'guide' foreign investments towards high-end manufacturing, high-tech industries, modern service industries, new energy and environmental protection industries.

Affirming this emphasis on science and technology, a Xinhua dispatch in mid-March publicized a report of the Chinese Academy of Science and Technology for Development (CASTED), which ranked China twenty first among the world's forty most innovative countries. The report asserted that by 2020, China will be an 'innovative country' with scientific progress expected to contribute 60 percent of the nation's economic development and R&D investment would jump to 2.5 percent of GDP. A 'National Exhibition of Major Scientific, Technological Achievements over the last Five Years' also opened in Beijing on March 9.

The NPC and CPPCC discussed issues of concern to ordinary people, including the impact of high prices of apartments on young citizens. CPPCC delegate Liang Bei, Director of the Real Estate Research Centre at Beijing University of International Business and Economics, wryly suggested that women over twenty whose boyfriends cannot afford housing should change partners in favour of men who are over forty and can afford housing!

Three Deputies represented the over 200 million migrant workers in China, highlighting this problem. The CCP leadership has taken major initiatives to ameliorate the living and working conditions of rural migrant workers. A major pilot project underway in Chengdu is planned to be expanded across numerous counties this year.

This NPC's composition reflected the economic changes in China over the past thirty years. It included 70 Deputies accounting for almost US$ 70 billion in wealth. Private businessmen and entrepreneurs represented at the NPC and CPPCC sessions were comforted when the NDRC report reiterated that "non-public sector" would be encouraged and government will create "an institutional environment for economic entities under all ownership forms to use factors of production on an equal basis in accordance with the law, compete as equals in the market and be equally protected by the law". Wang Wenbao, Vice Chairman of the All-China Federation of Industry and Commerce and CPPCC member, urged 'earnest implementation' of the central government's policies to encourage development of private business. By end 2010, he recalled, China had 42 million private and self-employed businesses and China's private sector created more than 75 percent of the jobs, 60 percent of the GDP and 50 percent of total tax revenues.

An online posting about the high personal tax liability, during the NPC, generated excitement among 'netizens'. It claimed that an individual earning 10,000 yuan a month would have barely 4,400 yuan left after taxes. The ensuing public debate prompted the Deputy Head of the Research Institute for Fiscal Science under China's Ministry of Finance to clarify that an individual earning 10,000 yuan a month pays only 780 yuan in taxes.

A development with potentially far-reaching implications quietly taking place in China over the past few years found reflection in the NPC. This is the increased activity of 'Left', or neo-Maoist forces, who are particularly critical of the rising incidence of corruption, widening gap between the rich and poor, growing instances of land grab, and collapse of faith in communist ideology. Public debate between the 'Left' and more liberal elements within China's power elite has increased, with the 'Left' website 'Utopia' posting a picture of Qin Xiao, Chairman of the 'Baoyuan Foundation' and a 'Princeling', among those of nine dissidents with nooses around their necks. Indicating the influence of 'Left' forces, the authorities did not erase this posting while removing almost three hundred and fifty million others labeled as 'offensive'. Attacks against proponents of greater political freedom and restraints on state sector enterprises also increased as the NPC and CPPCC drew near.

Ms Fang Ming, a NPC Deputy and China National Radio anchor, aired 'Left' sentiments during the session when she recommended a ban on advertising on CCTV-I and on local flagship TV networks to "prevent commercial interests from leading media around by the nose". She cited the example of Chongqing Satellite TV, which has recently gone 'Red' by removing all commercials and telecasting a steady stream of public interest programming.

Official Xinhua reports on the meetings of senior central leaders with NPC Deputies from various provinces similarly yielded interesting insights.

Significantly, Politburo Standing Committee member and CPPCC Chairman Jia Qinglin, while meeting delegates representing Taiwan referred only to "peaceful reunification and one country two-systems". No belligerent remarks by NPC Deputies or commentators was reported. Jia Qinglin did, however, speak of the need to realise "rejuvenation of the Chinese nation and national revival... in promoting the peaceful development of cross-Straits relations...".

Politburo Standing Committee member Li Changchun spoke to Guizhou Deputies of building "a system of public cultural services and development of Red Tourism". Official Chinese statistics reveal that "Red tourism" in Zunyi, has been growing each year. Xi Jinping has also, interestingly, traveled twice in six months to Mao's home in Shaoshan, Hunan. This March in Shaoshan, he praised Mao's 'spiritual legacy'.

There was a noticeable difference in tenor of remarks of central leaders to Deputies representing provinces and autonomous regions where large numbers of minority nationalities reside. This was the case with Ningxia-Hui, Xinjiang and Tibet.

He Guoqiang, Secretary of the Party's Discipline Inspection Commission and member of the Politburo Standing Committee, met Deputies from Ningxia-Hui Autonomous Region. He emphasized the importance of "building grass root party style and clean government" which, he said, "build the state's political power". He exhorted them to "step up supervision of the education and administration of the ideology and work style of the grass root cadres...".

China's Security Czar and Politburo Standing Committee member

Zhou Yongkang interacted with delegates from Xinjiang-Uyghur Autonomous Region. He stressed that the "socialist legal system with Chinese characteristics has provided a forceful legal guarantee for unifying the will and action of the people of all nationalities…". He urged continuance "of educational activities on the main theme of love the great motherland and build a beautiful home" and declared it necessary to "relentlessly pay close attention to the work to safeguard stability and strike against all kinds of separatist and sabotage activities according to the law in order to safeguard social harmony and stability..".'

Tibet merited special attention. The Chinese leadership again projected the Beijing-appointed Panchen Lama who duly greeted Tibetan delegates and urged people to work for "betterment of the motherland". An official propaganda blitz tried to diminish the Dalai Lama's stature. A lengthy article claimed that the Dalai Lama's nephew in Taktser was wealthy because of donations and that two of this nephew's three children were communist party members! Chinese President Hu Jintao met the Tibet delegation and stressed the need for '…stability to boost leapfrog development and maintain perennial stability in Tibet." He reiterated calls of the Tibet Autonomous Region (TAR) Party Secretary, Governor and other Deputies to relentlessly continue the struggle against the "Dalai Lama clique".

Wen Jiabao spoke of the need to strengthen national defence and asserted that the army should "…constantly enhance its capability to accomplish a range of military tasks, the most paramount of which is winning local wars under information age conditions". Priority must be given to "raising the overall ideological and political standards of the army". Retired Rear Admiral Yang Yi elaborated that "the issue of crisis escalation and even the danger of military conflict exist in many hot spots, especially those around China. China needs to strengthen its military forces to defend national security and keep peace and stability in the region". Chinese military commentators separately observed that a minimum of ten percent annual hikes in defence budgets would henceforth be the norm.

A preliminary plenary session of the PLA delegation attending the NPC was, significantly, chaired by the Director of the PLA's General Political Department (GPD), Li Jinai. The nomination of Central Military Commission (CMC) Vice Chairman Guo Boxiong as Head of the PLA delegation and Xu Caihou – who oversees political and ideological affairs in the CMC – and Li Jinai, as Deputy Heads reveals that the Central Military Commission (CMC) and PLA leadership are focused on modernization of military hardware and political and ideological education.

Major General Luo Yuan, former Deputy Director of the Military Research Department at the Academy of Military Sciences (AMS) and CPPCC delegate, clarified that the enhanced budget would be spent on: (i) countering threats of separatists in Tibet, Xinjiang and Taiwan; (ii) modernizing the military; (iii) handling the increasing number of diversified tasks, missions and threats; (iv) sharing the rewards of reforms and opening up; (v) coping with inflation; and (vi) making up for low and negative growth in military spending during the first decade of reform and opening up.

The importance of political and ideological education in the PLA, emphasized in Military Commission Chairman, Hu Jintao's interaction with PLA Deputies, was reinforced with the launch of a year-long political and ideological campaign in the PLA promptly after the NPC session.

This NPC plenum will have far-reaching implications. In addition to boosting China's economy it will give a quantum jump to China's scientific and technological capability, raising it equal to European levels. The disclosure that "construction of large scale hydropower plants will gain momentum in south west China", could imply diversion of the Brahmaputra. The double-digit hikes in China's defence budget, as GDP grows to an estimated $ 55 trillion by 2015, will mean acquisition of hi-tech weaponry by the PLA. Intensified training in joint integrated operations and enhanced emphasis on informatisation to 'fight and win local wars', will additionally need to be monitored by India. Finally, China's trading partners, like US and Europe and neighbouring countries like South Korea, are keenly watching implementation of the new economic plans since increased domestic consumption could facilitate export of goods by them. An unstated downside is that as China's plans succeed, its surplus savings will be reduced leaving it with less to invest in US Treasury Bills.

This was published as an Issue Brief by the Centre for Air Power Studies on May 15, 2011.

9. China: Initial Assessment of the Fifth Session of the Eleventh National Peoples Congress

The Fifth and final 10-day session of China's Eleventh National People's Congress (NPC)—China's version of a parliament—opened in Beijing on March 5, 2012, amidst predictable high security. In conformity with past practice, a 2-day meeting of the Chinese People's Political Consultative Conference (CPPCC), presided over by Politburo Standing Committee member and CPPCC Chairman Jia Qinglin, concluded in Beijing on March 3, 2012.

Restiveness in China's border regions of Tibet and Xinjiang was pushed to the forefront when the opening day of the NPC coincided with the immolation of the third Tibetan in three days in the Aba region of Sichuan province and trouble erupted in Kashgar where twelve Uyghurs were killed. The official media did not report these events, though the situation in both regions figured subsequently during panel discussions of NPC Deputies .

The NPC session, which will be the last before Chinese President Hu Jintao and Premier Wen Jiabao retire at the Eighteenth Party Congress in October 2012, commenced at 9 am in the Great Hall of the People with the presentation of a 30-page 'Report on the Work of the Government' by 69-year old Chinese Premier Wen Jiabao to 2,987 NPC Deputies. Other reports presented were the 'National Development and Reform Commission (NDRC) Draft Plan for National Economic and Social Development' and the Ministry of Finance's 'Budget Report'.

Premier Wen Jiabao's speech was shorter than in previous years and concluded in 70-odd minutes. Possibly reflecting the factional infighting within the Chinese Communist Party (CCP) for positions in its Politburo (PB) and Politburo Standing Committee (PBSC), none of the reports contained any bold assertions or initiatives. On close scrutiny the Government's Work Report and NDRC Report, however, reveal a pronounced bias in favour of reform indicating the Government's resolve. The reports this time also sought to largely equally balance the concerns of rural and urban residents. The association with this Work Report of PBSC Member and Vice Premier Li Keqiang and Vice Premier Wang Qishan, an upward mobile 'princeling' and reputed tough no-nonsense economist, would indicate the successor leadership's agreement with its contents.

Salient features this year included Chinese Premier Wen Jiabao's decision to: reduce GDP growth to 7.5 percent (for the first time since 2005); annually create 9 million new jobs in towns and cities; hold registered unemployment at below 4.6 percent; revise the poverty line at 2,300 yuan; ease registration requirements to allow rural workers to secure benefits and work in cities; contain any increase in the consumer price index (CPI) below 4 percent (it rose to 5.4 percent in 2011); and, increase the total volume of imports and exports by 10 percent. The RMB floating rate would be allowed to become more flexible and use of the RMB for cross-border trade and investment would be expanded. Allocations for agriculture, farmers, social security, medical insurance as also old-age pensions for rural and non-working urban residents were enhanced. Expenditure on education and S&T was increased.

Important recommendations in the Finance Ministry's Budget were: enhanced expenditure on security; revision of Individual Income Tax; raising of VAT; relieving small and medium businesses of the tax and fee burden; and halving the tax on small businesses.

The 40-page NDRC report noted the global economic outlook as "grim" and number of "new international and regional hot-spots" as increasing. Retaining last year's focus on S&T and Information Technology, it said spending on R&D as a percentage of GDP will increase. Significant among the proposals were to: restructure heavy and chemical industry to reduce their share in the national economy; boost sales of consumer goods by 14 percent; accelerate development of the central and eastern routes of the South-North Water Diversion Project (there was no mention of the Western Route possibly because of its sensitivity); and reform coal, natural gas and domestic fuel prices this year. It simultaneously assured that the government will adhere to the "basic economic system where public ownership is dominant and economic entities with diverse forms of ownership" would co-exist. Touching on an issue that has excited popular concern, it said land reforms will guide transfers of land-use rights which are "legal, voluntary and compensated".

Compared to the Work Report of 2004, where "Reform" was mentioned 56 times and more than in other years, it was mentioned 70 times in this Work Report along with calls for further deepening of reforms. China's official media took the cue and numerous media commentaries on the subject referred to "Reform". By March 6, at least 70 mentions of "Reform" were noticed.

This was preceded by calls over the past many months by reputed liberal academics, economists and some 'princelings' for more and deeper reforms. A Tsinghua University report authored by Professor Sun Liping, former doctoral adviser to Xi Jinping, current Vice President and successor apparent and released on 9 January, 2012, warned that "vested interests" are holding back reform and seeking to perpetuate the transitional system in which they can maximize their interests, thus leaving China in a "transition trap". It accused these interest groups of using "maintaining stability" as a pretext to resist reform. It cautioned that such "rigid thinking" will ultimately "fuel social conflicts and even turn daily conflicts into suspicions about and grudges against the system". Advancing radical suggestions it recommended that China break out of the trap by embracing values like democracy, rule of law and revitalizing "society through political reform". Such calls attracted opposition from high leadership levels in the Party, as evidenced by the China Youth Daily, People's Daily and others who published this report, removing it from their websites within hours of publication.

An earlier confidential Tsinghua University report released in 2010, had set the tone by disclosing that expenditure on internal security in 2010 had reached 514 billion yuan and that public safety expenditures, which increased by 16% last year, would be augmented by a further 8.9%. Arguing that with the increase in social conflicts social stability has become a "knot" in present-day society, the report said that to deal with social conflicts the State has to first, strengthen the capacity of the system in order to accommodate conflicts and clashes and, second, improve the capacity to use institutionalised modes to resolve these conflicts. Good institutions do not eliminate conflicts, but resolve them by applying institutionalised modes of resolution, it said. Therefore, it is necessary to first of all be able to accommodate contradictions and conflicts.

Nevertheless, the Finance Ministry's report revealed the Chinese leadership's anxiety at the growing incidence of popular protest by substantially increasing spending on police, state security, armed militia and other domestic security forces by 11.5 percent. For 2012, China set combined central and local government spending on domestic security at 701.8 billion yuan (US$ 111.4 billion), compared with 629.3 billion yuan in 2011. The bulk of these allocations are reflected under provincial and local government outlays. The central government's domestic security budget for 2012 is 182.3 billion yuan, a rise of 7.7 percent.

Defence spending more than doubled since 2006 and registered a 11.4 percent increase to touch 670 billion yuan (US$ 106.4 billion), exceeding US $ 100 billion for the first time ever. Like last year,

Premier Wen Jiabao said this was necessary to enhance the capability of the armed forces to "win local wars under information age conditions". He added that the PLA would strengthen ideological and political standards and adherence to the principle of "the Party having absolute leadership over the armed forces". Wen Jiabao also, pointedly and for the first time, declared "we will run the armed forces with strict discipline".

NPC Spokesman and former Chinese Foreign Minister, Li Zhaoxing, assured "China's limited military strength is aimed at safeguarding sovereignty, national security and territorial integrity and will not pose a threat to other countries." Claiming that China's military spending had actually decreased as a proportion of GDP, he said the defense budget would mostly be spent on daily necessities, training and equipment for military personnel and "research, experiment, procurement, repair, transport and storage of all weapons and equipment, including new types of weapons." The increased allocation reflects Beijing's concern on issues like the South China Sea, US activities in the Asia-Pacific, tension along the India-China border, etc., though Wen Jiabao's Report made none of the standard references to not ruling out the use of armed force for re-unification of Taiwan.

Interestingly, while share markets remained flat in Shanghai and elsewhere, defence-related enterprises listed on the Shanghai bourse promptly registered an increase in value. For example, the shares of China North Optical-Electrical Technology Co. (manufacturing military control systems and sensors) and China Dongfanghong Spacesat Co. (which builds satellites) immediately rose by 9.7 percent and 3.9 percent.

Education received a major budgetary boost and spending was increased by 16.4 percent to 378.132 billion yuan. China's National Bureau of Statistics publicised a secondary education boom in China where college education jumped 147 percent and 8,930 people of every 100,000 have attended university. Other reports disclosed that last year 128,000 Chinese students went to US universities.

S&T continues to receive special attention as does the promotion of innovation. Spending on S&T is being increased this year by 12.4 percent to 228.546 billion yuan. NDRC disclosed the launch of 'Innovation 200 Programme', and building of an additional 54 key national laboratories, 28 national engineering laboratories, 23 S&T infrastructure platforms, 88 enterprise technology centres and 173 laboratories and engineering research centres. Hi-tech industries grew 16.5 percent last year.

Apparently flowing from the Party Central Committee plenum last October where culture was the sole agenda item, a substantial allocation of 49.384 billion yuan has been made for culture and sports, including for "cultural resources related to the CCP".

Tibet and Xinjiang regions figured during the panel discussions of NPC Deputies. Wu Zegang, an ethnic Tibetan and head of Aba Prefecture in Sichuan, accused "the Dalai Lama clique and overseas separatist forces" of "leading Tibetan Buddhism onto the track of extremism." He said "to encourage self-immolations, they even offer a price of compensation for the dead. All these prove that self-immolations are pre-mediated political moves." PBSC member and CPPCC Chairman, Jia Qinglin asked authorities to, "resolutely crush the Dalai Lama clique's conspiracy of making Tibetan-inhabited areas unstable…", while Tibet Autonomous Region (TAR) Chairman Padma Choling assured Deputies that Tibet was "safe and stable".

China's official news agency 'Xinhua' attributed some interesting remarks to NPC Deputy and Xinjiang Governor, Nur Bekri. On March 5, he warned that China would "spare no efforts to prevent and crack down upon sabotage activities of the three evil forces of separatism, extremism and terrorism to ensure social stability". He said management of religious affairs would be strengthened in accordance with relevant laws. More interesting was Nur Bekri's remark on

March 7, that recent incidents of unrest in southern Xinjiang-Uyghur Autonomous Region stemmed from "Islamic separatists" with ties to militants in Pakistan.

During these discussions, Xinjiang Party Secretary Zhang Chunxian, asserted that authorities would "show no mercy to these terrorists and fight them unswervingly." The Administrative Commissioner of Kashgar Prefecture, Akbar Ghopur, said that "the three forces constantly try to infiltrate their extreme beliefs into the prefecture that borders Afghanistan and Pakistan."

Among the NPC's highlights was a very unusual disclosure, which was unmistakably linked to the infighting for positions in the PBSC at the forthcoming Party Congress. On the opening day of the NPC session, Chongqing Mayor Huang Qifan told Hongkong's Phoenix Television that Wang Lijun, Public Security Chief of the economically high-performing, centrally-administered Municipality, had gone to the US Consulate in Chengdu and was personally persuaded by the Mayor and other officials to leave peacefully and calmly. The disclosure confirmed speculation that Wang Lijun had attempted to defect. This statement by Wang Lijun's immediate superior directly indicted the Public Security Chief of espionage thus substantially deflecting responsibility from Chongqing Party Secretary and Politburo member Bo Xilai, a 'princeling' supported by Xi Jinping and who is viewed as likely to be promoted to the Politburo Standing Committee this October. The Mayor's statement is unusual because the CCP does not like to admit that its senior cadres have been caught spying. Quoting sources close to the CPPCC, Hongkong's South China Morning Post claimed that President Hu Jintao told Communist Party members among the CPPCC delegates in an internal briefing on March 3 evening, that Wang Lijun was a "traitor". These remarks hint at Bo Xilai's elevation to the PBSC this October.

China's second richest man, 66-year old Zong Qinghou, who is a NPC Deputy, called for an increased role for private business in the economy. He asked for a cut in taxes to allow private investment in the country's important industries. Zong Qinghou, whose personal net worth is US$ 10.7 billion, is Chairman of the Hangzhou Wahaha Group Co.

When the Chinese Premier encouraged Chinese companies to 'go global' and said restrictions would be eased to permit individuals to invest overseas, Zong Qinghou remarked that Xi Jinping was friendly to private business and would encourage them. He said Xi Jinping had gained experience of private business while serving in Zhejiang province.

Anticipatedly, there was no attempt to tinker with contentious issues and there was no suggestion to amend the 'one-child' policy.

The Work Report indirectly addressed the issue of profligate spending by Party and government cadres, which has been the subject of widespread critical comment in China including on micro-blogs. Premier Wen Jiabao announced that 98 central government departments, provincial and municipal governments including Beijing, Shanghai, Guangdong and Shaanxi had publicly declared expenditure on official overseas travel, official vehicles and official hospitality last year. He added that strict controls would be imposed in 2012 on official overseas trips, official vehicles and their use, and official hospitality.

Lu De, son of Deng Xiaoping's confidante and former culture minister Lu Dingyi and a 'princeling', had last year expressed regret that Party and government officials spent a third of all government revenue on luxury cars, travel, healthcare, banquets and other perks, adding "and yet we still call it the Communist Party and socialism." One report circulating inside China claimed the government annually spent US$ 15 billion on the purchase of luxury automobiles. Separately two Chinese scholars, Yu Liu and Dingding Chen, recently estimated that expenditure on foreign travel, healthcare, banquets, luxury cars etc by Party and government cadres in 2004 exceeded 900 billion yuan.

Concern was expressed in the Premier's Report, in order of priority, on the issues of social security, income distribution, and health care reform. Income disparity, income distribution and price regulation were identified as areas of concern. "Price" was mentioned 13 times in the Report and "housing prices" twice. The term "people's livelihood" received 13 mentions this year and "education" was mentioned 33 times, indicating the heightened attention to these issues. A reference to PM 2.5 (air quality index) appeared for the first time in this year's Work Report.

This NPC has been used by at least two aspirants to the PBSC to buttress their image. Wang Yang, a former Communist Youth League (CYL) cadre supported by President Hu Jintao and presently Party Secretary of Guangdong, suggested on March 6, that lengthy introductions and mandatory applause for speeches by seniors be abandoned. He suggested the strengthening of IPR and sought cuts in the authority of Ministers to veto projects recommended by provinces. On February 12, prior to opening of the NPC, CCP CC Propaganda Department Chief, Li Yunshan, released a book entitled 'On Cultural Construction' where he listed 6 points for cultural reform and development.

Days before convening of the NPC and barely a year before Premier Wen Jiabao's retirement, reports filtered out in late February 2012 that the Premier's younger son, Wen Yunsong, had been appointed Chairman of China Satellite Communications Co. (China Satcom), one of China's six largest telecommunications operators. Wen Yunsong, also known as Winston Wen, became Vice Chairman of China Satcom in 2010.

Unlike on earlier occasions, China's economic prosperity was manifest on the opening day of the NPC session. It was reflected in the increase in the personal worth of the 70 richest NPC Deputies, now estimated at US$ 90 billion, or a US$ 11.5 billion increase since 2010! Many NPC Deputies were fashionably turned out. Because of the media focus on this aspect, the CCP CC's Propaganda Department warned China's media, including the People's Daily and Xinhua, not to "hype the 'Two Sessions', gourmet food and the clothing and accessories of representatives." China's netizens, however, continue to monitor this aspect. One posting showed Li Xiaolin, daughter of former Chinese Premier Li Peng, in a US$ 2000 Emilio Pucci suit, observing it could outfit 200 children with warm clothes. Li Xiaolin, the CEO of China Power International Development Ltd., was perhaps targeted for her comment at this NPC session that "I think we should open a morality file on all citizens to control everyone and give them a 'sense of shame.'"

US@ 1 = RMB (Yuan)

This was published as an Issue Brief by the Centre for Air Power Studies on March 14, 2012.

10. China's Recent Policy of Assertiveness

China's current assertive posture has got alarm bells ringing in many world capitals, especially in Asia. Even countries usually careful not to offend China have expressed concern. What has aroused apprehension is the strong suggestion of military muscle in China's diplomacy and Beijing's demonstrated willingness in recent years to use force. This trend has become especially noticeable since late 2008. It reflects the Chinese leadership's assessment that national capabilities are now poised to merge with intentions, enabling China to overtly push on issues benefiting its national self-interest.

China's current policy, particularly towards its neighbours, however, has a history. In fact the formulation enunciated in 1979, that China needs a peaceful neighbourhood environment till it achieves its Modernisation goals, itself has inherent a time limitation. Deng Xiaoping's advice to successor leaders, to 'lie low, bide your time', supplemented this.

China's communist leadership has retained the ambition underpinned culturally by *Sanjiao*, or the Buddhist-Taoist-Confucian tradition preserved by a centuries-old bureaucratic legacy, that China must regain its self-perceived rightful role and influence in the world. Deng Xiaoping, along with other leaders of the Chinese Communist Party (CCP), believed that 'power flows from the barrel of a gun'. This was reflected in his decision to retain defence as an area of focus when he launched the Four Modernisations programme.

Deng Xiaoping brought in Geng Biao as Defence Minister with the objective of giving the PLA's senior echelons exposure to the advances made by foreign armies in military doctrine, tactics and technology. His directive to 'teach Vietnam a lesson', when senior

PLA Commanders remained complacent despite Deng's criticism of the condition and capabilities of the PLA, resulted in the PLA suffering severe unanticipated casualties and consequently being shocked into embracing efforts to modernize it. In a prescient move, which at the same time hinted at China's intention of using the PLA to robustly support its national security and foreign policy objectives, Deng Xiaoping took steps to modernize the fledgling PLA Navy. He envisaged that the PLA Navy would have to play an important role in future in safeguarding sea-lanes vital to China's commerce and recovering 'lost territories'. As far back as 1982, he appointed Liu Huaqing, then the only senior PLA officer with sea experience and the rank of Admiral, to modernize the PLA Navy and equip it with a doctrine. That a large role was envisaged for the PLA Navy in the future was underscored even then in Admiral Liu Huaqing's definition of the term 'coastal waters'. With Deng Xiaoping's approval he defined this to include 'the Yellow Sea, Eastern Sea (East China Sea), the Southern Sea (South China Sea), the Nansha Archipelago and Taiwan, the seas on this side and that side of Okinawa, as well as the Northern Region of the Pacific.' The role that the PLA would play in the future was, therefore, clearly not unanticipated.

Deng Xiaoping was equally conscious of the importance of the PLA in domestic politics. Particularly important was the PLA's role as the sword arm of the Chinese Communist Party (CCP). He ensured that the PLA remained the 'Party's army' and stayed subordinate to the Party. The PLA's usefulness to the Party in this role was demonstrated during the 'Tiananmen Incident' in 1989. He similarly sought to ensure that successor generations of Party Chiefs would secure the loyalty of the PLA. In 1987, he decided that the CCP Central Committee (CC) General Secretary would head the Military Commission, thereby combining in the Party Chief full powers over the Party, Army and Government. To prepare the Party General Secretary for this role it was decided he would initially serve as first Vice Chairman of the

Military Commission to familiarize himself with military affairs and build a support base in the PLA. He would later take over as Chairman. This policy was implemented for the first time with the appointment of Jiang Zemin as first Vice Chairman and subsequently as Chairman of the Military Commission. This was successfully repeated with his successor, Hu Jintao. Both leaders further strengthened the Party's already tight grip over the PLA to ensure that the military remained 'absolutely subordinate' to the Party and the Party General Secretary.

Successor generations of Chinese leaders inherited the ambition to 'recover' China's 'lost territories'. Modernization of the PLA was essential for realization of this ambition. The role of the PLA in implementation of national strategic and foreign policy was accordingly shaped. This was evident in the PLA doctrines as revised periodically. Though the US remained the prime source of threat and the PLA was being equipped to tackle it, by 2006 China had developed the doctrine of 'Winning short-duration Local Wars under Hi-tech Informatised Conditions'. The emphasis for the PLA was, therefore, to quickly 'win local wars' on its periphery. This doctrine suggested that China was preparing to, some time in the future, 'recover' its lost territories and areas of influence. Taiwan was for a while the primary focus. That focus expanded to actively include the South China Sea, described as a 'core national interest'. Modernisation of the PLA remained an unwavering central objective through the decades and was aimed at achieving this goal as well as acquiring the capability to deter, or delay, the US from assisting its allies.

The first change in doctrine, to that of 'winning regional wars under hi-tech conditions', occurred after Jiang Zemin took over as Chairman of the Military Commission. The US doctrine, tactics and firepower used during the First Gulf War in 1991, and later the US actions in Kosovo and Afghanistan (2001) and the Second Gulf War (2003), jolted the Chinese into realizing how backward they were in comparison. These US military actions provided considerable material for study to Chinese strategists as evidenced by the plethora of articles analyzing these wars in authoritative Chinese military publications. Jiang Zemin ensured adequate funds for the PLA and annual double-digit hikes in the defence budgets became the norm. This policy was continued by Hu Jintao as Chairman of the Military Commission.

Hu Jintao, however, has taken greater interest in the PLA's modernization than his predecessor. He has emphasized the importance of 'integrated joint operations' and, promptly after taking over as Military Commission Chairman, inducted the Commanders of the PLA Air Force, PLA Navy and Second Artillery as Members of the Central Military Commission. He has ensured that the growth in the defence budget, which has registered a double-digit percentage increase each year except one since 1993, has kept pace with the country's growing economy whose foreign currency reserves presently exceed US$ 2.4 trillion. Conservative estimates peg China's current defence budget at around US$ 90-100 billion.

It is also under Hu Jintao's leadership that China discarded Deng Xiaoping's policy of *taoguang yanghui,* or 'lie low, bide your time', in 2008. A more assertive national policy has since become evident and the number of stand-offs between China and the US and other countries increased noticeably.

The PLA Navy for the first time ventured into the Indian Ocean on an anti-piracy mission and has, significantly, sustained this effort. It plans to formalise agreements with Indian Ocean littoral countries for bases for its flotilla operating in the Indian Ocean. A vivid demonstration of Chinese assertiveness was the manner in which PLA Navy vessels confronted the US survey ship 'USNS Impeccable' in March 2009, described by US officials as the 'most serious' incident since that involving the EP-3 aircraft in 2001. Another incident occurred in June 2009, when a Chinese submarine hit an underwater sonar array being towed by the destroyer 'USS John

McCain'. This incident occurred in Subic Bay off the Philippines coast. The confrontations were intended to demonstrate the PLA Navy's capacity to defend China's territorial waters and willingness to confront the USA, if necessary, to safeguard its interests. They were also intended to clearly signal to Taiwan and other countries in the region, who have off-shore disputes with China, that they should not rely on US assistance. Coinciding with these incidents were the unpublicised clashes taking place between Chinese Navy vessels and Vietnamese craft since late 2007. China simultaneously began to prepare the legal basis for enforcing its maritime territorial claims in the South China Sea. These actions have aroused concern in Singapore, Malaysia, Vietnam, Indonesia, the Philippines and other countries.

It is during this period that China adopted an assertive posture with India too. While border negotiations and official-level contacts between India and China continued, military pressure along the 4,057 kms long disputed India-China border increased as did the number of intrusions. China re-opened the hitherto settled issue of Sikkim and enhanced the profile of its territorial claim on Arunachal Pradesh. It initiated a policy of declining visas to residents of Arunachal Pradesh and compelled international institutions not to extend loans for development projects in that state. More recently, it raised the ante in Kashmir when it began issuing loose-leaf visas to residents of the state and later declined a visa to the Northern Army Commander on the plea that he commands troops in the 'disputed territory of J&K'.

Suggestion of military muscle in diplomacy was evident in China's reaction to the US-ROK joint military exercises in mid-2010. Chinese official media and military and strategic analysts accused the US of threatening China. China's official media and military publications, quite unusually, publicized a series of military exercises conducted by the PLA, Second Artillery and PLA Navy at this time. These reports pointed out that the PLA was preparing for any eventuality.

A relatively new element has been added to China's diplomatic posturing. This is the tendency of former, or serving, military officials to offer comments which appear to deviate from stated policy. A number of such officers are employed in military-affiliated think-tanks and hold posts equated with military ranks. Had they not been given licence to speak they would have been punished. This particularly when the Party and the Party General Secretary, Hu Jintao, retain such a tight grip on the PLA. No reports have been noticed to suggest that any punishments have been awarded, but some of them are known to have received promotions.

As military modernization began to show results China's leadership became more confident. An example was the remark in May 2009 by a senior PLA Navy officer to US Admiral Keating. The officer suggested: 'as we develop our aircraft carriers why don't we reach an agreement, you and I. You take Hawaii East, we'll take Hawaii West and the Indian Ocean. We'll share information and we'll save you all the trouble of developing your naval forces west of Hawaii'.

Meanwhile, Hu Jintao allowed Chinese military and civilian strategists the freedom to continue redefining the country's strategic frontiers more boldly. These Chinese strategists began describing it as: 'China's entire continental shelf, the north Pacific contiguous to Russia and Japan, the Bohai Gulf, the Taiwan Strait, the East China Sea and even west-ward through the Malacca Strait into the Indian Ocean'. By the 1990s some strategists had stretched the definition to include the Persian Gulf. Huang Kunlun, a military commentator, later further expanded this by articulating the 'theory of boundless national interests'. He clarified this to mean: 'wherever our national interests have extended, so will the mission of our armed forces'. Maps depicting China's so-called traditional sphere of influence also remain in circulation in China and include areas well beyond the newly defined strategic frontiers.

There are other instances where China has assertively pushed its self-interest disregarding the articulated valid concerns of other nations. One example is that of rare earth exports to Japan. A more serious issue that impacts on the livelihoods of millions of people relates to the construction of dams on the upper Mekong River thereby reducing water flows downstream. Another serious issue having a similar impact and affecting India is the proposed diversion of the Brahmaputra river waters to China's arid, but populated, north.

The assertiveness seen in China's policies is reflective of the newfound confidence of the Chinese leadership and people. This has been generated by a combination of factors including China's consistent double-digit economic growth over three decades, military might and ensuant international adulation. In contrast, Chinese analysts assessed that the US military was over-stretched consequent to being embroiled in the wars in Iraq and Afghanistan and that the world's major economies, especially the US, had been considerably weakened because of the deleterious effects of the international economic crisis.

Chinese leaders, therefore, perceived the current time as opportune for China to make its bid for pre-eminence in the broader Asia-Pacific region. Its success in coercing European countries to resile from long-held positions on contentious issues, like Human Rights and Tibet, encouraged Beijing. China's assessment seemed to have been substantiated when Hillary Clinton, during her first visit to Beijing as US Secretary of State, failed to mention Human Rights, Tibet and Democracy in meetings with Chinese leaders. Obama's declining to meet the Dalai Lama during his visit to Washington was additional confirmation of apparent American weakness. In this backdrop the joint statements issued after the two summit meetings between Hu Jintao and Obama, in September and November 2009 respectively, took on greater significance for the Chinese. They assumed that the US was willing to let China exercise the role of regional hegemon while retaining for itself the mantle of global superpower.

China's assertiveness is, however, proving to be counter-productive and recently received a setback. The US-ROK military exercises were correctly interpreted in Beijing as indicative of US intention to re-enter the Asia-Pacific and maintain its dominance. US President Obama's speech recently in the Indian Parliament would have amply reinforced this assessment. The public offer of support by US Secretary of State Hillary Clinton to Japan in the current dispute with China over the Senkaku, or Diaoyu, islands together with US overtures to Vietnam, Indonesia and South Korea have not gone unnoticed. Commentaries in the official Chinese media have described these as attempts at 'containment' of China and specifically warned India, Japan, Vietnam and Indonesia against falling into USA's trap.

There is debate underway in China, though, as to whether discarding Deng Xiaoping's policy of *taoguang yanghui* , or 'lie low, bide your time', was premature. Some articles, interestingly, occasionally appear in the Peoples' Daily and Guangming Daily and these also explore the possibility of Beijing reverting to its earlier policy. A few Chinese commentators have candidly acknowledged that China's policy of 'peaceful rise', modified to 'peaceful development', had apparently not found many takers. They recommend that Beijing reverts to its earlier policy and bides its time.

Whether and how China's leadership will try to retrieve its position and refurbish the image it had so assiduously cultivated earlier is unclear, but it will not be easy. In fact, there are no indications yet to suggest a reversal in policy in which Hu Jintao's probable successor, Xi Jinping, would have been involved.

This was published as an Issue Brief by the Centre for Air Power Studies on November 12, 2010.

11. China's Expanding Maritime Ambition and Growing Naval Power

Symbolic gestures are most often a mix of intent and ambition. China's recent success in its bid for a bloc for exploration and exploitation of minerals and natural resources on the Indian Ocean sea-bed is at once an expression of intent, self-confidence and ambition. It additionally introduces an element of a sense of 'ownership' to its presence in the Indian Ocean.

China's long-standing bid to secure a presence in the Indian Ocean has not been deterred by the recent escalating tension in the East China and South China Seas, where China remains keen on establishing its dominance. Beijing first unambiguously expressed confidence that its Navy had such capability in May 2009. Early that year a senior officer of the People's Liberation Army Navy (PLAN), told the visiting US Admiral Keating, ostensibly half jocularly, that: 'as we develop our aircraft carriers why don't we reach an agreement, you and I. You take Hawaii East, we'll take Hawaii West and the Indian Ocean. We'll share information and we'll save you all the trouble of developing your naval forces west of Hawaii'. The proposal articulated long-held Chinese aspirations.

It reinforced China's effort of December 2008, when a PLAN flotilla unilaterally sailed to conduct anti-piracy operations off the Gulf of Aden in the Indian Ocean. PLAN ships have remained in the Indian Ocean ever since, displaying their capacity for extended stays and carrying out limited operations. Chinese Admirals subsequently voiced the need for China to have bases abroad. In December 2009, Paris-educated Rear Admiral Yin Zhou suggested that China establish a permanent base in the Gulf of Aden to support its anti-piracy operations. The proposal was posted on the Chinese Defence Ministry website. Rear Admiral Yin Zhou justified the proposal saying that supplying and maintaining the fleet off Somalia was challenging without such a base. The idea has been supported in China's official media and web forums.

China has been steadily developing its maritime capability since the early 1980s. The primary objective has been to deter and delay 'hostile' navies from disrupting any potential military operations against Taiwan, or China's attempts to 'recover' claimed territories in the South China Sea. China's naval modernization accordingly focussed on building submarines, in addition to surface ships. It currently has over seventy submarines including the recently added indigenously-built nuclear-powered submarines. It accelerated construction of advanced guided missile frigates, guided missile destroyers and attack submarines. It unveiled the Dong Feng 21D (DF-21) anti-Ship Ballistic Missile (ASBM) capable of hitting moving targets and aircraft carriers. Hinting at the effective deployment of this capability, China's strategic missile force, namely the Second Artillery, carried out exercises when Beijing felt under pressure because the US and South Korea held their largest ever joint naval exercises in the Yellow Sea in early 2010. Later, in July 2011, People's Liberation Army (PLA) Chief of General Staff, Chen Bingde, for the first time publicly disclosed that the Dong Feng 21D anti-Ship Ballistic Missile (ASBM) had a range of 2700-kms.

Plans were scaled-up once Beijing felt it was ready for a larger role, including in distant waters, and it commenced building an aircraft carrier. Many of the vessels necessary for forming a carrier group already exist in the PLAN. In January 2007 Huang Qiang, spokesman for the Commission of Science, Technology, and Industry for National Defense, reported that China possessed the capability to build an aircraft carrier. Then, in November 2008, Gen. Qian Lihua, director of the Ministry of Defense Foreign Affairs Office, declared that the world should not be surprised if China built an aircraft carrier.

After the deployment of two Chinese destroyers to the Somali coast for anti-piracy operations in December 2008, China's Ministry of Defense spokesman, Huang Xueping, reported that China would now "seriously consider" construction of an aircraft carrier.

On April 6, 2011, photographs of the 75,000-ton, 990-foot aircraft carrier were posted on Chinese websites. The photographs clearly depicted the armaments fitted on board, which included Type 1030 30mm CIWS guns and FL-3000N missiles systems (all 18 cell varieties) for defensive weapons and APAR and Sea Eagle Radar sensors being fitted with an Optical Landing System. The photographs revealed that the aircraft carrier, possibly to be named '*Shi Lang*', the name of an ancient Chinese Admiral who conquered Taiwan, was then seventy percent complete and could carry out sea trials by the end of the year. The aircraft carrier actually conducted five days of sea trials from August 10, 2011. Another indicator that the aircraft carrier was nearly ready was the appointment of 50-year old PLAN Captain Li Xiaoyan, an experienced navy, army and air force commander who has studied how to command an aircraft carrier. Presently holding the rank of Senior Colonel, Li Xiaoyan was assigned in December 2010 to Dalian, where the aircraft carrier 'Varyag' is berthed. China's *Dongfang Zaobao* reported that the aircraft carrier will see service in the East, North and South China Seas.

According to official Chinese media reports Li Xiaoyan was chosen as commander of China's first aircraft carrier because of his well-rounded tri-service military experience. Born in 1961 in Changchun City of Jilin Province in northeastern China, Li first joined the PLA Air Force (PLAAF) where he received aviation training at the Second Aviation Preparatory School in 1979. He later attended Russia's Kuznetsov Naval Academy for advanced command studies in March 1996.

Indicative of the plans to build more aircraft carriers – three nuclear carrier groups are expected to be inducted into service within the next five years – Bai Yaoping, another naval aviation pilot and course-mate of Li Xiaoyan, was on July 4, 2011, appointed Vice President of the Dalian Naval School to train the new generation of PLA Navy commanders. Li Xiaoyan and Bai Yaoping were among the ten outstanding pilots picked for training in the first and only 'pilot warship captain class' held at the Guangzhou Warship Academy in 1987.

Approval by the 162-member, Jamaica-based International Seabed Authority, of China's application for exploration of a 10,000 square kilometer polymetallic sulphide ore deposit bloc on the Indian Ocean sea-bed, is an important step. It confirms Beijing's plans to extend its influence on a long-term basis in to the Indian Ocean. It simultaneously expands the scope of China's search for scarce and much needed mineral and natural resources from the land to the ocean floor. China joins three other entities to be awarded such a contract, the others being two companies in Tonga and Nauru for the Pacific Ocean and the Russian government for the mid-Atlantic ridge. The venture, which also gives China a modicum of 'ownership' in the Indian Ocean, will permit China to map the sea-bed and identify suitable spots including for mining gold, silver, lead, zinc and copper. The bid was filed consequent to the discovery of clues by a Chinese government-sponsored expedition team in 2005 that an enormous belt of polymetallic sulphides existed.

China's application to the International Seabed Authority clearly signals its desire to maintain a long-term presence in the Indian Ocean. Mineral exploration activity, which will take a long time once it commences, will require Chinese scientific research and supply vessels to regularly ply the sea lanes to the designated spot. It will entail regular visits by PLAN vessels. Giving an idea of the envisaged time-frame, Han Xiqiu, a researcher with China's State Oceanic Administration's Second Institute of Oceanography based in Hangzhou, Zhejiang, said that mining activities will not start 'until we have solved the environmental issues. We may need to wait for years, if not decades'.

The bid simultaneously brings into focus China's underwater research and warfare capability. It is one of the few nations with deep-sea exploration capabilities and recently sent its first manned deep-sea submarine, the '*Jiaolong*' to a depth of 5,057 metres in the Pacific Ocean. The deep-sea rift south of Madagascar, which is the area where China has been awarded the bloc by the International Seabed Authority, reaches a depth of 3,000 metres. Plans are to test the '*Jiaolong*' to a depth of 7,000 metres next year.

While the People's Liberation Army Navy (PLAN) will continue to receive the major share of the country's defence allocations, maritime defence capability will be augmented by additional budgetary infusions to the Ocean and Fisheries Administration, provincial maritime administrations and to shipyards. The management of territorial waters in China is dispersed among the fisheries, customs, maritime, border armed police and other departments. In 2008, the State Council defined the charter of the State Oceanic Administration of China as to: "protect national maritime rights and interests according to law … … in the waters under the jurisdiction of regular rights of law-enforcement system, cruise, investigate illegal activities." Ocean surveillance is under the three 'Sea Corps' commands of the State Oceanic Administration of China. Together they have more than 120 law enforcement vessels of different types and a number of law enforcement aircraft. The 'Global Times' disclosed in July that the number of vessels with the State Oceanic Administration will increase to 350 by 2015 and 520 by 2020. Meanwhile, Chinese military analysts have called for a unified maritime force. An article in *Jiefangjun Bao* (July 27, 2011) stated that 'presently the People's Republic of China is facing a very grim situation in the protection of its rights and interests of the seas. More than half of the three million sq kms of waters that should fall under China's jurisdictions according to the UN Convention on the Law of the Sea are under demarcation disputes with peripheral countries. Large numbers of China's islands have been invaded and occupied and China's oil, gas and fishery resources have often been plundered...China's maritime law enforcement forces are scattered among the oceanic, maritime safety, fishery administration, custom, border defense and other departments...China should build a team of highly efficient and practical maritime law enforcement forces as soon as possible'.

In addition to the emphasis on the construction of new and more advanced missiles, ships and submarines, Beijing has been quietly focusing R&D efforts on strengthening its undersea warfare capability.

There has been unwavering focus on the design, development and manufacture of Unmanned Underwater Vessels (UUV). Of the countries in the region China already has the largest submarine fleet. The UUVs would be part of China's asymmetric subterranean warfare strategy. The UUV programme was initiated as part of the secret "863" Programme. US analyst Richard Fisher stated in a report that in 1996, China revealed a UUV featuring artificial intelligence and automatic controls which could reach a depth of 6,000 metres. It was developed with Russian assistance. A new unmanned patrol-cum-surveillance vessel was unveiled by China at the Zhuhai show in 2006. This vessel was described as useful for long-range reconnaissance, communication relay, electronic interference, target strike, submarine mines search, anti-submarine combat etc. In 2007, the official Chinese Television channel telecast visuals of a PLA Navy minesweeper using a UUV for counter mine operations. UUVs have a variety of potential applications and can be used to effectively hamper an adversary's operations. Possible uses of UUVs envisage using them in the mode that Chinese military literature favours, namely the "swarming concept". Lyle Goldstein of the China Maritime Studies Institute of the US Naval War College has assessed that the UUVs could be used in "swarms" as part of an undersea network that could be deployed for sensing, shooting or as communication relay stations. They would also be low cost.

China has designated a number of specialized institutes to work on UUVs, which suggests that it has invested a considerable quantum of funds along with the necessary research and development (R&D) effort in the project. The 702nd Research Institute of the China Shipbuilding Industry, Shipbuilding Engineering Institute of Harbin Engineering University and the Institute of Underwater Engineering of Shanghai's Jiao Tong University are among the research institutes involved in the design, development and manufacture of the UUVs. The Shenyang Institute of Automation Robotics Laboratory developed the Hairen-I remote-controlled undersea robot. Beijing University of Aeronautics and Astronautics developed the SPC-3 Robotfish UUV while Tianjin University fabricated glider-type UUVs. The Ningbo Jiayang Machine Company has manufactured and offered for sale a 'Mini Unmanned Submarine' of 3,000 m length with a maximum speed of 3M/s and which can reach a depth of 300 feet. The company advertises it as useful for 'lifesaving, military, engineering and cruise'. It is very probable that Chinese researchers have been working on advanced guidance systems for the UUVs so that they could be effectively used in maritime undersea warfare. Their usage would initially be in the Taiwan Strait and the waters surrounding the Spratlys and Paracels but, as their quality and capabilities improve, they can be used in more distant waters including the Arabian Sea and Indian Ocean. This effort to develop UUVs meshes neatly with China's policy of strengthening its asymmetric offensive military capability.

In the context of the South China and East China Seas, which are the central areas of rivalry, China has been systematically preparing a legal basis for its claims by legislating laws and flourishing ancient maps to reinforce its claims to sovereignty. On the sidelines of the Fourth Session of the Eleventh National People's Congress (March 5-13, 2011) held in Beijing, Liu Cigui, head of China's State Oceanic Administration, disclosed that an "island census is aimed at clarifying the total number, area and resources data of the country's islands". China had promulgated and put into effect a 'Law on Island Protection' on March 1, 2010, which Liu Cigui described as being "conducive to better island protection and the management of uninhabited islands". China last conducted an 'island census' in the 1980s which revealed that the country had over 6,500 uninhabited islands accounting for 93.8 percent of the total. The Twelfth Five Year Plan's (2011-2015) section on socio-economic development, approved by this NPC session, elaborated on accelerating the planning and development of the Xisha (Paracels) and Nansha (Spratlys) archipelagos and adjacent waters. The stated objective is to enhance the protection of the Paracels and Spratly archipelagos, promote tourism and construct fishery logistics facilities in the Paracels. There has been separate indication that China is pushing ahead with plans to develop its claimed maritime area. During the release of China's Marine Development Report 2010, Sun Zhihui, Director of the State Oceanography Bureau, said that China had 'entered a new phase in marine development and will need to formulate a new strategy and policy'. The report also disclosed that the total value of China's marine products in 2009 had reached Yuan 3196.4 billion.

Beijing's long-term naval plans were spelt out by PLAN Commander Wu Shengli in an interview with CCTV shortly before the Navy Review in Qingdao in 2009. He announced that PLAN had been directed to place 'preparations for maritime military struggle on the top of the national security and military strategy'. He added that China will seek to develop 'technology heavy' forces based around the aircraft carrier, implying an emphasis on power projection including aimed at land-based targets. Though following Chinese President Hu Jintao's visit to the US earlier this year the level of rhetoric has dropped, the PLAN's build up and activities confirm that Beijing intends, in due course, to 'recover' sovereignty over major parts of the South China Sea and establish its dominance in maritime territories of its interest. The present decade is likely to witness more instances of China asserting its maritime territorial sovereignty especially in the South China and East China Seas, leading to heightened tension in the region.

The potential sale of advanced UUVs to Pakistan will add another dimension to India's maritime security threat. India's military and security establishment need to take serious note. Major lapses like the undetected and unchallenged arrival of three ships, two of them large and one carrying over 25 people, on to India's western shores after traversing 2,320 nautical miles, can no longer be allowed.

This was published as an Issue Brief by the Centre for Air Power Studies on August 29, 2011.

12. China Looks at Troubled Waters

The turbulence that is roiling the waters off China's east and northeastern shores has far reaching implications. Two messages among those emitted by the just concluded US-ROK joint military exercises mandate attention namely: US strategy towards China is one of calibrated cooperation and not capitulation, and the status quo that had begun to settle in the waters of the Yellow, East and South China Seas has changed.

The military exercise has reinforced Beijing's apprehensions that the US has decided to re-enter the Asia-Pacific region and maintain a dominant presence there. With this military exercise, Washington has effectively put the brakes on Beijing's steady and persistent efforts to expand the definition of areas of its 'core interest' and bring these within China's suzerain. Washington, by participating in the joint military exercise with South Korea at this time of rising tension in North East Asia and appreciably raising its force-strength, has also reinforced its commitment to an ally in the Asia-Pacific region and a neighbour of China. The action has simultaneously given comfort to other US allies in the region as well as those wary of China's ambitions and, dispelled notions that US interest in the region was weakening or that commitments elsewhere would compel the US to reduce force deployments in the Asia-Pacific. Of particular interest is the low-key announcement that during the next round of exercises scheduled for September, the nuclear-powered aircraft carrier 'USS George Washington' will enter the Yellow Sea. This appeared to reverse an earlier decision to keep the 'USS George Washington' away from the Yellow Sea due to China's objections.

China has predictably taken serious note of US actions. The unprecedented, large-scale US-ROK joint military exercise

'Invincible Spirit', where elements of Japan's Self-Defence Forces participated, witnessed deployment of firepower on such a massive scale for the first time in 34 years in the region. The 97,000-tonne nuclear-powered 'USS George Washington' sailed in these waters for the first time. It was accompanied by twenty warships. It was also the first time that F-22 Raptor Stealth aircraft of the US Air Force flew over Korean skies. Two hundred other fighter aircraft participated. Chinese military analysts promptly pointed out that the F-22 flies for long stretches at supersonic speeds and is capable of destroying North Korean leader Kim Jong Il's office, nuclear facilities, missile bases and other military targets within 40-60 minutes. They said the F-22 could easily target China and its 'political centre' too. It was the first time ever that the US Air Force's latest Stratofreighter aerially refuelled US aircraft during joint US-ROK exercises. A number of modern missiles, torpedoes and artillery pieces were deployed. The stated objective of these joint military exercises was to demonstrate US strength to North Korea, exert pressure on it and warn Pyongyang against any rash action aimed at the Republic of Korea. There was obviously another equally strong message. That was to inform Beijing that the US would stay on as the dominant power in the region, that it would come to the aid of its allies, and that China would not be allowed to further its territorial ambitions unimpeded.

Chinese military strategists and military personnel were quick to note that the joint military exercises, though ostensibly intended to intimidate North Korea, were equally intended to apply pressure on China. Note was taken of Japan's participation, which they said had 'caused China disquiet'. Chinese military analysts and strategists have been uniformly critical of the US action, warning it would damage US-China relations. Chinese military experts described the Yellow Sea and Sea of Japan as equally important, adding that the conduct of exercises in either sea poses a threat to China. The Yellow Sea "is straight at the heart of China" and the South China Sea is related to

"China's economic lifeline". Chinese forces were urged to prepare for a response and deploy in both the seas. The use of China's strategic force, the Second Artillery, was recommended. A scholar of the China Institute for Contemporary International Relations, affiliated to China's Intelligence apparatus, analysed that the US had led a gradual build up of naval forces around China's periphery and that sea power rivalry in East Asia is increasing. He enumerated that the US is enhancing its Navy deployment in the Asia-Pacific region, that Japan is unwilling to be inactive and is striving to become an Asia-Pacific regional power, that Russia is trying to gain prominence, and that India is strengthening relations with Japan and ASEAN.

The US-ROK joint exercises come in the wake of increasing Chinese assertiveness and military activity in the South China Sea. It follows overt displays of China's growing confidence in its capabilities and insistence, at Summits between the Chinese and US Presidents, for an enhanced role in international affairs including regional issues on par with the US. In mid-2009 a senior Chinese Navy officer said to a ranking US officer: 'as we develop our aircraft carriers why don't we reach an agreement, you and I. You take Hawaii East, we'll take Hawaii West and the Indian Ocean. We'll share information and we'll save you all the trouble of developing your naval forces west of Hawaii'. More recently in March and May 2010 in Beijing, senior Chinese officials expanded China's areas of 'core interest' by including the South China Sea.

Countries in the Asia-Pacific region are particularly vulnerable to a superior sea power intent on asserting its sovereignty, including over disputed offshore territories. China's People's Liberation Army Navy (PLAN), which is being rapidly modernized, is playing a steadily growing role in China's security and been used to reinforce China's stand where the legality of off-shore oil exploration concessions granted to foreign companies by other countries has been contested. It has helped assert China's claims on the disputed Spratly and

Paracels archipelagos and in the off-shore territorial disputes with Japan. Chinese Navy ships have fought silent battles separately with naval vessels of the Philippines and Vietnam, resulting in casualties in clashes with Vietnam. Beijing has publicly asserted that it will protect its claimed territories by force if necessary and has enacted a maritime law to that effect.

The South China Sea territorial dispute has the potential to erupt into a major dispute between China and other countries in the region. The dispute encompasses the Paracels Islands, Macclesfield Bank and the Spratly Islands archipelago. Disputes exist between China and Japan over the Senkaku-Diaoyutai Islands and between Korea and Japan over the Tokdo/Takeshima Islands. Chinese vessels have additionally apprehended Indonesian fishermen off Natuna Island. The Spratly Islands have additional strategic importance as they lie between Vietnam and the Philippines and could potentially block ships transiting through the South China Sea. Aircraft and helicopters based in the Spratlys would have the range to block the Malacca and Sunda Straits, both vital choke points for shipping going from the South China Sea to the Indian Ocean.

As part of its new assertive foreign policy, China raised the profile of the dispute centering on the resource-rich Spratly and Paracels archipelagos which sit atop an estimated 130 million barrels of oil and gas. A 'Draft Law on the Environment Protection of Sea Islands', which stipulates that 'ownership of the uninhabited islands shall revert to the state' and that 'the State Council of the People's Republic of China shall exercise control' over them, is before the National People's Congress. The Draft appears to include the Senkaku (Diaoyutai) Islands disputed between China and Japan in the East China Sea and Nansha (Spratly) Islands disputed between China and a number of countries including Malaysia, the Philippines and Vietnam. Tension has predictably escalated. Malaysia reiterated its claim to sovereignty in March 2009. That month the Philippines promulgated the 'Philippines Baselines

Law' asserting sovereignty over some of the Spratlys. China reacted by dispatching fishing, survey and monitoring ships to the waters near these islands. Once it enacts the Draft Law, Beijing is likely to get more aggressive.

The South China Sea is important also as a strategically vital passageway through which sea lanes critical for many countries transit. More than 200 ships pass through it daily. The majority of oil, natural gas, other resources and commercial cargo flow through it to China, Korea and Japan from the Middle East and South East Asian countries. Japan receives seventy five percent of its energy supplies from the Middle East through the South China Sea. The area is strategically important for the US which uses the freedom of the sea lanes of communication and the safety of navigation and over flight in the area and is intent on maintaining these. The US Navy and US Air Force use the South China Sea passageway for transit between military bases in Asia and the Indian Ocean and Persian Gulf areas. Additionally, US interests are guided by their commitment to the security interests of Japan and South Korea. US Secretary of State Hillary Clinton's remarks in Hanoi earlier this August had this background.

Chinese official media reaction to the first phase of the US-ROK joint military exercises has been strong. Hongkong's 'Oriental Daily News', taking specific note of Japan's participation, observed that Japan is taking unfair advantage of the situation in the East China Sea and is preparing to send Self-Defence Forces to be stationed on the Diaoyu (Senkaku) Islands. Asserting that if China does not act decisively the problem may become grave, it urged China 'to strike hard and break through the strategic fulcrum of the Diaoyu Islands'. The authoritative 'Liberation Army Daily' warned that China faces a 'very grim situation' and that more than half of the three million square kilometers of waters that should legally be in its jurisdiction is under dispute. Regretting that numerous islands belonging to China were under foreign occupation and that China's oil, gas and fisheries resources have been 'plundered', it called for creation of a unified maritime law enforcement force just as other nations had done. Other official Chinese media articles highlighted that over the past months the US had established a 'forward presence' in the region, held the 14-nation RIMPAC joint exercises and joint exercises with Japan, Singapore and the Philippines. China, they reiterated, was being 'encircled'. Other articles noted the visits to Vietnam in mid-August by a US destroyer and aircraft carrier 'USS George Washington', cooperation between the US and Malaysia's Navy and US moves to resume military cooperation with Indonesia. There were warnings to countries of the region to beware of US designs and consequences, but especially to Vietnam. A commentary in the Beijing-owned Hongkong-based 'Wen Wei Po' declared that the exercises make China 'uneasy because whether it is the Yellow Sea or Sea of Japan, China's political core Beijing-Tianjin region and its eastern economic centre of gravity are within the US carrier's combat radius'. Accusing the US of 'reviving Cold War mentality', it asserted that 'China does not want to fight a war with the US in North East Asia' but that 'if the US-ROK military exercise is aimed at China, it means the US is deliberately creating for itself the world's most powerful enemy'.

China permitted its citizens and the nationalistic 'fenqing' (youth) to post articles and blogs critical of the US. On July 26, the PLA convened for the first time ever a seminar of military and legal experts, which concluded that the military exercises were against International Law. At a seminar organized by the Kissinger China Society in Washington on July 26, Prof Jiang Changjian of Fudan University, said that 'friendly feeling' for the US among ordinary people in China had risen from 33.8 percent in 2003 to 65.1 percent in 2009 and among Chinese students from 39.6 percent to 72.1 percent during the same period. He, however, added the caveat that 89 percent of Chinese students and 72.4 percent of ordinary people consider US as the 'greatest threat to Chinese interests'. Positive feelings for the US, he cautioned, could fluctuate due to current US actions in the Yellow and South China Seas.

In a calculated show of force the PLA publicized the conduct of a series of military exercises. On July 18-19 it held 'Warfare-2010', a military supply drill 'deep in the Yellow Sea'. It was conducted jointly by the PLA's General Logistics Department and Office of Transport and Combat Readiness. This was followed by large scale live-ammo exercises in the South China Sea by the Nanjing Military Region from July 26-28. Warships, submarines and combat aircraft from three PLA Navy Fleets participated. This exercise was witnessed by PLA Chief Chen Bingde, who declared that the PLA should 'pay attention to the developing international situation' and 'make preparations for military struggle' (translated in Chinese as 'battle' or 'war'). From June 30-July 5, a live-ammo joint military exercise was held in the East China Sea. On August 3, the Jinan Military Region commenced 'Vanguard-2010', a five day exercise involving 12,000 personnel, seven types of fighter aircraft, 'spy' planes and helicopters. It saw the deployment of new types of ground-to-air missiles, seven types of anti-air weapons and the PLA's most advanced anti-aircraft gun. Conducted with the scenario of defending Beijing, the exercise was described as the 'Jinan Theatre's largest' army air-defence exercise. The North China Sea Fleet's air arm, began drills on August 11 on the Liaodong and Shandong Peninsulas with two batches of fighters over the Bohai Sea. This included night-time simulated attacks and surveillance operations over the Yellow Sea. Chinese military expert, Ni Lexiong, was quoted by 'Liberation Army Daily' as saying that the PLA Air Force normally conducts training exercises in daytime, but since the US prefers to attack at night such night time exercises were necessary. Three more exercises in the South China Sea are planned and more military exercises are anticipated.

An important indicator of the seriousness with which the Chinese leadership views the developments is the directive issued by the

Central Military Commission in mid-August. Party Committees of all seven Military Regions were instructed to monitor the 'political thinking of military cadres to ensure their loyalty to the Party' at this time.

During this same period of rising tension the PLA conducted three military exercises opposite India in the Tibet Military District (TMD). From mid to late July an Artillery reconnaissance element of a Mountain Brigade under the TMD carried out an exercise under 'actual combat conditions'. Later in July, the Communications Repair detachment of a PLA Air Force Radar Regiment under the TMD carried out an exercise to repair wired, wireless and radar special lines of all radar positions under the Regiment. The exercise, it was clarified, was conducted between June-August because of the disruptions caused by rain, thunder and lightning in this period. Also in late July, the Emergency Support Brigade of a Logistics sub-department under Chengdu Military Region stationed in Chengdu maneuvered 500 kms to a Plateau area about 3500 metres above sea level in west Sichuan province 'to temper its troops in a strict way so as to cultivate the actual combat awareness of officers and men'. The exercises indicate accretion in military capability in Tibet and, in the backdrop of sustained Chinese pressure on India regarding Kashmir and Arunachal Pradesh, need to be taken note of.

While China's leadership under Hu Jintao continues to test the limits to which it can push its regional and territorial ambitions, it will seek to insulate Sino-US relations from undue damage. The first public comment on the rising tensions by a Chinese Defence Ministry spokesman, Senior Colonel Geng Yangsheng, urged that 'media should not over-interpret war games and make subjective speculation about any heightened situation'. Another cautionary note was sounded by Colonel Han Xudong of the National Defence University, who wrote in 'Liaowang' that the term 'core interests' should not be loosely used and that 'China's muscle is weak compared to the US'. A few analysts suggested caution and that China buy time and strengthen its Navy. The comments of Premier Wen Jiabao and Foreign Minister Yang Jiechi, China's senior most leaders to have spoken yet, were also carefully worded.

This was published as an Issue Brief by the Centre for Air Power Studies on August 29, 2010.

13. China: Emerging Cyber Power

The rapid development of technology, especially in the sector of communications, has facilitated the pace and conduct of commerce and government and added to the conveniences available to citizens. This is especially visible in what can best be described as the area of 'Critical Communications Technology', which includes all forms of modern communication including the internet and mobile telephone network. The latter two particularly are quickly getting blended for seamless operation. A mobile telephone today, for example, is a multi-media gadget which gives the user simultaneous access to the internet, video-streams, Facebook, Twitter and Kindle.

Development of the internet forty years ago was predictably driven originally by US defence requirements, but it is now indispensable to modern social, commercial and governmental activity. Latest figures estimate the current number of internet users worldwide at 3.3 billion and this number is rapidly increasing. Growth in internet usage in a ten year period between 2000-2009, for example, has been 362.3 percent. The number of mobile telephone users is also high and estimated at 4 billion. The rapid growth of the internet has simultaneously made it an attractive target for 'cyber criminals'. It has also become the arena for a silent, but potentially devastating, kind of warfare namely, cyber-warfare.

In view of the 'benefits' that cyber attacks give the attacking entity it has become an option that many countries and other entities are actively seeking to harness. Numerous countries are trying to develop their capabilities in various aspects of cyber-warfare and this has, in turn, triggered research not only on defensive measures, but also on methods of tracking, neutralizing and deterring 'attacks'. About 100 countries are assessed as presently having cyber warfare capabilities.

Since the advanced developed nations are the most 'wired' and consequently the most vulnerable, they have simultaneously initiated serious debate on the manner in which the victim of such an 'attack' could retaliate. China, which continues to harbour deep-rooted suspicions about US intentions towards it, is one country that has been striving hard to acquire a cyber warfare capability. Its objective is to possess a cyber warfare capability adequate to effectively cripple its adversaries and disrupt their critical communications.

Modernisation and strengthening of its armed forces has been a priority for China's leadership since it initiated the 'Four Modernisations' Programme in 1979. The Chinese leadership's deep-rooted suspicion of US intentions has dictated the modernization plans for the People's Liberation Army (PLA). These include the capability to deter US actions in the neighbourhood as well as those that could adversely affect China's national security interests. Recognising the asymmetry between the military capabilities of the Chinese and US armed forces, which were highlighted during the US involvement in the first Gulf War and later in Kosovo, Iraq and Afghanistan, the Chinese leadership searched for strategies to balance the inequality. The advantages offered by cyber-warfare were considered attractive and China's military leadership has focused on that aspect of warfare. Concrete steps to achieve the objective included China's secretive '863 Programme'. This programme has been based on the premise that technology is the key to rapid development and that China needs its own hi-technology base to become a world power. It also, importantly, erased the distinction between the civil and military. This programme and the focused scientific effort received a quantum push in July 2010.

The Chinese leadership's strategy for dominance of the high technology industry was comprehensive and overarching and included all aspects. These are technology, military and resource-supply. As part of this, the strategy was designed to ensure a captive, uninterrupted source of supply of rare earth metals. China declared rare earths a secret national top priority in the mid-1980s and in 1997, Deng Xiaoping observed that 'China would be for rare earth metals what the Middle East is to oil'. This was adopted as the guiding principle. Fifteen years later China has acquired virtually monopolistic control over the supply of rare earth metals to the world's market. Though about 42 percent of rare earth resources are elsewhere in the world, China is virtually the only country with a significant refinery capacity.

These rare earth metals include tertium, dysprosium, yttrium, thulium, intetium, noedymicum, europium, cerium and lanthanum. These rare earth metals and especially the group of 17 'lanthanide' elements, are critical for the hi-technology and 'green' industry. The metals are irreplaceable and are used in hundreds of technologies ranging from mobile phones, ipods and BlackBerrys to low-light energy bulbs, lasers and aviation. They are integral to the manufacture of wind turbines, electric motors of hybrid cars, superconductors, microscopes and missile guidance systems. Numerous US scientific organizations including the National Minerals Advisory Board and National Academy of Science have determined rare earths as crucial to US national security. Neodymium iron boron magnets (neo magnets), for example, are the world's strongest permanent magnets and are used in various hi-tech devices from guidance systems of smart bombs to computer hard drives. Other rare earth metals like lanthanum, samarium and praseodymium are critical to hybrid-electric battery production and nuclear submarine technology. Anti-missile systems, jet engines and satellite communications systems are some of the other technologies that use rare earth metals.

Causing serious concern to Japan and other countries is the recent proposal of China's Ministry of Industry and Information Technology calling for a total ban on rare earth exports like tertium, dysprosium, yttrium, thulium and lutetium. Exports of other rare earth metals like neodymium, europium, cerium and lanthanum will be restricted to 35,000 metric tonnes a year. This is far below global needs with Japan's requirements alone exceeding 38,000 metric tonnes a year. Japan, which was a victim in 2010 of China's policy of using economic levers to achieve strategic or foreign policy objectives, has accused China of treating rare earth metal exports as a '21st century economic weapon'. It is now looking for supplies from Vietnam and Malaysia. US Senators have also expressed concern at the potential scarcity of rare earth metals.

The military dimension to China's interest in cyber technology, which soon got incorporated into China's military doctrine, has got steadily emphasised. A major, though understated, contribution to the shaping of military doctrine was the quasi-official book published in February 1999, by two PLA Senior Colonels Qiao Liang and Wang Xiaogui, entitled 'Unrestricted Warfare'. The book was published with the approval of influential sections in the higher echelons of the PLA. Qiao Liang, incidentally, progressed in his career to reach the rank of Lieutenant General. As Qiao Liang writes in the book, 'the first principle of such warfare is that there are no rules and there are no limitations'. Following up on Chinese President and Military Commission Chairman Hu Jintao's exhortation in 2007 that the armed forces should focus on 'informationisation', China's Defence White Paper, 2009 also highlighted 'informationisation' as the goal of the country's armed forces along with 'integrated joint operations'. Interestingly, Sun Tzu's Art of War, written over two thousand years ago, and which continues to provide most of the general tenets of the PLA's plans to fight future wars, includes some of the advantages that accrue from cyber-warfare. Deception, stealth, ingenuity and evasion of war are among the features. Cyber-warfare anticipatedly became an area of intensive research and large sums of money were poured into cyber research and development, especially for military applications. Cyber espionage and cyber-war became priorities for the PLA with the US continuing to be the prime target.

This military dimension was fleshed out further by Major General Dai Qingmin, who strongly advocated that China develop its cyber warfare capability. He developed the conceptual framework that guides the PLA's Information Warfare (IW) strategy and which is called 'Integrated Network Electronic Warfare' (INEW) (wangdian yifizhan). Integrated Network Electronic Warfare (INEW) combines, as its name suggests, computer network operations and electronic warfare for use in a coordinated or simultaneous attack on adversarial C4ISR networks and other key information systems. Major General Dai Qingmin first outlined the use of INEW, to seize control of the electromagnetic spectrum, in a book entitled 'An Introduction to Information Warfare' and in articles published in 1999 while he was on the faculty of the PLA's Electronic Engineering Academy.

A report prepared for the US Government by the Northrop Group in October 2009 described the use of INEW in the battlefield. It said the INEW used 'techniques such as electronic jamming, electronic deception and suppression to disrupt information acquisition and transfer, launching a virus attack or hacking to sabotage information processing and information utilization, and using anti-radiation and other weapons based on new mechanisms to destroy enemy information platforms and information.' This description illustrates the range of action that INEW envisages. In 2000, Major General Dai Qingmin, who was backed by the PLA Chief of General Staff Fu Quanyou, was promoted to head the PLA General Staff Department's 4th Department, which is responsible for electronic counter-measures and the PLA's offensive Computer Network Attack (CAN) missions. Here he enhanced the GSD 4th Department's capabilities. In 2007, Major General Li Deyi, who was Deputy Head of the Department of Warfare Theory and Strategic Research at the Academy of Military Sciences, underscored the emphasis given to cyber warfare by China when he asserted that information deterrence is rising to a strategic level and will achieve a level of importance second only to nuclear deterrence.

It was in 2007 too, that China demonstrated the advances it had made in its ability to physically neutralise a space-based component of an adversary's cyber network. In January that year China successfully tested a direct ascent ASAT weapon that used a kinetic kill to destroy an ageing Chinese weather satellite. With this China became the third nation in the world to acquire this capability. A year earlier in 2006, the US military had accused China of using a laser dazzling weapon that temporarily blinded a reconnaissance satellite. Chinese researchers are currently working on various radio frequency weapons with the potential to target satellites and other components of the US C4ISR architecture.

Cyber-warfare is an attractive option for a weaker power confronting a more powerful nation. China's strategists assessed that the more 'wired' a nation, the more vulnerable it is to cyber attack. USA, which has been viewed by successive Chinese leaders as the country's main adversary, was considered a target against whom this new weapon could be used to considerable effect. Cyber-warfare also flowed from the country's efforts since the mid-1980s to develop a competitive indigenous industry in computer hardware and software. After the 1990s, China poured considerable resources into developing its information and communications technology industry. It sought and obtained technology, expertise and assistance from abroad and succeeded in building a national base for cyber research and development. China simultaneously forged an overarching strategic policy for information and communications technology. This combined military, civilian and strategic requirements. It envisaged a globally dominant role for China in this field in the future. To achieve the latter, China had to build a manufacturing base for Information Technology-related hardware and software and by 2004, it had overtaken the US in exports in this sector. This has given it an edge in enhancing its cyber-warfare capabilities, particularly against countries that purchase its software, routers, switches etc. This is equally applicable in cases where Chinese companies maintain or operate telephone communication networks.

The advantages of a cyber attack are considerable and initial success in a pre-emptive cyber attack, considered a distinct possibility in the initial phase of a conflict, can afford the initiating power success in the form of considerable and widespread material damage to the adversary. For example, a cyber attack retains a very high degree of stealth and can be initiated at lightening speed with minimum warning to the adversary. Resultantly, a counter-offensive would in most cases be launched after damage has at least begun to be inflicted. Cyber-attacks are difficult to detect prior to initiation as they require little physical preparation and are launched at the speed of light. The appeal of cyber-attacks for a weaker nation is heightened by the camouflage it affords and the difficulty in precisely ascertaining the identity of the attacker. This is because cyber-attacks can be launched through a multiple series of computers located in different countries and there is invariably a residual doubt as to the actual origin of the attack. Finally, cyber-warfare is a useful weapon for attacking and weakening the 'popular will', or resolve of the citizenry of the attacked nation. National resolve can be placed under severe strain by a cyber-attack because it can quickly confuse and disorient the adversary by disrupting, if not destroying, his communications network and public utility systems. Essential services like water works, electricity grids, transport systems including the underground rail network, financial systems etc. are likely to be the first targets of a cyber attack. In cases where the adversary is highly 'wired', like the USA or developed nations, the damage caused by cyber-attacks can be devastating. It is precisely because of the latter factor that a debate has been generated in the West as to whether a cyber-attack can be considered adequate provocation for attacking the perpetrator nation, including with precision strikes on equivalent targets from ballistic missiles.

While the US favours considering it an act of provocation adequate for launching a war against the country that mounts the cyber-attack, Russia is advocating a degree of restraint and recommends taking the matter before the UNSC.

The issue has begun to steadily grow in importance as China enhances its cyber-espionage and cyber-warfare capability and numerous cyber-attacks worldwide are being attributed to it. Hundreds of Chinese nationals are being imparted training in hacking, cyber-espionage, cyber-attacks and cyber-warfare. Many are being trained in academies run by the People's Liberation Army (PLA). Indication of the PLA's involvement in training 'cyber warriors' includes the 'informationisation' military courses offered in Wuhan University entitled 'An introduction to US and Taiwanese social information systems' and in Chengdu. It is apparent at first glance that the course would be designed to educate the students about the spread and vulnerabilities of cyber networks in these countries and as a guide to conducting cyber-espionage and cyber-attacks. This cyber force, which is increasing in strength, has numerous targets including USA, UK, France, Germany, Taiwan, Japan, India etc. Estimates are that at least 50,000 trained hackers are deployed by China against Taiwan and they are based in the Fujian and Guangdong provinces. Estimates similarly peg an equal number of Chinese hackers as targeting India and another of China's prime targets, namely the Dalai Lama's establishment, and based in the Xinjiang-Uygur Autnomous Region. USA, UK, Germany, France, India etc are among the countries that are regularly subjected to cyber attacks by China.

The PLA has, since 2002, steadily augmented its cyber force by creating cyber-capable Information Warfare (IW) militia units. These militia units comprise personnel from the commercial sector and academia. Militia units are being created within Chinese hi-tech and Information Technology commercial entities so that technically qualified and trained individuals with advanced education in software design are available. While the details of such efforts are obviously not publicized, a few examples have been discerned from the official Chinese media by the report recently released by the Northrop Group of the US. It has cited the case of a Political Commissar of the Guangzhou People's Armed Police Force garrison, advocating in 2003, the direct involvement of urban militia units in information warfare, electronic warfare and psychological warfare. He proposed making information warfare one of the primary missions of the Guangzhou Militia. In 2004, a Tianjin-based militia garrison restructured its subordinate units to increase capabilities for operations under 'informationised' conditions and created a dedicated 'Information Operations' unit. In 2007, militia units subordinate to a Henan Province military sub-district were organized for communications and network warfare and a year later, in 2008, an Anhui Province militia unit recruited personnel from large private enterprises for specialized technical training.

In March 2008, a militia battalion in Yongning County in Ningxia-Hui Autonomous Region within the operational jurisdiction of the Lanzhou Military Region established an Information Warfare Group. The Lanzhou Military Region, incidentally, now has an active support, reinforcement and operational role in military operations against India along with the Chengdu Military Region. Recent reports suggest that it now has an active role in India's western sector in event of conflict with India. This Information Warfare Group was tasked to conduct network warfare research and training and to "attack the enemy's wartime networks". This information was posted on the unit's website on March 19, 2008. The Yongning unit comprises an information warfare centre detachment (xinxi fendui zuozhan zhongxin), information gathering detachment (minbing wangluo zhan fendui), and a militia network protection unit (minbing wangluo fanghu fendui). The unit's composition indicates it is equipped to tackle the entire range of Computer Network Operations (CNO) missions. In February 2009, a PLA television program publicized that a Division in the Lanzhou Military Region conducted an opposed informationisation warfare exercise featuring computer network attack and defence scenarios while countering electronic warfare attacks, a common feature of informationised warfare training. Similar exercises have been held by units –usually at the Brigade level or above – in other Military Regions.

The PLA additionally has six Technical Reconnaissance Bureaus (TRB) in the Lanzhou, Jinan, Chengdu, Guangzhou and Beijing Military Regions, which are responsible for Signals Intelligence (SIGINT) and are apparently also tasked for computer network operations (CNO). Indications are that the TRB included Information Warfare (IW) in their tasks from around 1997. The First TRB in Chengdu, for example, received a series of commendations for 'substantial achievements in 'informationisation building'. The Chengdu Zhangji Bao on August 20, 2007 reported that Chengdu Military Region Unit 78006 was praised for breakthroughs in 'cutting edge IT research'.

US cyber security experts first detected penetration attempts by Chinese hackers of US computers and cyber networks in 2002. The objectives were primarily to test for vulnerabilities, cyber espionage and cyber attacks. Official US estimates in 2008 noted that Chinese hackers have mainly targetted US defence computers and downloaded 10 - 20 tetrabytes of data. Chinese hackers, or cyber warriors, are assessed as downloading intellectual properties estimated at US $ 60-70 billion each year from the US. US cyber security experts have concluded that China can clandestinely access the Non-secure Internet Protocol Router Network (NIPR Net) which carries unclassified US military traffic. This traffic includes administrative messages, schedules and time-tables of General Staff officers, deployments of US Navy ships etc. which could be useful to an opponent. They also successfully target networks of US defence sub-contractors and civil logistics firms obtaining data that could be used for assessing military-related deployments and movements. The US-China Security Review Commission estimated in 2008 that there are 250 hacker groups active in China and confirmed that China has an active cyber espionage programme. Most of the hackers are trained in Chinese military cyber academies.

While no substantiated evidence has yet been reported confirming that the Chinese government has enlisted the services of hackers, there are indications that at least some such informal arrangements exist with the security authorities. Many former hacker groups, which have disbanded, have formed themselves into legitimate security companies. Prominent examples are the Xfocus and Black Eagle Base groups. Xfocus now annually sponsors XCon, one of the largest 'hacker' conferences in China in partnership with NSFocus and Venus Technology. NSFocus, which was formerly the Green Army Alliance, is now a prominent commercial information security firm. The Black Eagle Base has appreciated the 'educational guidance' provided by the Commission for Science and Technology in National Defence (COSTIND now renamed SASTIND) to their leadership while they were in custody.

A few indications of the Chinese security authorities adopting a more active approach to recruit from the domestic hacker community are also available. Between July 2007 and November 2008 an individual calling himself 'City_93' posted job vacancy announcements for the Ministry of Public Security's First Research Institute. Peng Yinan, the founding member of the Chinese hacker group 'Javaphile', reportedly has a formal consulting relationship with the Shanghai Public Security Bureau.

After detecting that it is subject to regular cyber attacks from China, the US began meticulously monitoring hostile internet and cyber activity. US cyber security experts have since identified a range of techniques used by the attackers to penetrate US computers and the internet system. A few of particular concern, that have the potential for use against other targets, need mention. The 'security exploit', or 'zero day exploit', is a piece of software, data or commands that use a bug, glitch or vulnerability to cause the computer software, hardware or electronic devices to behave in an unanticipated manner. This allows the attacker to take control of the computer. Once detected these 'security exploits' can be neutralized through 'patches', but it is also for this reason that the attackers endeavour to keep the compromise of the computer via this method a secret. An idea of the disruption it can cause can be gauged from the fact that Taiwan was 'hit' by thirteen 'zero day attacks' in 2006 for which it took Microsoft 178 days to develop 'patches'. Also in 2006, Chinese hackers used this method to infect computers of the Bureau of Industry and Security of the US Department of Commerce, which manages the export licensing of military use products and information. The Department had to spend millions of dollars on the purchase of new, 'clean' hardware and software. The 'port scanner' is a two-layered system that combines reconnaissance and attack functions. In the reconnaissance mode it automates the process of finding weaknesses on computers on a network. They check to ascertain which ports on a specific computer are 'open', or available to access, and detect which programme or service is listening on that port. In the attack mode it can overload the computer and cause it to crash. Experts have calculated that the cost of reconnoitering computer networks is low and does not require much manpower. The 'Trojan' is another frequently used technique and deployed to gain remote access to a computer and download or destroy data. They are usually embedded in e-mail attachments. In 2005, the sensitive Oak Ridge National Laboratory and Los Alamos National Laboratory in the US were attacked by Trojans. Later in 2008, the Pentagon, defence-related think-tanks and defence contractors in the US were also subjected to Trojan attacks. Such attacks continue to be regularly detected each year.

'Worms' are another and preferred form of attack because of their easy availability. The Chinese used these to good effect in 2001 when nationalism was high, coinciding with the collision of a Chinese air force fighter aircraft with a US EP-3 'spy' plane. The Code Red and Code Red II worms were used on the occasion to deface numerous US military and computer industry websites. Over 60,000 computers in USA were affected and damages were estimated at over US$ 2 billion. The worms were assessed to have originated from a university in Guangdong, China. This attack was countered by attacks by US 'patriotic hacker' groups, who used the Code Blue worm to re-programme the Code Red worms and launch counter-attacks against targets in China.

Tracing the attacking computers and establishing the identity of the country, or entity, perpetrating the attack is very difficult and usually cannot be categorically confirmed. The primary method to trace the source of attack is the IP address, which is unique to each computer. The global IP address allocation is done by the 'Internet Corporation for Assigned Names and Numbers (ICANN)'. The attackers can, however, mask their identity and blur their footprints by using proxy servers. For example a Chinese cyber warrior, or hacker, can route his attack activity on a target in USA via a computer in Brazil, which in turn routes it through Russia. Attempts to trace the source of attack would initially lead investigators to the computer in Russia. If they persist they could track it further to Brazil, but reaching the original computer in China might be difficult. There can be a number of computers in different locations used for the purpose. In any case there is invariably a residual doubt as to whether the Chinese computer was actually the originator of the attack or merely another link in the chain of computers. This form of attack is complicated by the use of 'botnets', or a network of computers under the control of a single attacker. Each computer in this network, also called a 'zombie', is actually one that has been infected by a Trojan or virus. These 'zombies' are used remotely to attack targetted computers and can be quite effective as they usually are not used for normal hostile activity and therefore remain undetected till activated. Estimates are that there are 750,000 'zombie' computers in the US.

Prompted by the magnitude of the problem and the rapid strides made by China in cyber warfare capability, the US President early this year announced the creation of a US Cyber Command while the British Prime Minister declared that Britain would establish a cyber defence organization. South Korea has similarly established a cyber command. This is the first step towards these countries building a potentially robust response to cyber attacks that have the potential to disrupt their military and public utility services. It indicates also that the advanced nations have decided to establish organizations dedicated to securing the defence of their cyber-based and critical communications systems, while simultaneously developing technology to disrupt and destroy the systems of their opponents.

Russia independently demonstrated its ability to wage cyber-war. In 2007, it unleashed a concerted denial-of-service attack on the Estonian Government, media and bank servers crippling Estonia's internet services and forcing it to cut itself off from the internet. Estonia had to seek US assistance. The following year Russia launched a similarly crippling cyber attack on Georgia preparatory to the advance of Russian troops. Georgian Government and media websites and telephone lines were rendered non-functional and President Saakashvili's website had to be shifted to a US server.

Simultaneously, the Pentagon has initiated research to develop technology and systems to defend its computer systems from cyber attacks before the latter penetrate the US servers. This includes pre-emptive actions such as knocking out parts of an adversary's computer network overseas. Efforts have begun to develop a range of weapons capabilities, which include the capability to allow "attack and exploitation of adversary information systems" and which can "deceive, deny, disrupt, degrade and destroy" information and information systems. The US Deputy Secretary of Defense William J. Lynn III, referred in mid-August 2010 to a "fundamental shift in the U.S. approach to network defense", amplifying this to state that the strategy hinges on the "active defense" of military computer systems. Lynn clarified that this approach means "reaching out" to block malicious software "before they arrive at the door" of military networks, adding that "we need to be able to retain our freedom of movement on the worldwide networks." Keith Alexander, the one-star General who heads the Pentagon's new Cyber Command which comprises 1,000 proficient military hackers, addressing an audience at Tampa (Florida, USA) that August declared "we have to have offensive capabilities, to, in real time, shut down somebody trying to attack us." His statement reflected military thinking that cyberspace is the fifth domain - along with land, air, sea and space - and is crucial to battlefield success.

There are, however, obstacles to implementation of this 'offensive doctrine'. Operationally, experts feel that because the precise configuration of an adversary's computer is difficult to discern through the Internet, it can be very difficult to disrupt that computer's ability to attack without affecting other computers that might be connected to it. For example, the military's dismantling in 2008 of a Saudi website that U.S. officials suspected of facilitating suicide bombers in Iraq also inadvertently disrupted more than 300 servers in Saudi Arabia, Germany and Texas. The Obama Administration wants to avoid recurrence of such eventuality and has put a moratorium on such network warfare actions until clear rules are established. Other countries can be expected to establish similar outfits.

Especially pertinent for India are two independent reports released in March 2009 on China's cyber espionage attempts. These reports released separately by the Munk Centre for International Studies,

University of Toronto and Shishir Nagarajan and Ross Anderson, two researchers from the University of Illinois (USA) and Cambridge (UK) respectively, are very disturbing. Both investigations were triggered by suspicion in the Dalai Lama's office that their computer network was compromised. The two reports were released within days of each other. This may raise doubts about the purpose in publicizing the information and they have, predictably, been denied by the Chinese authorities. Their findings, however, should be equally disturbing to the less advanced countries, who are trying to upgrade IT applications in their infrastructure but tend to purchase equipment from sources that sell them cheaper. They should be even more disturbing to countries with a low awareness of security. Both the reports confirm reliable independent information that China is investing large sums and resources for cyber warfare and has been actively targetting computers, including specific computers, located in other countries.

The reports reveal, after investigation, that 1295 computers in 103 countries were targetted and affected. While the Munk Centre report assessed that the perpetrators of the attacks were based in China, the second report categorically identified the cyber attacks as emanating from China. The reports said that thirty percent of the affected computers were high value targets with many belonging to Embassies, Foreign Ministries of foreign governments and the Dalai Lama's offices in India, Brussels, New York and London. A NATO computer, one in the Indian Embassy in Washington and computers in nine other Indian Embassies viz. UK, US, Germany, Serbia, Cyprus, Belgium, Italy, Kuwait and Zimbabwe were identified as affected. The second report provided more details and stated that at least three government offices in the Philippines (Dept of Foreign Affairs, Dept of S&T, International Trade Bureau in the Dept of Trade), two computers in the Thai Embassy in the Philippines, and computers in the Associated Press office in London and the

ASEAN Secretariats in Indonesia and Malaysia were infected. Other computers affected by these attacks by Chinese hackers were in the Foreign Ministries in Iran, Brunei, Bangladesh, India and Indonesia. The report asserted that infected nodes stretch in an arc from India, Bhutan, Bangladesh, Vietnam, Laos, Brunei, Philippines, Hongkong and Taiwan. Many of the high value targets, it concluded, are linked to offices or individual officers working on Chinese foreign and defence policy matters especially in South and South East Asia.

The reports confirm that the Chinese military establishment has been training hackers and has constituted them into so-called 'patriotic' groups to carry out systematic attacks against selected targets. At times China launches coordinated attacks. The People's Liberation Army (PLA), some years ago, adopted the doctrine of 'active defence', which includes pre-emptive attack as an integral component. The PLA's doctrine also allows for asymmetrical warfare. Cyber warfare fits conveniently into this military philosophy as it can clandestinely probe a potential enemy's vulnerabilities in peacetime and be unleashed at a time and place of China's choosing when hostilities are imminent or when China chooses to convey a warning. Advanced countries, where information technology applications are more extensive and varied, are far more vulnerable. In the case of these countries their public service utilities are very vulnerable to cyber attacks and a capable adversary can disable public transportation, railroads, electricity grids, water supplies, dams, financial systems etc. Advanced countries like the US already have a high level of security awareness and spend large sums on security including cyber security. Timothy Thomas, a US military expert, wrote early in this decade that Chinese strategic thinkers consider that a state of information warfare already exists between China and the West.

The second report, 'Snooping Dragon', gives additional details and assesses that few organizations outside the defence and intelligence establishments would be able to withstand a Chinese cyber attack. The report details the sophistication of the Chinese cyber espionage effort and mentions that the hackers can take over a computer and use its video and audio functions to listen in to conversations and activities in a targetted room. It identifies China as the source of the systematic cyber attacks referred to in the Munk Centre Report and states that the Internet Service Providers (ISPs) based in mainland China and targetting the Tibetan movement are located mainly in the Xinjiang-Uygur Autonomous Region. The other base from which the Chinese hackers operate is in Sichuan province.

Though there could be some skepticism that both the investigations on which the two reports are based were prompted by suspicion in the Dalai Lama's office that the Chinese had possibly taken over some computers or the system, the findings are worrisome. The reports have been viewed seriously by many Intelligence organizations and governments.

India is trying to expand its internet and wireless telecommunications coverage. It is also trying to bring governance and public delivery systems 'on line' and this will increase its vulnerability to hostile cyber attacks. The Indian Railways and the Metro rail transport system, for example, are highly computerized. India has already been the target of cyber attacks in the past few years and earlier this year over 600 computers in the Ministry of External Affairs were detected as infected. The source of attacks was suspected to be China. Similar sustained cyber attacks can be expected to continue. This is equally applicable to the Indian armed forces, which are switching to increasingly sophisticated remotely controlled and guided weapons systems. Sophisticated services like the Air Force are especially vulnerable. These have inherent the risk of vulnerability to attack and disruption. For India, in the context of Chinese cyber warfare capability and preparedness, it is necessary to continually and closely monitor the activities of Chinese hackers and Chinese IT companies on governmental, public and private corporate networks to assess the identities and sophistication of the cyber attackers. It is necessary to acknowledge that China is a global leader in the computer, IT and wireless communications hardware and software industry. The Chinese system of pricing products makes them exceedingly competitive for developing nations who are tempted to purchase Chinese manufactured equipment or spares. This could have serious consequences in the context of cyber espionage, cyber reconnaissance and cyber war. In fact, purchasing computer hardware and equipment like connectors, switches and routers for use in systems increases their vulnerability to cyber-attacks from the manufacturer.

The vital area of 'Critical Communications Technology' is another potential Achilles' heel for many countries and especially the developing nations. The term is used in this context to refer to the sophisticated forms of communication including the internet, namely the mobile and satellite telephone networks. Vulnerabilities in this area will increase globally as the number of mobile phone users worldwide, estimated presently at 4 billion, is expected to touch 4.5 billion by 2013. Moreover, advances in modern communications technologies are effecting a blending between mobile telephones and the internet thus heightening the quantum of disruption that could be caused by a hostile 'attack'. This potential for damage to a vital system has been highlighted in the warning issued by the Chairman of Britain's Joint Intelligence Committee. He asserted in a confidential document that equipment installed by the Chinese telecom company, Huawei, in British Telecom's new communications network could be used to halt critical services like power, food and water supplies. A ready example is Russia's successful action in immobilizing Georgia's telecommunications. The potential for disruption of vital services is accentuated in rapidly developing countries like India, where the number of mobile telephone users is estimated at around 400 million and steadily rising.

The threat is enhanced by the efforts of the PLA to co-opt the Chinese telecommunications companies in their cyber warfare programme, as confirmed by the recent report of USA's Northrop Group. In 2003, the Guangzhou Military Region decided to establish Information Warfare (IW) militia units using local telecommunications companies as a base from which to draw personnel, financial support and infrastructure. In other words, civilian commercial IT expertise was being used to augment the PLA's IW capabilities. PLA officers surveyed Guangzhou's Dongshan District where the IT sector is concentrated to identify suitable personnel with advanced degrees, major scientific research achievements and computer networking expertise. The Guangzhou Military Region established four 'Militia Information Technology Battalions' in local telecommunications companies. These Battalions combined offensive and defensive Electronic Warfare (EW) units in the form of a computer networks operations (CNO) company with attack and defence platoons and an EW company with electronic reconnaissance and deception platoons. The Battalion was tasked to research operational methods for launching hacker attacks, propagating viruses, jamming information channels and disrupting nodes of enemy networks. In 2006, the Academy of Military Sciences (AMS) published an article explicitly officially endorsing the establishment of such IW militia and directed the PLA to make their establishment a priority. Garrison level commands were directed to establish such units with personnel from local commercial IT companies and universities and, where necessary, to relax the age and physical fitness criteria. Measures were taken to prevent exposure of these units to avoid any possible fallout from unintentional disclosure.

The rapid growth of China's telecommunications companies, including in international markets, has facilitated the enhancement of the PLA's cyber warfare capabilities. Some firms like Huawei, ZTE and Venus are leaders in this sector and are closely associated with Chinese government security organisations. Chinese IT and telecommunication companies are part of China's military-industrial-espionage conglomerate and, to an extent, reflect the strategy envisaged by China's leadership while drafting the '863 Programme' and formulating the kind of base required for China to gain global dominance in Information Technology. These companies constitute the defence portion of China's IT sector, which is preponderant alongside an aggressive civilian business side. The close organisational links that exist between China's leading communications enterprises and the PLA are evidence. In addition a number of the senior management, or founders, of these companies are former employees of the PLA or PLA-run research institutes. China's leadership, which has deftly combined the country's military and economic strengths to achieve strategic goals, has similarly used its capabilities in the sector of hi-tech critical communications technology to further, or consolidate, strategic objectives. Huawei and ZTE are two examples of how Chinese hi-tech telecommunications companies work to supplement China's strategic foreign policy goals.

The hi-tech Chinese telecommunications company, Huawei, is closely associated with the PLA and, like others, is a spin-off from a PLA research institute. Its founder CEO is 61-year old Ren Zhengfei, formerly a senior official of a PLA telecommunications research institute. He founded Huawei in 1988 and the company has received national preferences within the system in sales to the PLA. Huawei is a well established supplier of specialized telecommunications equipment, training and related technology to the PLA. It has, along with others such as ZTE and Datang, received direct funding for R&D on C4ISR systems capabilities. All these firms originated from state research institutes and continue to receive preferential funding and support. Huawei's accounts ledgers are secret and it is reported to have supplied Baghdad with 'illicit' communications just prior to the US invasion. Huawei has partnered with 'Beto', a Russian telecommunications company that is affiliated to the Russian military and was earlier involved in the production of missiles. Since Huawei commenced international marketing operations its expansion has been rapid. The Chairperson of Huawei is Ms Sun Yafang, who joined it in 1989 from China's Ministry of State Security.

The Zhongxing Telecom, or ZTE, is the other PLA-affiliated major Chinese telecommunications company that is making inroads into markets abroad. It emerged from the No 691 Electronics Factory under the China Aerospace Corporation which is subordinate to the PLA. Like Huawei, ZTE enjoys national preferences within the system and both companies are among the five that supply routers, switches and computers to the PLA. Founded in 1984, ZTE currently has 27,000 employees and has operations in 33 countries. In the subcontinent these include all of India's neighbours namely Afghanistan, Pakistan, Nepal, Bangladesh and Sri Lanka. According to provincial level Communist Party military newspapers, the ZTE Corp, which is also one of China's large telecommunications manufacturers, provides certification training and related engineering training to PLA personnel assigned to communications and IW related positions.

Julong is another Chinese telecommunications and IT company that is expanding. Located in Luoyang, Henan Province, it has deep links with the PLA. It manufactures routers, connectors, transmitters, mobile phones, networks and digital devices, SDH and DWDM systems, wireless local loop systems, high speed Ethernet switches and telephone systems. Julong is actively targetting the markets in Bangladesh, Pakistan, Vietnam, Cuba, North Korea, Columbia and Russia.

Venus Technologies Inc. is a far smaller and specialised Chinese telecommunications company. It has close ties to the commercial security companies formed by former hacker groups and called XFocus and NSFocus and is also a well known provider of information security and computer network operations expertise to the PLA and dozens of other entities in the PRC government. Venus' customer list published on their Website includes all PLA service branches, all PLA Staff departments (i.e. the General Staff, Armaments, Logistics, and Political Departments) and the defense consortiums China North Industries Group (NORINCO), China Aviation Industry Corp I (AVIC I), China Aerospace Science and Technology Group (CASIC), China Shipbuilding Industry Corporation, and the Jiuquan Satellite Launch Base, China's oldest space launch facility located in Inner Mongolia.

Tianrongxin, also known as Beijing TOPSEC Network Security Technology Company Ltd was founded in November 1995, and is China's largest provider of Information security products and services. Its Chairman is He Weidong. It was started as a small research institute under the '863 programme'. TOPSEC provides services and training to the PLA. TOPSEC is presently a China Information Technology Security Centre (CNITSEC) enterprise and credited with launching China's first 'Firewall' in 1996 along with other IT products like virtual private networks, intrusion detection systems, filtering gateways and security auditing and management systems. In September 2000, He Weidong founded 'Tianweichengxin' to develop business Public Key Infrastructure Certification Authority approved by China's Ministry of Industry and Information Technology (MIIT). The Chinese government owns fifty percent of TOPSEC. TOPSEC also operates and maintains China's National Evaluation and Certification Scheme for IT Security. TOPSEC has extensive linkages with the PLA. In 2004, for example, Yang Hua, a GSP Communications Department's 3rd Communication Regiment officer of the PLA's 61416 Unit was trained by TOPSEC in network security training. TOPSEC is also reported to have recruited hackers and from June 2002 till March 2003 had Lin Yong, owner of the Honker Union of China, on its rolls.

The efforts of Huawei, ZTE and other Chinese telecommunications companies to expand into the US, European and other telecommunications markets need to be viewed in this backdrop. They are enlarging their international presence by securing large contracts, often turnkey, for establishing telephone networks in developing countries and those where China has long term strategic interests. Huawei and ZTE are maintaining, or setting up, country-wide land-line or mobile telephone networks in the countries surrounding India namely, Afghanistan, Pakistan, Nepal, Bangladesh and Sri Lanka. Chinese telecommunications companies are well established in Myanmar. Both, Huawei and ZTE have, surprisingly, been able to develop major interests in the Indian telecommunications market despite the obvious implications for the country's security. Both companies have large offices in Bengaluru and Delhi. Huawei has a major software research centre in Bengaluru—an area in which India is a leader. It also claims to have provided 'cutting edge technology to all the telecom operators' in India. ZTE has registered a sales volume of US$ 1 billion in India in 2009. It has tied up with the Russian telecom company Sistema, which recently launched operations in India.

Huawei and ZTE are together the 'main service providers' (MSPs) for the majority of Indian mobile telephone networks and in most cases also maintain the network operations. The vulnerabilities are obvious. Mobile telephones are used by all levels of politicians, bureaucrats, armed forces and security officials. Corporate and industrial tycoons use them too. Confidential subjects are routinely discussed on these lines. Both Huawei and ZTE have the access to eavesdrop and monitor conversations of persons of interest. If considered necessary they are in a position to selectively disrupt, or terminate, communications of certain phones. In times of crisis or hostility these companies could suspend the country's entire mobile telephone network which are operated or maintained by them causing widespread confusion, systems breakdowns, damage and financial and material loss. Similar concerns prompted UK's Joint Intelligence Committee to issue a warning about Huawei. Other areas vulnerable to attack include those entities using Chinese computer software and hardware. India is undoubtedly a prime target of Chinese cyber attacks and such attacks could be launched by Chinese IT companies from within India.

It is evident that China's leadership has focused on development of an overarching architecture for cyber warfare and network operations. This combines the capability for attacking cyber-based communications and information systems as well as space-based communications like mobile and satellite telephone networks. The inclusion of Lanzhou, Chengdu and Guangzhou among the five Military Regions selected for enhanced Information Warfare capability is noteworthy. Significant also are the efforts of the Chinese commercial telecommunications companies, all of whom are linked to the People's Liberation Army (PLA), to penetrate and dominate the communications infrastructure of countries which are of strategic interest to China. The continuous cyber attacks on targets in various countries similarly point to China's efforts to upgrade its capability.

Cyber warfare is fast developing into the preferred battlefield of the future. It will involve space-based assets and weapons, a high competence in cyber-related hardware and software development, and numbers of technically competent cyber warriors. As more countries opt for e-governance systems to promote transparency in government and accelerate delivery of public services, their populations' vulnerability to cyber attacks will increase. There is little doubt that China will continue to invest resources to rapidly acquire the required capabilities. India and countries falling within what Beijing considers as its sphere of influence will be particularly vulnerable.

This essay, while not published in its entirety earlier, was written in March 2010.

14. India and China: The Way Forward

This decade is witnessing major geopolitical changes as the US, the sole global superpower, readjusts policies to ensure that its pre-eminent status remains unchallenged and its strategic interests world-wide are not threatened. The steady rise of regional powers and especially China, which has acquired the ability to challenge the US' hitherto largely unrestrained exercise of power, has compelled Washington to undertake a reappraisal of US strategic policies. Economic factors, including the perceived decline of US economic strength, have been a significant factor. Perceived, because the current economic decline is something the US will in course of time come out of. It has the advantages of vast underestimated economic assets worldwide, sizeable untapped–or unexploited–natural resources and an unmatched lead in very advanced scientific and military technologies and capabilities. A major determinant for virtually all countries, including India, in shaping their strategic and foreign policies will be the nature of the US-China relationship that finally emerges.

There can be no doubt that China's growth has so far been steady and has the approval of the vast majority of Chinese people. China's rapid economic rise and military modernization have enabled it to command increasing influence in the Asia-Pacific region, Europe and international fora. While many countries in the Asia-Pacific are dependent on China's huge economy for their exports and their physical proximity to China inhibits a definitive independent stance, even European governments, weakened by their domestic economic condition, have capitulated to Beijing on matters like Human Rights, IPR and Tibet—all issues which they traditionally used to castigate Beijing.

China today is a very self-confident nation and this self-confidence is translating into growing assertiveness. The mix of assertiveness combined with a strong dose of nationalism, or nationalist jingoism, is now part of China's strategic calculus and is visible in China's foreign policy initiatives with the US, Europe and in the region as also in its uncompromising stance on issues affecting its "core national interests" and sovereignty. Pronouncements on the latter by Chinese military academics and serving and retired People's Liberation Army (PLA) officers indicate the views of the CCP leadership and are not, as suggested by some analysts, off-the-cuff remarks by a pushy PLA. This is borne out by the fact that such remarks have often been published in the official Chinese media and none of those who made such strong remarks have been contradicted or penalized. In fact, many have been promoted. The Chinese Communist Party (CCP)'s grip on the PLA has also, in recent years, been getting increasingly firm.

This self-confidence is similarly reflected in the content of the Chinese media and comments in the millions of micro-blogs posted daily. The mushrooming of Chinese government-sponsored Confucius Centres worldwide and infusion of billions of dollars to revamp and expand outreach of the official Chinese print (the People's Daily is set to launch a US edition) and visual media is reflective of this. The Chinese Communist Party (CCP) Central Committee (CC)'s Propaganda Department has concurrently tightened control on all content in the Chinese media and websites and these are strictly monitored and censored. It is, of course, adapting to changing situations and has reduced the number of topics that are off-limits to the official media.

India-China relations specifically need to be viewed in this backdrop. The Chinese leadership's view of India is significant. While discussing India in interactions with foreign strategists and diplomats, Chinese officials and members of Chinese government-controlled think-tanks list three main items as issues of concern.

These are, in the Chinese-listed order of priority: the Dalai Lama and Tibet issue; the border dispute; and India's geopolitical ambitions. These can be classified as tactical and short-term, medium-to-long term and strategic. For example, during the US-China Strategic Dialogue in Washington a few months ago, when the US proposed a US-China-India trilateral, China vehemently rejected the idea and questioned how the US could place India anywhere near on par with China when the two were not at all comparable. Noteworthy also is the omission by China of vital natural resource issues like water and food, which will become serious factors that bedevil the relationship in the next ten to fifteen years.

For India, dealing with China will be a major challenge through this decade. China's growing economic strength, military might and attitude towards India, are factors that India will have to contend with. Catching up with China's economy—far from overtaking it as various economists and academics have suggested—is out of the question, unless the CCP stumbles and its grip over the administrative apparatus and society is weakened. Going by the internal political developments of the past some months this might not be such an outlandish idea. Many observers would be aware of the new high in political infighting in the CCP, with Beijing being awash with rumours on the 14th March night that Bo Xilai has been removed as Party Secretary of Chongqing. This comes within a day of Wen Jiabao saying at a press conference on 14th March that the Chongqing leadership should learn lessons from the Wang Lijun incident. However, the CCP is unlikely to get too debilitated and will last for the next five years and probably through the decade.

Given China's attitude towards India, the unresolved border issue and other foreseeable areas of competition, it is evident that India will need to fashion a policy which allows it to resolutely withstand persistently increasing Chinese pressure while simultaneously seeking areas of cooperation to defuse tensions. It will need to deftly balance safeguarding of national interests with the shortfalls in capabilities. Policies will require to be designed to meet short, as well as long term, interests and predicated on India's 'going it alone' as the US, and any other country will, in event of conflagration, only be a distant witness.

It is important for India not to forget, or dismiss as an aberration: the close Sino-Pak relations; China-brokered missile-for-technology deal between Pakistan and North Korea; China's close support to Pakistan including on the Indo-US Civilian Nuclear Agreement; their joint effort to get NSG to veto the deal; ignoring of the Indian Prime Minister's phone call; opposition to India's entry to the UNSC as a regular Permanent member; steady upgrading of the border dispute and claims in Arunachal Pradesh and J&K into an international dispute in keeping with the principles of 'Sanzhong Zhanfa' or 'Three Warfares'; ignoring Indian concerns regarding water (Brahmaputra); etc. This attitude is buttressed by the warnings to India by Chinese academics and strategists that China may need to "teach it a lesson". Similarly, any thinking that India-China relations will improve in case India is able to broker a thaw between the Dalai Lama and Beijing is unreal. The initiatives taken by Beijing confirm that it has decided to wait the Dalai Lama out. Realistically, the current unease in relations is unlikely to dissipate at least in this decade.

India, however, has options that will consolidate its position without the adoption of a politics of confrontation. These will need to be implemented within the next five odd years. A few are mentioned.

The first step should be to consolidate our legitimate sovereignty over the states which abut the borders, thereby simultaneously calling into question China's claims. This can easily be done by aggressively abolishing the requirement of 'inner line' permits in the border areas of the Himalayan belt and the north-east and encouraging tourism by facilitating hotels, visas and connectivity. In this age of Google Maps the requirement of 'inner line' permits is archaic. Connectivity in the region is currently very poor. There should be multiple and upgraded road and air links between Delhi, the major metropolis and each of the states and regions like Ladakh, Sikkim, Arunachal Pradesh, Assam, Meghalaya etc in the north-east. Traffic will pick up in a short while, but in the interim, fares in these sectors must be subsidized for Indian citizens. Such a move will automatically severely retard China's efforts to internationalise the border/territorial dispute and acquire legitimacy.

Upgrading of defence and cargo related transport infrastructure in the border areas has not made an appreciable dent despite the passage of over five years since a crash programme was initiated. This needs to be done urgently and comprehensively by building a border roads network augmented by satellite and network communications and airfields or helipads. If necessary, private companies should be invited to participate.

India needs to seriously build its indigenous defence capability and factor in adequate deterrence. India's defence capability will be taken seriously only once it appreciably reduces the need for defence-related imports. The current programme for upgrading the armed forces also needs to be objectively reviewed. More importantly, Beijing will change, or pause in, its policy towards India only when India has a demonstrable capacity for imposing costs. China's current military doctrine is clear that any conflict will open with an overwhelming cyber and electronic jamming offensive followed quickly by a barrage of targeted missile strikes aimed at military command and communications centres, airfields, airfield repair units, troop concentrations and political centres of power. In the second stage they will strike public utilities, government networks and population centres. The stated objective is to overwhelm and destroy the will of the military and political leadership and compel them to capitulate. Long range missiles are India's only quick, affordable and effective option. India should rapidly develop and operationalise a missile strike capability to target Beijing and other major cities in China's heartland. China will not be deterred by missile strikes in Tibet, Xinjiang or elsewhere in the peripheral regions.

China is rapidly strengthening its maritime capability and has plans to induct three aircraft carriers into the PLA Navy (PLAN) soon. The Varyag, which will be renamed, is going to be operationalised in the PLAN on PLA Day on 1 August. An under-assessed aspect is the PLAN's submarine warfare and Unmanned Underwater Vessel (UUV) capability. Added is the adverse and disturbing impact of China selling UUVs to Pakistan. India has a few years to strengthen the Navy, including as the third leg of its nuclear triad, if it wants to secure its shores, sea-lanes and retain dominance in the Indian Ocean.

Cyber warfare is a critical component of China's strategy and, in this context, India needs to beware of the activities of Chinese telecommunications companies like Huawei and ZTE.

The study of all aspects of contemporary China is imperative and India is severely deficient in this. Required are many more think-tanks dedicated to the study and analysis of China with the focus on specific subjects of national interest. Government needs to encourage the start-up of such think-tanks and fund them generously so they can hire and retain competent and knowledgeable individuals, Chinese language knowing researchers and, travel without seeking foreign funding or non-reciprocal hospitality to relevant countries. There should be a sharing of non-classified information — like data on personalities, visits exchanged and details of meetings — between government and think-tanks. Analysis by a think-tank with an ideological bias will not be objective or independent and, in fact, prove misleading. Analyses provided by the think-tanks will supplement those by government departments.

At the same time, Government needs to very quickly acquire relevant capability to analyse China-related developments in-house and, more importantly, get advance information regarding China's military exercises, movements and missile deployments and operational readiness. Present day military operations give extremely short reaction times and the Government agencies must be ready to meet the new demands.

In addition to these measures, India should send a large number of young scholars between 20-25 years old to Taiwan, Singapore, and some to China, to study Chinese. While a number of them today are lured to the travel trade by higher remunerations, if they are sent in large numbers then many will be available for government, think-tanks, China-related research, industry and media. As a beginning, a hundred scholarships a year would begin to meet the requirements.

India can also ease visa restrictions to welcome groups of tourists and students from China. This will expose large numbers of Chinese to an entirely different, democratic environment and way of life. In the long run it should undercut long-held propaganda or prejudices about India. Finally, India and China should explore areas of long-term mutually-beneficial cooperation. A major area that offers itself for long-term joint endeavour is the harnessing of a dependable and secure source of alternate energy with a minimal carbon footprint. China has unveiled an ambitious plan for harnessing solar energy in space to tackle its need for a secure and abundant source of energy. Plans are to build a facility in space with 100MW capacity to capture solar power and relay it to earth to generate electricity. It envisages that a space solar energy station will be completed and ready for commercial use by 2040. India has similarly been investing in science and made remarkable progress in space science and technology. The project offers the leadership of both countries the opportunity to invest resources and scientific know-how in a venture that has the promise to substantially alleviate their national energy concerns. Participation by China and India in such a joint solar energy project, anticipated to become operational in 30 years, will provide adequate time to promote understanding and dispel suspicion.

The investment of high grade scientific resources, huge amount of finances and the anticipated mutual benefit, should deter disruption of the project. Finally, in addition to the numerous beneficial diplomatic spin-offs, the project will usher a technical revolution in the fields of new energy, new material and solar energy leading to the emergence of several industries and simultaneously elevating the manufacturing technology and capabilities of both countries. Such cooperation would be a long-lasting, beneficial, confidence-building measure and, if suspicions are not dispelled in thirty years they never will be!

This is the text of a valedictory address delivered by the author at a National Seminar on "India & China: The Way Forward", organised by the Chennai Centre for China Studies on March 16, 2012.

15. High-Level Visits from China: New Diplomatic Strategy

By the end of this year India would have played host to two of China's senior most leaders. The first visitor, Zhou Yongkang, arrived on a 3-day (Oct 31-Nov 2, 2010) visit in early November. His ranking at the bottom of the list of the 9-member Politburo Standing Committee, the Chinese Communist Party's all-powerful and apex body, belies his true importance and influence as China's Security Czar. In that capacity he oversees the country's entire Party, government and military security apparatus. Chinese Premier Wen Jiabao is the other dignitary scheduled to arrive on December 16. Both these leaders are due to demit office on retirement at the next Chinese Communist Party (CCP) Congress scheduled to held around October 2012. The visits occur at an important juncture in India-China relations and when the geopolitical situation in Asia and the Asia-Pacific is in a state of flux.

Both the leaders are also traveling to India at a time when there is a visible assertiveness in China's policies, which is reflective of the newfound confidence among the Chinese leadership and people. This has been generated largely by China's consistent double-digit economic growth over three decades and ensuant international adulation. The Chinese Communist Party (CCP) leadership's confidence particularly, stems from its view that: (i) the Party's successful policies have raised the nation to its present level of military strength and economic prosperity; (ii) that the country is much wealthier as visible in its high share of international trade, huge US$ 2.4 trillion foreign currency reserves etc. and that the majority of the people are vastly better off than before as evidenced by their approximately US$ 4,000 annual per capita income; (iii) that the Party has generally maintained stability and law and order in society, including to a fair extent in the restive Autonomous Regions of Xinjiang and Xizang (Tibet); and (iv) that the Party's pre-eminent position currently remains unassailable.

Chinese analysts have concurrently assessed that, in contrast, the US military is over-stretched consequent to being embroiled in the wars in Iraq and Afghanistan and that the world's major economies, especially the US, have been considerably weakened because of the deleterious effects of the international economic crisis. China's leaders, therefore, perceive the current time as opportune for China to make its bid for pre-eminence in the larger Asia-Pacific region.

Zhou Yongkang, in his capacity as China's chief of security has considerable say in matters concerning maintenance of social stability and order. His inputs are particularly important in decisions and policies regarding the national minorities and autonomous regions, especially concerning the Uyghurs in Xinjiang and Tibetans in Xizang, or the Tibet Autonomous Region. He, in fact, headed the preparatory groups for the two major Work Forums on Tibet and Xinjiang held in the first half of this year. His responsibility for policies relating to China's minority nationalities was not lost on the Tibetan community in India, who staged a protest when he was in Delhi on Nov 1. Significantly, Zhou Yongkang has additionally been entrusted with a major role in formulating China's new Asia policy, which includes India, and is in the last stages of finalization. His visit to India was also in this connection.

Others involved in formulation of the new Asia policy include Dai Bingguo, China's Special Representative for Talks with India as also separately with Russia and USA. He is understood to be an advocate of a hard line stance on India. Vice President and newly appointed Vice Chairman of the Central Military Commission, Xi Jinping, is another important member of the team. He is Deputy Head of the Party's Leading Group on Foreign Affairs Work. He is also a member of the Party's Leading Group on National Security Work. His proximity to Zhou Yongkang and his background strongly suggest that he would side with Dai Bingguo. Foreign Minister Yang Jiechi, also a member of this policy formulation body, is believed to favour a moderate position. He will, however, be outnumbered. China's Commerce Minister, Chen Deming, a Doctorate in Economics and Business Administration, is another member of the Party's Leading Group on Foreign Affairs Work.

The highlight of Zhou Yongkang's visit to India was his address to the Second India-China Conference convened by the Congress Party. The last of the five points that he recommended at this conference incorporated a new formulation. He said 'for controversial issues and disagreements, the two countries should properly handle them on the basis of mutual respect, consultations on equal basis and mutual understanding and mutual accommodation, so as not to let specific issues affect the overall relations'. The formulation expands the scope of discussions to include all controversies and disagreements, including the border, implying that negotiations could be protracted. During his visit he met the Prime Minister, External Affairs Minister, Congress President Ms Sonia Gandhi and her son Rahul Gandhi as also leaders of the main opposition party, the BJP and leaders of the three Left parties. Meeting Sonia Gandhi, the Chinese visitor described her as one who knew China well, was a friend and had visited China five times. The border issue, according to the official Chinese news agency Xinhua, was discussed with Rahul Gandhi. Zhou Yongkang briefly visited the Infosys campus in Bangalore on his way back to China.

Coinciding with Zhou Yongkang's stay in India, the People's Daily on Nov 2 published an article by its editor, Li Hongmei. Commenting on the Indian Prime Minister's visits to Japan, Malaysia and Vietnam, the article described India's 'Look East Policy' as 'Look to Encircle China'. It concluded with the veiled warning that 'India's leadership will not rashly board the ship of

Japan without giving a glance at China's expression'.

During his interaction with the Prime Minister, CCP CC Politburo Standing Committee member Zhou Yongkang predictably mentioned the issue of the Dalai Lama and Tibet. Both are important items on his agenda. When the Prime Minister raised the issue of the Chinese government issuing stapled visas to residents of Jammu and Kashmir, however, Zhou Yongkang side-stepped a reply observing that it would be better discussed with Premier Wen Jiabao. Xinhua's domestic service despatch of Nov 2, while reporting this meeting, did mention the Indian Prime Minister's assurance that India regarded the Tibet Autonomous Region as part of China and that India would not let Tibetans in India engage in anti-China activities, but omitted any reference to the Prime Minister raising India's concerns regarding Kashmir or the issue of stapled visas.

The deft manner in which the Chinese have been handling this question, with senior leaders declining to directly give a response, is pertinent. At the same time, Beijing has reiterated its unyielding official position on the issue of stapled visas to residents of J&K at every opportunity.

A day prior to Prime Minister Manmohan Singh's meeting with Chinese Premier Wen Jiabao on the sidelines of the ASEAN Summit in Hanoi on October 27, 2010, the Chinese Foreign Ministry spokesman at the official press briefing on October 26 stated, in reply to a question, that: "China and India are staying in close communication on the issue. Once there's any update, information will be released in due course. China's visa policy toward residents of the India-held Kashmir is consistent and remains unchanged". When the Indian and Chinese leaders met a day later and the Indian Prime Minister raised the subject, the Chinese Premier replied that it could be taken up when they met in India.

Similarly, just prior to the meeting between the Indian and Chinese Foreign Ministers at the India-Russia-China Tripartite Meeting in

Wuhan, China, on Nov 14-15, 2010, the Chinese Foreign Ministry spokesperson clarified that the issue of stapled visas to residents of Jammu and Kashmir was official policy. According to the briefing by Indian officials on Nov 15, 2010, during his meeting with Chinese Foreign Minister Yang Jiechi, India's External Affairs Minister SM Krishna for the first time ever drew a parallel between the 'territorial red lines' of both countries. He told China that just as New Delhi had been sensitive to its concerns over the Tibet Autonomous Region and Taiwan, Beijing too should be mindful of Indian sensitivities on Jammu and Kashmir. The statement was intended to underscore the depth of India's concerns over recent Chinese attempts to question the country's sovereignty in Kashmir. Clarifying the context to the press, Foreign Secretary Nirupama Rao said the two Ministers reviewed the state of bilateral relations, which Yang Jiechi described as in "very good shape." External Affairs Minister Krishna said there was a need for both sides to be sensitive to each other's core concerns. Foreign Secretary Nirupama Rao said "in that context the External Affairs Minister spoke of Jammu and Kashmir and expressed the hope that China would be sensitive to J&K just as we have been to the Tibet Autonomous Region and Taiwan". Chinese Foreign Minister Yang Jiechi, however, did not deviate from current policy and replied that 'China always believed the problem of Jammu and Kashmir could only be resolved through dialogue and negotiations between India and Pakistan and that there has been no change in its policy'.

Chinese Premier Wen Jiabao's upcoming visit to India on December 16, will be his second, the last being in April 2005. He will combine it with visits to two other countries including Pakistan. Anticipating that the matter of China issuing stapled visas to residents of J&K will be raised when he visits India, he will come prepared. But the Chinese are unlikely to grant any meaningful concession. Chinese Premier Wen Jiabao could also choose to mainly discuss economic and trade matters and raise the subject of the Dalai Lama and Tibet in a pro forma manner to avoid the discussions becoming contentious and marring the atmosphere of his visit.

This visit by Wen Jiabao takes place before his scheduled retirement in October 2012. It also occurs after a couple of telling incidents. During the Sichuan earthquake in 2008 when Wen Jiabao was personally leading the national disaster relief operations, the PLA and PAP forces did not render any assistance till instructions were issued by Military Commission Chairman and PRC President Hu Jintao after his premature return from the G-20 Summit. More recently, Wen Jiabao's comments on 'democracy', made in an extensive interview on Oct 3, 2010 with CNN's Farid Zakaria, were blanked out by the official Chinese media. This is most unusual in the case of the third highest ranking leader in China who, in any case, probably referred to 'socialist democracy' and not democracy as understood by Westerners.

The visits by Zhou Yongkang and Wen Jiabao to India take place when bilateral relations are under strain because of China's actions and insensitivity to India's concerns. They coincide with China adopting an assertive posture with India. While at the superficial level border negotiations and official-level contacts between India and China continue, military pressure along the entire 4,057 kms undemarcated India-China border has been constant with no decline in the incidence of intrusions. There has, on the contrary, been a steady increase in pressure on a range of issues. Illustrative are China's: opposition to the Indo-US Civil Nuclear Agreement; ducking receiving the telephone call from the Prime Minister; attempts to frustrate India's bid for a permanent seat at the UNSC; continuing assistance to Pakistan militarily and for expanding its nuclear capabilities; augmenting of China's military infrastructure in Tibet; re-opening the hitherto settled issue of Sikkim; and enhancing the profile of its territorial claim on Arunachal Pradesh, which it refers to as 'southern Tibet'. It initiated a policy of declining visas to residents of Arunachal

Pradesh and compelled international institutions not to extend loans for development projects in that state. More recently, it raised the ante in Kashmir by inviting a Hurriyat 'leader' to China through an NGO, designating the entire state as 'disputed' by issuing loose-leaf visas to residents of the state and later declining a visa to the Northern Army Commander on the plea that he commands troops in the 'disputed territory of J&K'.

Another issue with the potential to cause serious discord is the proposed diversion of the Brahmaputra river waters. Work on the Western Route, which directly affects India, began this year and is scheduled for completion in 2050. There is talk of a mega construction at the Great Bend just north of where the Brahmaputra enters India. Though Chinese President Hu Jintao officially denied plans to divert the Brahmaputra while meeting Indian Prime Minister Manmohan Singh in Delhi in 2006, and kept silent during the Prime Minister's subsequent visit to China, there is evidence – including satellite photographs – that construction of dams at various points along the river has started. Available reports suggest there are plans for constructing 17 dams along the course of the Yarlung Tsangpo river. Construction of the dam at Zhangmu commenced last year and, according to an announcement by the TAR Governor in March 2009, four dams are planned on the Brahmaputra. Despite India seeking clarification regarding Chinese plans for diverting the waters of the Brahmaputra none has been forthcoming. In fact, China steadfastly denied it was constructing any dams till a couple of months ago when, confronted with data, it admitted to building a hydel project at Zhangmu. Beijing, however, described this as a 'run of the river' project similar to that being built by India on the Sutlej river.

Deep seated suspicions in Beijing of US intentions could well influence the India-China relationship. The growing warmth in US-India relations is a source of apprehension for Beijing and has generated numerous critical references in China's authoritative official media and by its military and strategic analysts. The large-scale joint US-ROK military exercises, second phase of which commenced on November 28, and escalation of tension on the Korean Peninsula has added to the pressure on China. These concerns were reflected during the tension in US-China relations this July when the US-ROK joint military exercises were staged in the Yellow Sea. A Hong Kong-based Chinese language paper at that time observed '…the issue of China's territorial disputes with neighbouring countries will ignite the flames of war sooner or later. If a country must be chosen for sacrifice, India will be the first choice…India's long term occupation of southern Tibet (Arunachal Pradesh) is indeed worrying…If armed force is used to resolve border disputes, China must pick a county to target first, and it will definitely pick a big country, which means choosing between Japan and India…'. Numerous other critical references to India were noticed in China's official media in the period between July-August 2010. Similar references earlier to Japan and India had added that China's relationship with both these countries have limits imposed by history. Numerous critical references were again seen during US President Obama's visit to India. These harped that the US was trying to draw India into an alliance and that US, Japan and India were trying to contain China.

The visits to India by Zhou Yongkang and Wen Jiabao sandwich that by US President Obama last month. The visits are part of China's two-tiered diplomatic strategy of overtly portraying normalcy, by exchanging high level official visits with nations where there are strains in the relationship, while simultaneously pushing assertively on issues perceived as affecting sovereignty or territory. Examples are the number of high level visits exchanged with Vietnam recently and Chinese President Hu Jintao's meeting with Japanese Prime Minister Naoto Kan on the sidelines of the APEC Summit in Tokyo, despite strained ties with Japan and the Dalai Lama's presence in Japan at the time. China's relations with both these countries are strained. The objectives of this strategy would be to keep the door open for negotiations, portray China's 'reasonableness', induce a sense of complacency in the other country, and exert pressure – including military – to extract concessions. The recently concluded important fifth plenum of the seventeenth CCP Central Committee reiterated the objective of 'winning short-duration local wars under hi-tech informatised conditions'.

Indications are that China will continue to exert pressure on India on a range of issues and be unyielding in its stance on the border. The Chinese authorities will urge the Dalai Lama's representatives to get the Dalai Lama to resile from his declared position on the border issue including Tawang. During Wen Jiabao's forthcoming visit India's leadership should clearly assert India's interests and enumerate the various areas of concern indicating that Kashmir is not the only one.

This was published as an Issue Brief by the Centre for Air Power Studies on December 6, 2010.

16. China's Actions in Kashmir: Implications

Increasingly regarded during the past few years as the potential cockpit of future conflict in South Asia, Kashmir and the disputed India-China border have been brought into sharper focus by China's recent actions. More importantly, it reveals that in addition to its policy of trying to keep India under pressure and contained within the subcontinent, Beijing has decided to follow a definitively assertive policy regarding its claims in both, the eastern and western, sectors. This could well be reflected in official talks, including on the border issue. In a deliberate move Beijing had earlier publicly re-stated its claim on Arunachal Pradesh, through a statement by its Ambassador, just days prior to Chinese President Hu Jintao's arrival in Delhi in 2006. China's actions have now focussed the glare of media attention on the Kashmir issue as well as the latent tensions in India-China relations.

Events centering on Kashmir have gained in momentum and gravity over the past couple of years. US and Chinese interests also converge in Pakistan. While the US continues to exert pressure from behind the scenes on Islamabad and New Delhi to work towards a compromise arrangement on Kashmir and nudged India into taking concessionary conciliatory steps, China has now chosen to opt for more assertive and direct action. Particularly in recent weeks China has publicised its hardened stance on the Kashmir issue, thereby raising the ante. This is a qualitative departure from its policy of maintaining pressure on India by steadily increasing the number and nature of intrusions across the remote terrain through which the Line of Actual Control (LAC) runs. Significantly, Beijing's decision to publicise its new stance has been timed to coincide with the volatile situation that began developing in Kashmir since June this year.

Beijing's reluctance to accept a routinely proposed visit of the Northern Army Commander demonstrated its hardened stance on the Kashmir issue. Beijing would have been aware that its cited pretext, that the Army Commander's operational jurisdiction includes the 'disputed area of Jammu and Kashmir', would become public knowledge and raise objections. China has expressed similar reservation in at least one other case recently. Beijing has thus expanded its objections to the inclusion of residents of Jammu and Kashmir and Arunachal Pradesh in official or quasi-official delegations while reiterating the 'disputed' status of both these states of the Indian Union.

That the decision not to accept the Northern Army Commander's visit was deliberate and taken by the highest echelons of China's Party and Government is reinforced by another action reported to have occurred in Shanghai last month. On that occasion personnel of China's Public Security Bureau strode in to the India Pavillion in 'Shanghai Expo-2010' and seized printed material depicting India's territorial boundaries. This action, which occurred almost four months after the Shanghai-Expo opened, was timed to attract attention and taken when the exhibition was open to the public.

China's latest actions regarding Kashmir follow a predetermined pattern, which has consistently reflected a pro-Pakistan bias. They were preceded by the decision, implemented since the beginning of last year, to issue loose-leaf, or stapled, visas to residents of Jammu and Kashmir. With this Beijing signalled that it considered the entire state of Jammu and Kashmir as 'disputed'. Delhi-based Chinese diplomats and 'well-informed' Chinese journalists sought to peddle the story that this decision was taken by the Embassy in Delhi without consulting Beijing. Beijing, however, has not rescinded this decision despite repeated protests by India at various levels. In any event, such a major policy decision, which would undoubtedly impact on Sino-India relations, can only have been taken at the highest levels of the Chinese Communist Party and Government. In fact, the Chinese Foreign Ministry spokesperson reiterated in early September that the policy regarding 'stapled' visas for residents of Jammu and Kashmir would continue. Since October last year, maps and brochures distributed to visitors and journalists invited to Tibet by the Chinese government depict Kashmir as an entity separate from India. Media kits providing 'basic information' about Tibet describe Tibet as having 'borders with India, Nepal, Myanmar and Kashmir area'. For many years China's defence attaché in Delhi has declined to participate in visits to Jammu and Kashmir organized by the Ministry of Defence on the plea that it was a 'disputed area'. A visit by the Commander of the Lanzhou Military Region to Jammu and Kashmir a while ago was cancelled due to Pakistan's objections regarding the status of Kashmir. In stark contrast, visits are exchanged between high officials from China and Pak-occupied Kashmir (PoK), Chinese military delegations visit PoK and Chinese state-owned companies are engaged in an estimated over 60 projects in PoK in addition to repairing the Karakoram Highway. By neglecting Indian sensitivities Beijing has 'de facto' narrowed the dispute only to the portion of Kashmir within India. Beijing can be expected to emphasise Kashmir's 'disputed' status by taking steps like objecting to financial assistance by international organisations.

Two summit meetings between US President Obama and Chinese President Hu Jintao constitute the backdrop for these overtly assertive actions by Beijing on the Kashmir issue. The five-part joint statement issued on November 17, 2009 and quickly welcomed by Islamabad, includes two paragraphs seriously impinging on India's interests. US and China, one paragraph observes, would work for the "improvement and growth of relations between India and Pakistan...". It asserts "both sides are ready to strengthen communication, dialogue and cooperation on issues related to South Asia and work together to promote peace, stability and development in that region". There is no specific mention of Kashmir, but the context is clear. Pertinent to the joint statement was the exchange between US President Obama and Chinese President Hu Jintao at their earlier summit meeting in Pittsburg on September 22. China's official news agency 'Xinhua' reported that Hu Jintao urged Obama, in the context of the China-US bilateral relationship, that "the two countries should push for a proper resolution to the regional issues relating to the Korean Peninsula, Iran and South Asia".

Beijing's attitude on Kashmir became visible soon after the September Summit last year, suggesting the subject had figured in earlier discussions between Washington and Beijing. Just days prior to the Hu-Obama Summit, Chinese Vice Foreign Minister He Zhengyue announced China's willingness to mediate between India and Pakistan if requested, and the offer was repeated twice soon after the Summit. Hurriyat 'leader' Mirwaiz Umar Farooq's assertion, made promptly after issue of the Joint Statement, that China has a role in settlement of the Kashmir issue and disclosure that he will be travelling to Beijing soon after Eid – the first time any Hurriyat member would go there – reinforces suspicion that Washington and Beijing have discussed the Kashmir issue possibly keeping Islamabad in the loop. Hurriyat 'leaders' have, in any case, invariably been received at the US State Department during their visits to the US when they also separately meet personnel of the Pakistan Embassy. China's desire to keep cordial relations with India has dictated some ambiguity on the Kashmir issue in recent years, but Beijing is now apparently preparing for a proactive role.

The situation in Afghanistan and US desire to pull out by mid-2011 has again contributed to convergence of US and Chinese short term interests. The US pressured China to conclude the US$ 3.5 billion deal to develop the Aynak copper deposit in southern Afghanistan. US expects China, with its huge foreign exchange reserves and hunger for energy resources, to be attracted by Afghanistan's estimated

US$ 1 trillion mineral resources and spur mineral development thus generating a legitimate source of revenue for the Afghan government. This would facilitate US withdrawal.

China's plans for Afghanistan are, however, long term. It has taken up numerous projects in areas infested by the Taliban. While China's earlier security ties with the Taliban regime have got diluted, it expects to benefit from Pakistan's links with the wide spectrum of forces in Afghanistan and Taliban. It has also ingressed Afghanistan's telecommunications sector and ZTE and Huawei, both affiliated to the Chinese People's Liberation Army, have set up digital telephone services in the country and provided almost 200,000 subscriber lines. Both are prominent in Pakistan's telecommunications infrastructure. China has also participated in the Parwan irrigation project and restoration of public hospitals in Kabul and Kandahar.

Afghanistan is at a geo-strategically sensitive location. Apart from immense reserves of oil, gas and precious and rare metals, it sits astride important trade routes that inter-link Central and South Asia. Afghanistan and Central Asian countries are within a region that is not under the dominance of a single major power and the region has become the scene of major power competition. China too has a multiplicity of interests. It is intent on insulating its north-western border from the spread of extremist Islamic ideas and stopping the trans-border support received by separatist Uyghur outfits from Central Asian countries. Expansion of influence in the region will be a buffer in event of any future deterioration of relations with Russia. It will be a deterrent against possible inimical plans by the US to encourage Tibetans and Uyghur 'separatists' to undertake adventures inside Tibet and Xinjiang. Finally, development of a transport network across the region will open new economic opportunities and markets for its land-locked hinterland provinces. The China-dominated Shanghai Cooperation Organisation (SCO) is well placed to play an active role in future.

The freight railway line from western China through Tajikstan into Afghanistan and on to Pakistan has immense strategic implications for China and the region. It will be Afghanistan's first long distance railway and link it to other markets, primarily China. It will bring Afghanistan into the orbit of the Central Asian Republics. The railway line will augment China's ability to transport cargo and passengers from western China to Gwadar. It will upgrade China's military logistics capability, facilitating movement of troops to the borders with Russia as well as into Afghanistan and Pakistan. It will enhance China's influence in Tajikstan as the latter will get an alternate trade route instead of the present sole route through Russia. Its investments and influence in Afghanistan, and particularly the railway line, will give China dominant influence in Central Asia and the Persian Gulf. China's strategic analysts and official media articles have frequently mentioned the importance of China acquiring a foothold in Central Asia.

China has also invested huge amounts in Pakistan, especially in its western areas from Gilgit to Gwadar. Beijing plans more investments including upgradation of the Karakoram highway and extension to Gwadar, a China-Pakistan railway over the Karokaram and a gas pipeline running along the same alignment. Ongoing developments in Pakistan are, however, a source of concern and China would be preparing to safeguard its investments against any future adverse eventuality. The well informed Chinese-language 'Hong Kong Economic Journal', which has credible reporting on China, implicitly endorsed this by stating: 'even though China has accumulated relevant experience in building the Qinghai-Tibet railway, the question of how to overcome political instability in some areas of Pakistan will be the key to success of the construction of the (proposed) railway. The constant struggles among domestic political factions and unresolved religious and secular conflicts in Pakistan will create a huge test for the normal operation of the China-Pakistan railway. If the China-

Pakistan railway, which will cost billions of Yuans to build, cannot be used effectively because of domestic chaos in Pakistan, it will no doubt have a negative effect on China's strategic intentions'. Well before the New York Times report by Selig Harrison, claiming that Chinese troops are in northwest Pakistan, surfaced, a report hinting at the development had appeared in this Chinese paper. It disclosed that: 'Chinese special forces may be invited to Pakistan to assist in counter-terrorism and stabilizing the situation...If the Chinese army enters Pakistan, this will be a major variable in Central Asia...By reaching Pakistan, they will draw closer to the Iranian border...This news has reportedly attracted Washington's close attention and was also one of the reasons why the Yellow Sea exercises were halted temporarily...It is only a matter of time before Chinese troops head west into Central Asia and the most likely breakthrough point is indeed Pakistan with special forces acting as the vanguard...'. China and Pakistan have held three joint counter-terrorism exercises since 2004 and, viewed with these reports, it seems Beijing is preparing for a more robust role in the region. Its stance on Kashmir is inextricably linked to this. China's actions will benefit Pakistan and be coordinated with Islamabad.

The recent warmth in US-India relations has become a source of apprehension for Beijing, generating numerous critical references in China's authoritative official media and by its military and strategic analysts. A Hong Kong-based paper observed '...the issue of China's territorial disputes with neighbouring countries will ignite the flames of war sooner or later. If a country must be chosen for sacrifice, India will be the first choice...India's long term occupation of southern Tibet (Arunachal Pradesh) is indeed worrying...If armed force is used to resolve border disputes, China must pick a country to target first, and it will definitely pick a big country, which means choosing between Japan and India...'. Similar references to Japan and India had added that China's relationship with both these countries have limits imposed by history. More critical references were noticed in recent weeks when tensions were high because of the US-ROK exercises in the Yellow Sea.

China has additionally injected a military component to stiffen its actions. During this period the Chengdu Military Region conducted at least three military exercises inside Tibet across India's borders. Additional types of fighter aircraft were deployed this year at Gonggar airfield and China has operationalised seven modern airfields in Tibet. Border defences and road and rail networks are being extended and upgraded. Plans envisage a railway running along China's border with India from east to west. Interestingly, the number of Lieutenant Generals and Major Generals (in the PLA and PAPF) in the Chengdu Military Region have registered an increase. This is particularly noticeable in the Tibet Military District. (Table below).

Chengdu Military Region

	2005	2007	2008	2009 (till Jul 2010)
Gen	1	–	–	–
Lt Gen	8	10	6	10
Maj Gen	54	48	53	70

Tibet (Xizang) Military District

	2005	2007	2008	2009 (till Jul 2010)
Gen	–	–	–	–
Lt Gen	–	–	–	1
Maj Gen	8	9	7	12

China's strategy of trying to confine India within the subcontinent and keeping it under pressure by bolstering Pakistan, Bangladesh and Nepal remains unchanged. Keeping pace with its modernization programme, China has become more forceful in asserting its territorial claims. This includes reinforcing diplomatic and political pressure with military muscle. The evolving geopolitical situation in the region has simultaneously put China under some pressure. With reference to India, China has asserted itself regarding Arunachal Pradesh and Kashmir will henceforth be the additional source of pressure. The window for India to respond has a limited time horizon. India will have to respond to Chinese pressure, also to prevent a coalescing of Sino-Pakistan collusion on Kashmir. Options are available. A beginning was made in demonstrating resolve when the Prime Minister visited Tawang and the Dalai Lama later travelled to Arunachal Pradesh and Tawang. This was again evidenced when the Prime Minister met the Dalai Lama. India now needs to send an unequivocal signal that its territorial sovereignty will not be compromised in Kashmir. This will necessitate fresh reappraisal of the Kashmir policy to eliminate outside interference. India will simultaneously have to build defences and assert its 'core national interests'.

This was published as an Issue Brief by the Centre for Air Power Studies on September 13, 2010.

17. Myanmar: Chink in China's Armour

The traditional 'paukphaw' between China and Myanmar – a Burmese term for the tight embrace of friendship – has been showing signs of fraying at the edges since the latter part of last year. The altered US policy towards Myanmar has contributed to this. Greater strain has been imposed on the relationship following the clashes between the Myanmar Army and Kokang rebels of northern Myanmar in August 2009. Beijing, which has considerable investments in Myanmar and views it as of strategic importance, including as a buffer with India, remains understandably nervous at the prospect of the clashes widening and drawing in the other rebel outfits in northern Myanmar, which could unsettle China's southwestern border. In a rare rebuke, Beijing advised Yangon to 'properly handle domestic problems and maintain stability in the China-Myanmar border region' to cool matters down.

China's relations with Myanmar, after a turbulent interregnum when Beijing supported Burmese communist rebels in the 1960s, improved steadily after the military junta seized power in 1988. Confronted by tough economic sanctions imposed primarily by the West and Japan and faced with isolation, Myanmar's military regime adopted an open economic policy to generate revenues and looked towards China despite its suspicion of the communist leadership in Beijing. The split in the Communist Party of Burma (CPB), due to conflict between the Burmese leadership and ethnic cadres in 1989, helped the rapprochement. Chinese assistance in military hardware, trade and investment grew within a decade from US$ 15 million to US$ 800 million. Military training and hardware which, between 1991 and 1995 totalled almost US$ 740 million, was an important ingredient. Prompted by strategic interests, China commenced investing in infrastructure projects. These include a port, road and railways to link China's landlocked Yunnan province with a deep water port on the Indian Ocean. As part of efforts to enhance energy security and avoid vital imports transiting the Malacca Straits, China recently invested in a major US$ 2.5 billion Sino-Myanmar oil and gas pipeline project linking Madnay Island off Kyankpyu on the west coast of Myanmar to China. This pipeline, once completed in 2013, will carry 85 percent of China's POL imports from the Middle East and Africa. By the end of 2009, at least 69 Chinese companies were involved in Myanmar's energy and mining sector and had invested in 90 completed, current and planned projects. 45 of the Chinese companies were engaged in 63 hydropower projects and 16 in 21 onshore and offshore oil and natural gas projects. In contrast, in 2007 only 26 Chinese companies were involved in such projects. Beijing has emerged as Myanmar's largest trading partner and fourth largest foreign investor with investments presently totalling US$ 1.331 billion. Two-way trade in 2008 amounted to US$ 2.6 billion. China has also been a dependable ally and supported Myanmar by exercising its right to veto in international forums like the United Nations when resolutions critical of the State Peace and Development Council (SPDC) regime were put to vote.

Despite this decades-old close relationship, the people of Myanmar and sections of the military junta have reservations about their dependence on China and have sought to explore alternate sources of investment and trade. China's continuing support to rebel groups in northern Myanmar has also not escaped notice and some years ago prompted a critical public remark by Senior General Than Shwe while on a visit to northern Burma. The memory of China's support to the communists over four decades ago has not yet been erased.

Other factors contributed to Yangon's tentative search for ways to reduce dependence on China. These include the overtures made by India, following a change in policy, since 1995-96. These were reinforced by ASEAN's decision to include Myanmar, first as an 'observer' and a year later in 1997 as a full member, allowing cooperation between Myanmar and ASEAN member-nations. Meanwhile Myanmar liberalised foreign investment regulations so that the regime could earn hard currency to support the country's ailing economy. Foreign investment resultantly flowed in from ASEAN. Important areas of interest comprised the extraction of natural resources such as timber, gems, and offshore oil exploration. Key investors included Thailand, Singapore, and Indonesia.

A major incentive to Myanmar's military junta to broad-base trade and investments has been the US decision in early 2009 to review its policy of isolating Myanmar. After concluding that its erstwhile policy served only to push Myanmar closer into the Chinese embrace, Washington initiated steps to engage Yangon. In March 2009, Stephen Blake, a Director in the US State Department's Mainland South East Asia Office visited Myanmar. Though a fairly low ranking official, he was, in a marked departure from protocol, received by Myanmar's Foreign Minister Nyan Win and other high officials. Later, in July that year the US agreed to sign the ASEAN Treaty of Amity and Cooperation, which it had declined to since 1997, mainly, because of Myanmar's presence. In mid-September US Senator Jim Webb was accorded an uncharacteristically warm reception when he was received by Senior General Than Shwe and permitted to meet Aung San Suu Kyi. The Myanmar military regime additionally released incarcerated US national John Yettaw. This visit was followed by that of Kurt Campbell, US Assistant Secretary of State, in November 2009. Campbell, who was the highest ranking US official to visit Myanmar since US Secretary of State Madeline Albright's visit in 1995, was received by Myanmar's Prime Minister Than Sein. Campbell's visit paved the way for the first meeting in 43 years between a US President and Myanmar Prime Minister. US President Obama met Myanmar's

Prime Minister Than Sein on the sidelines of the ASEAN Summit in Singapore on November 15, when Obama urged the release of Aung San Suu Kyi and called on Myanmar to ensure that the upcoming elections in 2010 are free and fair.

The US plans to upgrade its diplomatic representation in Yangon to the level of a full fledged Ambassador. This will probably occur around March 2010. US business is expected to enter Myanmar shortly thereafter, sizeably boosting Myanmar's economy and opening a slew of foreign policy and trade options for the regime. An indication that Myanmar's regime is aware of the potential new opportunities was the visit in mid-December 2009 of Nobel Prize-winning economist Joseph Stiglitz to Yangon to advise Myanmar's Generals on economic reforms. He is understood to have advised the Generals to spend more on education and less on weapons. He also advised them on the sale of natural resources including oil and natural gas for revenues, but cautioned that these should be used wisely so that opportunities are not lost.

The recent tension in Myanmar's northern territories between the Myanmar Army and ethnic rebel armies comes amidst this backdrop of a changing scenario. It has aroused concern in China's foreign policy and strategic establishment as it has the potential to jeopardize China's considerable strategic interests in Myanmar and open the way for interference by other powers. An additional complication is that because of their Han ethnicity the Kokang rebel armies get a lot of media attention in the Chinese media. This coverage has prompted numerous nationalistic comments in Chinese cyberspace.

The Kokang, who are the only Burmese Chinese feudal state in Myanmar, are the remnants of the last Ming Dynasty and have consequently received considerable aid from China. The other ethnic rebel armies in Myanmar's northern areas are the United Wa State Army (UWSA), Kachin Independence Army, Shan State Army and the Mongla-based National Democratic Alliance Army-Eastern Shan State (NDAA). Together they can field almost 40,000-45,000 fighters.

A number of leading cadres of these groups are erstwhile members of the Communist Party of Burma (CPB). These groups have been involved in the drug trade and consequently been the target of anti-drug drives regularly launched by the Myanmar Army.

On this occasion, the rebel groups declined to comply with the Myanmar Army's directions to provide a specified number of people for the proposed Border Guards Force (BGF) programme. While the specific provocation for the latest operation against the Kokang rebel army is unclear, analysts feel it could be a follow up to the successful operation launched in June 2009 by the Army against the Karen rebels located along the borders with Thailand. It has been noticed that the Myanmar Army has chosen to fight the weakest of the rebel armies perhaps to pick them off one by one. Analysts suggest that the offensive could have been mounted to eliminate these armed opposition groups before the elections are held in 2010, as well as to test the limits of China's resolve to support the ethnic rebel groups. So far the Myanmar Army has not encountered Chinese interference.

The current fighting, which commenced in mid-August 2009, has demonstrated the Myanmar Army's ability to move quickly and effect a rapid advance. This round of fighting has simultaneously exhibited the limits of Chinese influence. Beijing had requested Yangon not to mount any offensive against the rebels till its 60th anniversary celebrations were over in October, but Yangon did not wait. The military offensive escalated tension between China and Myanmar as an estimated 30,000 refugees fled to China's Yunnan province. In an unusual criticism of Myanmar's military regime the authoritative English-language weekly, 'Beijing Review', published photographs of the refugee camps and said that 13,000 refugees had been housed in seven refugee camps and that the Yunnan province had provided Yuan 10 million (US$ 1.46 million) for aid to the refugees. A provincial Chinese TV station also reported the clashes in Kokang. Though a report in a dissident paper cited a confidential document to claim that the majority of soldiers in

China's Chengdu Military Region were 'spoiling for a fight', Beijing has confined its reaction to low-key criticism and responded carefully. It deployed 700 PLA troops along the border to prevent clashes and maintain the peace in border townships and advised Yangon to cool down the situation. It simultaneously allowed remnants of the rebel armies to enter Yunnan and discard their weapons and uniforms. China is talking to the various rebel armies in a bid to defuse tensions. It does not want problems on its southwestern border and is concerned that protracted fighting between the Myanmar Army and estimated 40,000-45,000 fighters of the rebel groups could disturb the region where oil and gas reserves are located and jeopardize China's strategic interests.

Reports indicate, though, that survivors of the Chinese volunteers, thousands of whom formed the bulk of the Communist Party of Burma (CPB) during the 1968-79 heydays, are regrouping inside China to discuss ways to assist the ex-CPB rebel groups. They have already formed a committee to raise funds. An estimated 15,000 Wa soldiers from China have joined forces with the United Wa State Army (UWSA) and most have combat experience as Chinese soldiers in the war against Vietnam. The Wa, incidentally, are an ethnic Chinese minority people.

The strains in Sino-Myanmar relations are visible. In addition to Myanmar ignoring Chinese requests to defer action against the rebels till after the 60th anniversary celebrations in October, Yangon's official media publicized reports of the visits to Yangon by US personages. Particularly galling to the Chinese leadership would have been the article in 'Myanmar Times' in early September. This article, cleared by the official censors, reported on the Dalai Lama's visit to Taiwan. It assumes significance as this was the first mention of the Dalai Lama in Myanmar's official media in 20 years.

China is concerned that the relationship with its long-term ally has encountered turbulence. This was reflected in a recent (Dec 15) article in the Beijing-owned Hong Kong-based influential paper 'Ta Kung Pao', which described the relationship after the firing at Kokang as 'quite tricky'. The unusually candid article suggested that apparently 'Burma is undergoing delicate changes' consequent to 'America's hard-soft strategy', and expressed apprehension that the Kokang incidents 'are a premonition of worsening Sino-Burmese relations'. An unidentified senior Chinese official separately described the relationship as based on mutual self-interest. He said: 'we are in it for what we can get out of it, and they are also in it for what they can get out of it'.

The altered US policy towards Myanmar has introduced fluidity in the geo-strategic situation in the region. China-Myanmar relations are, however, likely to be adversely affected only gradually. China is well entrenched in Myanmar's economy and infrastructure. Chinese companies have a major presence in core sectors in Myanmar and virtually control Myanmar's telecommunications network. China is unlikely to easily allow any loosening in its relationship with Myanmar. The 2-day visit to Yangon in mid-December 2009 by Chinese Vice President Xi Jinping, widely tipped to succeed President Hu Jintao, was an indication of Myanmar's importance to China. 16 agreements were signed during the visit when Xi Jinping was received by Senior General Than Shwe.

The US is also handicapped by domestic legislation that will limit the scope of its overtures and material assistance to Myanmar. Myanmar's military junta is, additionally, suspicious that the US maintains covert links with the ethnic rebel groups in the north, a majority of whom are Christians. These suspicions prompted Myanmar's military regime to deny the US Navy permission to send relief supplies directly to the affected areas in the aftermath of Cyclone 'Nargis' in May 2008.

A potential complication is the developing clandestine relationship between Myanmar and North Korea in which China has been complicit. This relationship was raised to a higher level by the MoU signed in November 2008, by Shwe Mann, the regime's third-most powerful figure and Chief of Staff of the Army, Navy and Air Force and Coordinator of Special Operations. He secretly led a 17-member delegation to North Korea via China and visited Pyongyang and Myohyang, where secret tunnels have been built into mountains to shelter aircraft, missiles, tanks and nuclear and chemical weapons. The MoU formalizes military cooperation and provides that North Korea will build or supervise the construction of special military facilities for Myanmar, including tunnels and caves. Indications are that the tunnels being constructed in Myanmar could be linked to North Korea's clandestine nuclear weapons programme.

India has a short window of opportunity to expand influence in Myanmar, which it must seize now. This would be best done by encouraging large Indian business houses and industry, if necessary with incentives, to move in to Myanmar with their good practices especially in projects which require long gestation periods. Priority should be accorded to projects which will be in operation over the longer term, like in the natural resources sector and those in the manufacturing, health and power sectors. This should be reinforced by substantially increasing financial assistance to Myanmar offering scholarships and opening Cultural centres. India should simultaneously push for enhanced military cooperation and offer training slots to larger numbers of Myanmar armed forces officers. In view of China's robust policy to enhance influence in India's neighbourhood, evidenced by the accords signed during Nepalese Prime Minister Madhav Nepal's recent visit to Beijing, India has to formulate effective policies so as not to lose further space. This includes substantially increasing fiscal assistance to its neighbours and reinforcing diplomacy with the strength of its indigenous industry.

This was published as an Issue Brief by the Centre for Air Power Studies on January 1, 2010.

18. China's Increasing Inroads Into Nepal

The delicate balance between India and China that existed till the past decade in landlocked Nepal, now threatens to gradually tilt in China's favour. Prompted mainly by the internal security imperative of quelling unrest in the Tibet Autonomous Region (TAR), elevated now to a high national priority, Beijing's strategic planners some years ago accorded Nepal a higher profile and adopted a more assertive foreign policy. This synchronised, perhaps coincidentally, with the growing political uncertainty in Nepal. Nepal has, in any case, always been important in China's South Asia policy.

China's strategic objectives in Nepal are clear. These are to neutralize and eliminate Indian influence, secure China's borders by ensuring that the Tibetan refugee population is effectively curbed, and recover what it considers as one of its 'lost' territories seized by 'imperialists'. After China took over Tibet in 1951, it viewed Nepal, along with Ladakh, Sikkim, Bhutan and Arunachal Pradesh, as a 'new buffer' between India and China. Till recently its efforts in Nepal were, however, effectively circumscribed by culture and geography. This balanced the triangular relationship between Kathmandu, Delhi and Beijing, despite occasional turbulence, for over half a century. The situation began to alter about a decade ago.

Till recently China followed a cautious policy, which included supporting Kathmandu's effort to designate Nepal a 'Zone of Peace' and signing a Treaty of Peace and Friendship in 1960. A boundary agreement followed. Gradually, as its modernization programme began to yield results, China's policy towards Nepal became confident and political efforts were supplemented with economic content. Chinese officials simultaneously began increasingly alluding to India's 'hegemonism' and assured Nepalese dignitaries that China will continue to support Nepal's effort to safeguard national independence, sovereignty, and develop its economy.

As imbalances between China's coastal areas and the hinterland got accentuated consequent to implementation of economic reforms, China's leaders sought to assuage domestic discontent by encouraging the landlocked, hinterland provinces to explore economic opportunities. Trade was encouraged between the Tibet Autonomous Region (TAR) and Nepal and it increased remarkably between 1983-89. A five-year trade agreement was concluded, followed by an agreement on economic and technical cooperation during Nepalese Prime Minister G.P. Koirala's visit to China in 1992. The following year Koirala visited Lhasa, becoming the first Nepalese Prime Minister to ever visit Tibet. China began providing Nepal grants and assistance and in 2006, offered a grant of Yuan 100 million (US$ 13 million) and concessional loan of Yuan 200 million (US$ 26 million). The advent of the Maoist government under Prime Minister Prachanda, who was openly critical of India, elevated China-Nepal ties. He made revision of the India-Nepal Trade and Transit Treaty an issue. China increased the grant offered to Nepal to Yuan 150 million (US$ 21 million) and allowed duty free access to 500 Nepalese goods. As part of its policy where strategic interests are involved, China identified infrastructure projects for cooperation and particularly eyed Nepal's estimated 83,000 megawatts of hydro-electricity. It extended a loan of US$ 187 million for the construction of two power plants.

China soon expanded the relationship to include the sensitive defence sector. In June 1992, it offered Nepal anti-aircraft guns worth US$ 70 million. This was a none too subtle gesture 'unfriendly' to India. Though not accepted, the offer paved the way for further contacts. The next year Nepal's Defence Secretary led a delegation to China, described by China's then Defence Minister Chi Haotian as 'a major event in the history of contacts between the armed forces of the two countries'. In mid-1994, Nepal's Inspector General of Police visited Beijing for the first time ever, during which Beijing voiced its concern about 'anti-China' activities by Tibetans inside Nepal. China was assured that such activities would be stopped. Chinese defence supplies to Nepal and military exchanges escalated appreciably after the visit of the Royal Nepal Army Chief to Beijing in 1999. The shift in Nepal's weapons procurement policy was enunciated in June 2005 by the Royal Nepal Army's Master General of Ordnance. He identified China as the only country which continued to supply arms and ammunition to Nepal, adding that Nepal was entirely dependent on China for military supplies. Major deals for the purchase of ammunition and military equipment were signed the following years, ousting India from the position of solitary supplier of ammunition. In December 2008, the visiting Deputy Chief of General Staff of the Chinese PLA, Lieutenant General Ma Xiaotian, pledged US $2.6 million as military assistance for Nepal. The previous year China had announced military aid worth $ 1.3 million, the first such assistance to the Maoist government in Nepal. Beijing also supported the Maoists' proposal to integrate approximately 19,000 Maoist guerrillas with the Nepal Army. Meanwhile, China ingressed Nepal's critical telecommunications sector, thus ensuring long-term leverage in the country. Within two years Chinese companies were engaged in 27 projects and ZTE and Huawei, both intimately associated with the PLA, made major inroads. Huawei set up the mobile telephone networks in Kathmandu and other cities while ZTE secured an over US$ 50 million turnkey contract for upgrading Nepal Telecom's nationwide mobile phone capacity.

Overall, Beijing adopted a watch and wait policy amidst the fast paced political developments which witnessed consecutively the removal of King Gyanendra, rise of the Maoists, gathering momentum of the pro-democracy movement and protracted impasse over the Constituent Assembly. China moderated its stance and veered to supporting pro-democracy forces. Chinese State Councillor Tang Jiaxuan's visit to Kathmandu in March 2006, signalled this shift and marked the commencement of a more assertive policy. He urged reconciliation between the contesting forces and, departing from the earlier practice of only meeting Palace officials, met prominent leaders of the 'anti-King' Seven Party Alliance. China additionally initiated contact with the Maoists, whom a Chinese Ambassador had, in 2003, described as an embarrassment to the image of China's Chairman Mao!

Significant visits were those of Wang Hongwei in July 2006 and Wang Jiarui the following year. Wang Hongwei, a retired Major General of the People's Liberation Army (PLA) and Research Fellow at the prestigious Chinese Academy of Social Sciences (CASS), expanded China's political base in Nepal and quietly met Maoist cadres. China already had contact with the then almost 30,000-strong Nepal Communist Party (United Marxist-Leninist). He expressed the hope that they would participate in the interim government in Kathmandu. Wang Hongwei was later instrumental in inviting a number of senior Maoist leaders to China. Similarly reflecting China's newly assertive policy, Wang Jiarui, Minister in the Chinese Communist Party's powerful International Liaison Department, met a number of senior Nepalese leaders including Prime Minister Koirala and Nepal Communist Party (United Marxist-Leninist) leader Madhav Nepal. He emphasized that stability in Nepal would benefit China's bordering regions, that Nepal should hold elections early, and requested assistance in curbing the activities of Tibetan refugees who could plan to enter China to disrupt the Olympics.

Political interaction accelerated during the period Prachanda was Prime Minister. He broke with tradition and travelled to Beijing on his first visit abroad. He went twice more. An estimated 38 Chinese delegations visited Nepal in 2008-09 while 12 high-level Nepalese economic, technology and defence delegations travelled to China. China cultivated a spectrum of political parties including the Communist Party of Nepal-Maoist (CPN-M), the Nepal Communist Party (United Marxist-Leninist) and the Madhesi People's Rights Forum. In April 2009, a NCP-UML delegation led by Jhala Nath Khanal visited Beijing and was informed that China wants "a new kind of relationship" with Nepal. The pronounced pro-China tilt was corrected with the installation of GP Koirala as Prime Minister.

A network of China Study Centers (CSCs), set up to popularise the Chinese language and, more importantly, disseminate anti-India propaganda, reinforce traditional Chinese diplomacy. At least 35 China Study Centres, entirely funded by Beijing, are strategically established in southern Nepal along India's border. China's propaganda offensive includes the China Radio International's local FM radio station in Kathmandu and a Nepal-China Mutual Cooperation Society (NCMCS), funded by the Chinese Embassy in Nepal.

The real game changer in China-Nepal relations is, however, the Qinghai-Lhasa railway which was operationalised in July 2006. China's decision to extend the Qinghai-Tibet Railway line – capable of carrying an estimated 7 million tons of cargo a year – from Lhasa to Zhangmu, bordering western Nepal and Yadong in the east, by 2015 underscores China's strategic interests. The railway is augmented by all-weather expressways radiating out of Lhasa and stretching up to Yadong, on the border with India's Sikkim and, connecting with the Western Highway which runs to the north of the border along western Nepal. To enhance connectivity, China built a road link between Lhasa and Khasa, a border town located some 80 kilometres north of Kathmandu and is constructing another road along the shortest route from Tibet to Kathmandu. Though built to cater to the need of military logistics, the expressways fulfill important strategic objectives. Completion of these major infrastructure projects inside China, coincidentally when Nepal was undergoing historic political changes, has given China a crucial immediate advantage. China's new transportation network has provided alternate trade routes to a landlocked Nepal. China moved quickly to exploit Nepal's sensitivities and reopened the Kathmandu-Lhasa highway in 2008 and designated Zham in TAR as a dry port for Nepal. Next year it agreed to open two more custom posts bringing the total to seven. Chinese Ambassador Zheng Xianglin observed in August 2008 that "Nepal is situated in a favourable geographical position in South Asia, and a passage linking China and South Asia". Separately, Chinese Foreign Minister Yang Jiechi indicated that both countries were working towards a 'strategic partnership', while Liu Hongcai, a Vice Minister in the CCP's International Liaison Department, reiterated the caution (Feb 2009): 'we oppose any move to interfere in the internal affairs of Nepal by any force'.

The priority target of China's revised policy towards Nepal was its 20,000-strong Tibetan community which, anticipatedly, was the first to feel the impact of China's rising influence in Nepal. After King Gyanendra assumed power in a Palace coup in 2001, two offices of the Dalai Lama were shut down at Chinese insistence and only sustained international pressure ensured that the government in Kathmandu allowed the Dalai Lama's establishment to retain one office. Beijing coerced Kathmandu into prohibiting activities that were sponsored by pro-Dalai Lama elements or organized by the Dalai Lama's representatives in Nepal. The Nepalese police and border posts were instructed to apprehend Tibetans attempting to illegally cross over into Nepal from Tibet, either to escape or visit Dharamsala for a glimpse of their exiled Tibetan religious leader, the Dalai Lama. Those apprehended were detained and handed over to the Chinese authorities, who either incarcerated or executed them.

Chinese pressure increased once Prachanda took over as Prime Minister. A visible result is the drastic reduction in number of Tibetans entering Nepal and the severely curtailed activities of the Tibetans resident in Nepal. From the 2,900 Tibetans who escaped into Nepal in 2006 en route to India, the number dropped to 658 in 2008 and 752 in 2009. The Chinese Embassy in Kathmandu became more active and started monitoring Tibetan activities very closely. There was enhanced interaction between the Chinese Embassy and Nepalese authorities on the Tibet issue. Annual commemorative functions organized by Nepal's Tibetan community or the Dalai Lama's official representatives began to be disallowed.

China's interference in Nepal became more noticeable with the beginning of the 'Year of the Tiger', which marked the unveiling by China's leadership of a new, tougher policy towards Tibetans inside the Tibet Autonomous Region (TAR) and Tibetans resident elsewhere in China. The new policy clarifies too that Nepal, as a country bordering the restive TAR, is now viewed by Beijing as a 'frontline' state in its struggle against Tibetan 'separatist' elements. Nepal is seen as a possible base for US-sponsored anti-China activities involving Tibetans. There has been appreciably increasing pressure on Nepal since December last year, when a Counsellor in China's Embassy in Kathmandu expressed concern at the number of Tibetans illegally entering Nepal. He urged Nepal's Home Secretary to heighten vigilance along the borders. In February 2010, during bilateral talks at Kyirong in the Tibet Autonomous Region (TAR)'s Xigaze prefecture, the Chinese authorities renewed their appeal. This time, however, they expanded the scope of their effort to include palliatives to the local populace in a bid to co-opt their support. Among the measures discussed to strengthen vigilance along the border, the Chinese for the first time undertook to provide commodities and goods worth Nepalese Rupees three million to the people of the area. The offer will be attractive to people who live in areas where transportation links are poor due to difficult terrain.

The pressure applied by the Chinese prior to March 2010, to obviate the possibility of anti-China activities and demonstrations by Tibetans in Nepal on the anniversary of the Tibetan Uprising on March 10, was considerable. China's Defence Attache in Kathmandu, Chen Chong, was noticeably active and suggested to Nepal's Home Ministry a list of measures to curb activities by the Tibetans, which he said were on the rise. He especially identified the Dolakha district, which he had visited the previous month. On March 7, the Chief Coordinator of Tibetan Refugees in Nepal, Thinley Gyatso, who is a functionary of the Dalai Lama's establishment, was arrested in Kathmandu to prevent him from organizing any anti-China or pro-Dalai Lama functions. In another pre-emptive move the Nepalese authorities conducted a series of raids on Tibetan hotels, restaurants and homes in Tibetan areas across the country. Joint efforts to curb activities by the Tibetans continue. This includes visits for senior Nepalese officials to places along the China-Nepal border for studying the ground situation.

Another factor which is disturbing in the backdrop of Beijing's strengthened policy towards Nepal, is the negative opinion regarding India that is circulating among Parliamentarians and in governmental circles in Kathmandu. This asserts that India is 'overbearing' and cites around 'forty five points of confrontation'. These refer to alleged territorial intrusions by India ranging from a few square kilometers to larger areas. Such negative impressions in influential circles will facilitate Beijing's efforts to expand influence in Nepal. They could make it easier for Beijing to deepen inroads into Nepal's political, bureaucratic, security and military establishments. In the event of a Maoist government coming to power in Nepal, the development would be to China's benefit.

An interesting, but little-noticed, development with a potential for exploitation is that the 128-130 Buddhists, who are members of Nepal's parliament but are affiliated with the Maoists, are gradually coalescing into a pressure group. These individuals, who continue to be staunch Buddhists and belong mainly to northern Nepal, have joined the Maoists as they feel they have no alternative. This group maintains quiet contact with the Dalai Lama's establishment in Dharamsala.

Koirala's demise in February 2010, particularly before the new Constitution has been finalised, re-introduces a high degree of uncertainty in Nepal's politics and in India-Nepal relations. A lot will depend on the support that Prachanda and the Maoists are able to garner and their determination to alter the agreements and treaties that bind India-Nepal relations. Nevertheless, compulsions of culture, geography that inhibits easy travel, and similarities among the people of India and Nepal will continue to impose limits on Nepal-China relations for at least a few more years. There is also the unsettled question of the Chinese occupation of three villages in Nepalese territory in the disputed area of Dhongbasain bordering Mustang and TAR, which has remained unpublicised in recent times.

This was published as an Issue Brief by the Centre for Air Power Studies on May 25, 2010.

19. China Crowding India Out of Sri Lanka

Traditionally close Indo-Sri Lankan ties forged by shared culture and ethnicity and reinforced by history and legend, are showing signs of coming under strain. Partially caused by New Delhi's failure to provide more forthcoming policy responses to Colombo's requests, India's diplomatic influence is now getting eroded. China stepped in to occupy the space and has, of late, begun expanding its presence in Sri Lanka. It is acquiring a meaningful presence in the political, commercial and cultural sectors. It is already influential in Sri Lanka's defence establishment.

The development assumes significance in the backdrop of China's uncompromising efforts to secure global acceptance of its pre-eminence in the region, which coincides with India's shrinking influence in its immediate neighbourhood. The latter could get accentuated following establishment of full diplomatic relations between China and Bhutan and imminent resolution of their boundary issue.

In keeping with the practice followed by it in many countries, Beijing sought to first exploit the economic and trade route. China's investments in Sri Lanka till 2004, were estimated at under US$ 250 million. China's financial involvement increased when it extended assistance valued at around US$ 300 million in the immediate aftermath of the tsunami in 2004. By 2006, China had followed through with an additional US$ 300 million in loans and aid. There has been a noticeable spurt in Chinese lending after the defeat of the LTTE in 2009, with almost US$ 6.5 billion being invested primarily in infrastructural projects. China provided almost 50 percent of all foreign loans and credits received by Sri Lanka in 2009 and 40 percent of all such assistance in 2010. Bilateral trade similarly registered an increase and in the first six months of 2011, totalled US$ 1.28 billion, or an increase of nearly 40 percent over the previous year. The enhancement of investments in Sri Lanka has coincided with increased Chinese economic and political activity in other countries neighbouring India, like Nepal.

Already burdened by domestic and external debt in excess of SL Rupees 5.5 trillion, Sri Lanka is eager for loans for its projects. China's loans to Sri Lanka, though, are neither at preferential rates and nor as grants-in-aid, but they do offer a grace period of 4-5 years for repayment. China is learnt to have been pressurizing Sri Lankan President Rajapakse to increase government spending on infra-structure to at least 6.3 percent of the GDP to enable Sri Lanka to move from a low income country to a middle income nation. Sri Lanka recently announced that it would spend US$ 21 billion in the period 2012-2015, or 6.5 percent of the GDP each year. China is expected to contribute more than half this amount. Additionally, in 2011, the China Development Bank Corporation agreed to provide US$ 1.5 billion over a three year period for roads, power plants and irrigation schemes.

Chinese companies have secured a number of infra-structure contracts. It is noticed, however, that they often by-pass the tender process emerging suddenly as single bidders. Cost over-runs of projects is also high. An instance is the project for construction of a 350-meter high transmission and communications tower on seven and a half acres of prime property along the picturesque Beira waterfront in central Colombo. Construction of the tower, which is estimated to cost US$ 108 million, is being funded by China's Exim Bank. There is speculation that the Chinese telecommunications company ZTE is involved. To ensure occupancy of the tower and revenues for its owners, the Sri Lankan government has already asked the three main telecommunications service providers namely, Airtel, Etilsat and Dialog, to move into the tower once it is completed. This will additionally facilitate security monitoring of all communications, including by the Chinese company. Interesting, albeit unrelated, is the scandal brewing in Pakistan of a Chinese telecommunications company also emerging suddenly as the sole candidate for supply of a telecommunications trunk system with integrated security-related software.

China has at least fourteen major infra-structure projects in hand in Sri Lanka. These include the Hambantota Port Development, Colombo Port Expansion Project, Norochcholoi Coal Power Project, irrigation projects valued at over US$ 700 million, and the Sapugaskanda Refinery Expansion and Modernisation project. Chinese companies are additionally involved in the development of schools.

The Hambantota Port Development project which, according to reliable inputs was awarded to China while India was still in talks with Sri Lanka, is a prime example including of cost over-runs in projects. China lent US$ 400 million for the first phase of the new port in Hambantota and China's Exim bank lent US$ 77 million for an oil bunkering facility. The cost of the first phase, originally estimated at US$ 360 million, escalated by US$ 40 million. The cause was pinpointed as the large rock slabs blocking the harbour's entrance and limiting access to ships with a draft of only 8 meters as against the planned access for ships of draft of 17 meters. The cost of phases two and three of the port's development, including the oil bunkering facility, is estimated at US$ 600-750 million. Analysts assess, however, that the final cost would exceed US$ 2 billion and there is suspicion that the Chinese deliberately concealed the initial cost estimates. The final expenditure makes Hambantota port commercially unviable and few ships call there. In order to salvage the situation the Sri Lankan authorities have directed that all automobiles will be imported only through Hambantota port, resulting in the addition of SL Rupees

40,000 in the cost price of each vehicle.

An international airport, the second in Sri Lanka, is being built at Hambantota and China has lent US$ 190 million for the project. Preliminary talks are underway between Sri Lanka and China for construction of a new railway line linking Omanthai in the north to Trincomalee and further south to Batticaloa. The estimated cost of the project, if it materialises, is US $ 1 billion. China's Exim Bank has separately committed US$ 102.5 million for the purchase of 13 new diesel engines by Sri Lanka from China. China has also supplied 15 power sets at a cost of US$ 2.46 million each.

The Norochcholoi Coal Power Project is an instance of where labour imported from China is used. Phase One of the three phase, 900 MW Coal Power project is already on stream. The project costs over US$ 1.5 billion.

Of special note is the Sapugaskanda Refinery Expansion and Modernisation (SOREM) project in which China has strongly indicated a willingness to invest US$ 2 billion to upgrade the existing capacity of 50,000 barrels per day to 100,000 barrels per day. The estimated cost of the SOREM project when Sri Lanka was participating with Iran was US$ 1.49 billion. China has additionally sought numerous concessions like duty-free import of machinery, tax-free income for the 2500 workers proposed to be employed and who will be brought from China, allocation of land free of cost, and preferential terms for distributing refined products in the domestic and export markets. In case the project is awarded to China, then Lanka IOC's market share will be adversely affected.

Sri Lanka is keen to exploit its wind power generation potential estimated at approximately 1,643MW and plans to commence generation of 643 MW within the next ten years. The big Chinese wind generation companies like Goldwind, Dongfang Electric and Sinovel, in their search for new markets are working aggressively to secure these contracts. Mannar, Jaffna and Puttalam, all incidentally close to the Indian coast, have been identified as areas with 85 percent wind generation potential. If the Chinese companies get the contract for the project, then Chinese technicians will be conducting extensive feasibility studies in these areas and later working there for at least ten years to complete the projects.

China has shown interest in the development of off-shore oil and natural gas exploration in the Mannar Basin. They are unhappy with the block in the Mannar Basin awarded to them and are keen to get a block in the Cauvery Basin. Allocation of a block in the Cauvery Basin, which has a depth of 100 metres, will make exploration cheaper. The prospects of a find in this area are also better.

China has exhibited interest in a number of other projects. It has agreed to extend US$ 760 million for construction of roads across the country. China's Exim Bank has granted a loan of US$ 310 million for construction of the Colombo-Katunayaka Expressway, which will connect Sri Lanka's capital with the international airport and work is well underway. China is also involved in the education sector. The Chinese company CATIC, which is primarily in the aviation sector, recently received Sri Lankan cabinet approval awarding it a contract worth US$ 89.55 million to relocate and develop the Institute of Technology presently situated within the Moratuwa University campus. Talks are underway for additional Chinese involvement in other secondary school development projects.

More insidious are the inroads being made by China's 'soft power' in Sri Lanka. As a first step, China Radio International recently obtained a licence to operate a 24-hour FM Radio channel in Sri Lanka. It currently has an hour-long programme in Sinhala which is directly broadcast daily from China. This service is channeled through Sri Lanka's 'Youth FM'. China's CCTV has also decided to telecast Chinese soaps and programmes with sub-titles in Sinhala. Sri Lanka's state-owned ITN started telecasting popular Chinese programmes three months ago. At the same time an unbearably high rate of tax was imposed on Sirisa TV, which used to show popular Indian TV serials. 'Xinhua', which as China's official news agency is known to combine espionage functions, is learnt to be contemplating expanding its operations in the island with the active support of the Chinese Embassy in Colombo which has 27 diplomats. Efforts are in hand to bring more Chinese journalists to Colombo. Beijing has taken active steps to promote people-to-people understanding. In addition to increasing the number of scholarships for Sri Lankan students to study in China, an agreement was signed in October 2011, to establish Confucius Centres at various locations in Sri Lanka. At the level of opinion-moulders, the China Institute for Contemporary International Relations, affiliated with China's intelligence establishment and specifically the Ministry of State Security, has proposed a long-term partnership with the Bandaranayake Centre of International Studies.

China used the opportunity offered by Sri Lanka's war with the LTTE to develop close military ties with Sri Lanka's armed forces. A number of Sri Lankan armed forces officers have been going to China for training in Chinese military institutions for the past many years. China has supplied and maintained aircraft, tanks, artillery guns and radars. Later, in 2009, an agreement was signed between the Government of Sri Lanka and two Chinese defence entities namely, Polytechnologies Inc and NORINCO for the supply of arms and ammunition valued at S$ 410 million. More recently the Sri Lankan government earmarked US$ 6.01 million for supplies for the armed forces for a year and entered into an agreement with CATIC of China for the purchase of six MA-60 aircraft at a cost of US$ 105.4 million for use by the Sri Lankan Air Force for VIP duties. Reports suggest that China has offered to assist build off-shore patrol craft for Sri Lanka's Navy. China has also indicated interest in a US$ 100 million project for construction of family accommodation for Sri Lanka's military personnel in the North and Wanni and East. It separately announced a grant of US$ 1.5 million for modernization of the Defence Services

College in Colombo and offered assistance for modernization of other training establishments including in Diyatalawa.

There is a similarity in the way Chinese companies operate in Africa and Sri Lanka. In both cases the process by which projects are awarded to Chinese companies is often opaque with the procedure of tenders being by-passed and Chinese companies suddenly emerging as single bidders. In the case of many of the projects there are cost over-runs, which while ultimately adding to Colombo's financial burden seem to be overlooked by the authorities. Procedural opacity allows for high cost over-runs which, in turn, leaves the companies with readily available surplus cash funds. Chinese companies also try and channelise business through well connected individuals. For example, 'Youth FM', which is owned by MP and President Rajapakse's son, Namal, is used by China Radio International to beam its hour-long radio broadcasts to Sri Lanka directly from Beijing. There are also reports of Chinese investment in Carlton TV, owned by Yoshita, a Navy officer and another son of the Sri Lankan President. Chinese companies also import Chinese labour for some projects, especially when these are located in rural areas where they are unlikely to attract adverse attention.

India needs to evolve steps to ensure that its influence in the region does not shrink and its foreign policy objectives and national aspirations are not compromised. Incidents like the harassment of Indian fishermen should be effectively discouraged as they undermine domestic and international perception of India's ability to safeguard its interests. India must, among other measures, capitalize on its inherent advantages and increase its lead as the largest source of tourism, direct foreign investment and export market for Sri Lanka.

This was published as an Issue Brief by the Centre for Air Power Studies on July 15, 2012.

20. China's Influence in Indo-US Relations

China's uninterrupted double-digit growth over the past three decades and rapid increase in military power today ensures it occupies centre stage in every conversation concerning geopolitics or international finance. This is the case whenever the US is discussed and is unavoidable in the context of India-US relations. The rapid increase in China's economic and military strength has also contributed to the newfound confidence among the Chinese people and leadership making China a truly 'aspirational' major world power.

In this backdrop the dynamics between China, India and the US are crucial and have the potential to substantively influence the future. India and China are two Asian powers rising simultaneously for the first time in history. Both countries are trying to build a durable and strong relationship with the US, which they consider essential for their development. Both view the US as a large market and source of capital, hi-technology, scientific infusions and defence equipment. China, however, has a considerable head start. The US too views a partnership with each of these countries as useful, but for quite different reasons. A common feature, though, is the attractiveness to the US of their large and growing unexploited markets.

US President Obama's recent visit to India took place in this backdrop. It materialized when apprehensions in Asia have been raised consequent to China's assertive behaviour and demonstrated willingness to use force in the past couple of years. The veritable U-turn effected by the Obama Administration in its China policy coincided with this development. The latter was demonstrated in recent months by the new vigour injected by the US in its relationships with countries in Asia. Recent examples are US President Obama's visit to Indonesia, the first by a US President since 2006, and his visits to South Korea and Japan at this juncture when there are strains in their relations with China. The US simultaneously underscored its commitment to defence treaty obligations to its allies. It broke new ground with the assertion, of US Secretary of State Hillary Clinton a month ago in Hanoi, that the US would preserve the freedom of navigation and over flights in the 'global commons' of the South China Seas, thereby making implementation of its sovereignty claims, over the Nansha (Spratlys) and Xisha (Paracels) archipelagos, difficult for China.

These developments overlapped with a phase of enhanced self-confidence among China's leaders. They feel the time is now opportune for their country to regain its rightful position and influence in the world and play a pivotal role in global affairs. They happen to, coincidentally, have a leadership under Hu Jintao that is willing to seize this opportunity. Accordingly, in 2008 the formula enunciated by Deng Xiaoping of '*taoguang yanghui*', or lie low bide your time, was discarded in favour of more overtly assertive policies. There is now an unmistakable suggestion of military muscle in diplomacy.

The US' capacity for maneuver with regard to China is, however, constrained by the nature of its bilateral relationship with China developed over the years and China's permanent membership of the United Nations Security Council. A proper appreciation of the breadth of China's relationship and exchanges with the US is important in the context of the developing India-US relationship. Beijing currently has over 80 points of contact and approximately 60 platforms for engagement with the US. Of particular importance are the 'Strategic Economic Dialogue' and 'Senior Dialogue on Global Issues'. These encompass subjects as diverse as those ranging from monetary policy and trade to space, cultural, educational and military exchanges. Also, during their summit meetings Presidents Obama and Hu Jintao discuss a range of global and regional issues including Iran's nuclear issue, resolution of problems in South Asia—a codeword for Kashmir—and the North Korean nuclear stalemate. Official communiqués issued after their last meeting a few weeks ago on the sidelines of the ASEAN Summit, however, omitted mention of South Asia while reporting the discussions.

In economic terms, almost all 'Fortune 500' companies are present in China and by 2008, US companies had invested in excess of US$ 50 billion in over 50,000 Chinese companies. Important in the US' current domestic climate is that low cost Chinese manufacturing helps US taxpayers save an estimated US$ 70 billion annually. China's holding of US Treasury Bills was estimated in July 2010 at US$ 894.8 billion. China's direct investments in the US also rose to US$ 6.4 billion by the end of last year. The US and China together account for over 30 percent of global GDP. The extent of this economic relationship not only reveals a bipartisan consensus on USA's China policy, but also emphasizes the mutual limits on independence of action imposed by this interdependence.

The US is now concerned at the pace of China's economic and military growth and rapid spread of its influence. Expanding Chinese influence in South East and South Asia has begun to, albeit very gradually, undermine US influence. China's steadily increasing military strength is beginning to give it a capability adequate to deter US forces from going to the aid of allies in the region, like Taiwan and Japan. US efforts are underway to check China's growth and enmesh China in international political and economic systems so that its rise is non-threatening.

During his visit to India a few weeks ago, US President Obama, in his speech to Parliament, offered India a 'global partnership in the twenty first century in Asia and the Indian Ocean'. The implication was evident – to check China in both these regions. His remark that the US would welcome India as a permanent member in the United Nations Security Council was, however, high on rhetoric and short on substance. There are many impediments in India's path to permanent membership of the UN Security Council including, the lack of consensus on the issue in the US, opposition from China and Pakistan to India's inclusion, and the glacial pace of the reform process itself which has yet to formalize a view on whether future permanent UNSC members would have the right of veto.

Other factors that cause India and US concern include the 9-10 percent annual rate of growth of China's economy which, in terms of PPP, is already half that of the US. Budgetary allocations for modernization of the People's Liberation Army (PLA) are increasing proportionately. China's foreign currency reserves of US$ 2.4 trillion are also growing, adding to its heft in international economic policy and in South East Asia, the Pacific Islands, South Asia, Africa and South America. China is presently trying to expand its footprint in Europe and the railway network planned to link China with Spain via Turkey is reflective of China's ambitions.

China has actively used its economic and political influence to further national interests. Examples are its activities in Nepal and South East Asia. Beijing is increasing pressure on Kathmandu to rein in the Tibetans while simultaneously enlarging influence by establishing China Study Centres, undertaking infrastructure projects, unilaterally distributing old age pensions in the poorer northern border areas of Nepal etc. Visits by senior Chinese leaders to Nepal have increased. During at least their last three visits to Kathmandu, Chinese leaders have recited their usual formulation of respecting Nepal's sovereignty and territorial integrity, but significantly added that China will not allow other countries to interfere in Nepal's affairs either. In South East Asia, the countries are dependent on China's economy for their growth and this circumscribes their scope for action whether on issues relating to reduced flows in the Mekong River caused by China's actions in the upper reaches, or with regard to contested claims in the South China Sea.

India-China relations will be in a critical stage for the next 5-10 years. A relationship already bedevilled by a 4,057 kms-long disputed border and China's lack of sensitivity to Indian concerns, including questioning its sovereignty over Arunachal Pradesh and Kashmir, will additionally be confronted by serious challenges in the coming decade. These include water, energy resources and food, which will impact on the populations and their livelihoods in both the countries. Their resolution will require a high degree of statesmanship, which will have to balance inescapable domestic demands with national imperatives, as otherwise the trajectory of upward growth of both countries could be adversely affected.

In addition to the extant Sino-US relationship, it is imperative to take note of areas where US and Chinese interests converge and impact on India's sovereignty and territory. Both countries, for example, have a stake in Pakistan as candidly acknowledged by Obama during his recent visits to Mumbai and Delhi.

US interests and involvement in Pakistan are symbolized by the over US$ 18 billion Washington has handed out to Islamabad, in addition to military and other supplies, since September 2001. China has similarly invested huge amounts in Pakistan, especially in the western areas from Gilgit up to Gwadar. Beijing envisages additional investments including upgradation of the Karakoram highway and extension to Gwadar, a China-Pakistan railway over the Karokaram and a gas pipeline running alongside. More than 60 Chinese companies are engaged in at least 200 projects in Pakistan's northern areas. The developments in Pakistan are, however, a source of concern and China would be preparing to safeguard its investments against any future adverse eventuality. Neither the US nor China will exert unrelenting pressure on Pakistan to eviscerate the sources of terrorism against India despite protestations to the contrary.

Their positions also converge on Kashmir. While the US has chosen to nudge India strongly from the sidelines to offer concessions on

Kashmir, China has opted for an assertive pro-active stance by declining visas to residents of the state of Jammu and Kashmir and declaring the entire state as disputed. India will come under increasing pressure on the issue in the near future and will have to formulate its independent stand on both these matters.

Another area where US and China's interests converge, at least in the medium term, is Afghanistan. To pave the way for its pull out by mid-2014, the US is facilitating China's involvement in Afghanistan. It anticipates that China, lured by the estimated US$ 1 trillion mineral deposits in Afghanistan, will commence their exploitation yielding a steady revenue stream to the government in Kabul. Beijing, however, has its own strategic agenda and has drawn up plans for a railway to link Afghanistan with China through Tajikstan and to Pakistan.

The railway line from western China through Tajikstan into Afghanistan and on to Gwadar in Pakistan is a major venture with immense strategic implications for China and the region. It will be Afghanistan's first long distance railway and will simultaneously ensure China's ability to transport cargo and passengers from land-locked western China up to Gwadar. It will upgrade China's military logistics capability, accelerating and facilitating movement of troops, munitions and missiles to the borders with Russia as well as into Afghanistan and on to Pakistan. China's extensive involvement in Afghanistan will ensure it a place on the negotiating high table thus reinforcing Pakistan's position. The China-dominated Shanghai Cooperation Organisation (SCO) will also be well positioned for the future.

The US has over the years toyed occasionally with the idea of allowing China a larger role in the wider Asia-Pacific region while retaining for itself the mantle of the world superpower. In recent years this has meant cooperating with China in certain areas even if it meant ceding space to it. These include areas impacting on Indian interests.

The first occasion was in 1974, when then US Secretary of State Kissinger visited Beijing and met Vice Premier Deng Xiaoping. In a thinly concealed reference to the clandestine Sino-Pak nuclear collusion Kissinger said, "One of my colleagues said he was not only in favour of giving arms to Pakistan, but arms and nuclear weapons to Pakistan and Bangladesh". It could not have been coincidence that China's involvement in Pakistan acquiring nuclear capability was not questioned by the US and that subsequently in 2005, when China signed a civil nuclear cooperation agreement with Bangladesh, there was no protest from the US. China's recent move to enhance Pakistan's nuclear programme and sell it additional nuclear reactors has similarly evoked only muted US protest. If China succeeds in overcoming international objections it will have shown itself as an alternative world power to the US

A second instance was in June 1998, when US President Clinton, in a speech in Beijing, outlined the possibility of the two nations sharing responsibility in different areas of the Asia-Pacific to preserve world peace including nuclear non-proliferation. He singled out India and Pakistan for special mention as also Kashmir.

In 2008 China took this suggestion a step further. A senior PLA Navy officer told visiting US Admiral Keating, albeit half jocularly: 'You take Hawaii East, we'll take Hawaii West and the Indian Ocean. We'll share information and we'll save you all the trouble of developing your naval forces west of Hawaii'. The timing of this disclosure coincided with US efforts to co-opt Saudi Arabia and China in bailing out Pakistan, and when Beijing had adopted a visibly tougher stance against India.

This was followed by two summit meetings between US President Obama and Chinese President Hu Jintao in September and November 2009. Reporting on the summit meeting in Pittsburg on September 22, 'Xinhua' said Hu Jintao urged Obama that "the two countries should push for a proper resolution to the regional issues relating to the Korean Peninsula, Iran and South Asia". This was the first time that this suggestion was made by China at the highest level. The five-part joint statement, issued at the conclusion of US President Obama's visit to China on November 17, 2009, asserted: "both sides are ready to strengthen communication, dialogue and cooperation on issues related to South Asia and work together to promote peace, stability and development in that region". These reflect the US Administration's view that China will be a locus of power in the emerging new world order. The summit meetings also constitute the backdrop to Beijing's recent attitude on Kashmir. Other areas where India will come under pressure in the near future are Afghanistan and the Nuclear issue.

Nevertheless, India must utilize the present advantageous international situation to build and expand relations with the US. As India consolidates relations with the US and broadens areas of cooperation, it will safeguard its strategic and territorial interests, including staying relevant in the larger Asian region and South Asia.

India can take initiatives in keeping the 'global commons', namely sea lanes of communication and over flights, safe and open; in securing and policing cyberspace; and in the neutrality and disarmament of space. Cooperation would mean visibly enhancing cooperation with US and other navies in securing vital sea lanes in the South China Seas, Straits of Malacca and the Indian Ocean. India should strengthen the Andaman and Nicobar Tri-Command by augmenting air and sea power to facilitate long range aerial and sea patrols and adding a submarine base. Securing and policing cyberspace will yield multiple benefits. In addition to enhancing security of communications and essential services, it will facilitate the husbanding of resources and technology. The disclosure in mid-November that all US Federal civil and military internet traffic had been hijacked to China-based Chinese servers for an entire eighteen minutes represents an opportunity. Another area is science and technology and space. Cooperation in these areas would be of mutual benefit and put India on a higher plane of research and development.

Deep seated suspicions in Beijing of US intentions could impact on the India-China relationship. The growing warmth in US-India relations has become a source of apprehension for Beijing and generated numerous critical references by China's authoritative official media and analysts. This was reflected during the tension in US-China relations this July when the US-ROK joint military exercises were staged. A Hong Kong-based Chinese language paper then observed '...the issue of China's territorial disputes with neighbouring countries will ignite the flames of war sooner or later. If a country must be chosen for sacrifice, India will be the first choice... India's long term occupation of southern Tibet (Arunachal Pradesh) is indeed worrying...If armed force is used to resolve border disputes, China must pick a county to target first, and it will definitely pick a big country, which means choosing between Japan and India...'. At least six other critical references to India were noticed in China's official media between July-August 2010, when tensions remained high because of the US-ROK exercises. Earlier references to Japan and India had added that China's relationship with both these countries have limits imposed by history.

It is in India's strategic interest to consolidate and expand its relationship with the US. Its physical proximity to China will be an important consideration as will the challenges anticipated to emerge over the next decade in India-China relations. India will need to recognize that in such situations the US will be a distant witness.

This was published as an Issue Brief by the Centre for Air Power Studies on November 29, 2010.

21. The Emerging US-China Accommodation

The unusually lengthy 4,228-word joint statement issued on November 17, at the conclusion of US President Barack Obama's four day visit to the People's Republic of China, reflects the changing global geopolitical balance of power. It is an acknowledgement of China's rise as a major world power and an attempt by the US to co-opt it into accepting greater responsibility in international affairs. Its objective is to enmesh China in a web of international obligations and agreements in the hope that it would not behave as an aggressive power. The US President's visit to China so early in his term and broad scope of the joint statement, however, also confirm the importance of this bilateral relationship to both countries and, that China will be a locus of power in the emerging new world order.

Soon after installation of the Obama Administration, Washington began signalling that it was contemplating recasting its China policy. In addition to the preferential treatment accorded to China at international gatherings during the past couple of years because of its economic strength, US Secretary of State Hillary Clinton's visit to Beijing in February 2009, clarified the new US Administration's changed tack on China.

Other suggestions of heightened US sensitivity were the move to curtail funding for Radio Free Asia and Voice of America transmissions to China, which were successfully resisted by the US Congress, and President Obama's failure to meet the Dalai Lama during his visit to Washington in October. After an interval of three years Washington received Xu Caihou, Vice Chairman of China's Central Military Commission, in late October just prior to Obama's visit to Beijing, marking the resumption of high level military exchanges. Seven agreements were signed during the visit, when Cu Xaihou reportedly agreed that China will undertake landmine clearing operations in Afghanistan and train Afghan police and military personnel. Finally, Obama avoided mentioning Tibet and Human Rights issues during meetings with Chinese leaders in Beijing recently, though he urged resumption of a dialogue with the Dalai Lama.

Also pertinent to the Joint Statement was the exchange between US President Obama and Chinese President Hu Jintao, at their second Summit meeting in Pittsburg on September 22. China's official news agency 'Xinhua' reported that Hu Jintao urged Obama, in the context of the China-US bilateral relationship, that 'the two countries should push for a proper resolution to the regional issues relating to the Korean Peninsula, Iran and South Asia'. He mentioned Taiwan, Tibet and Xinjiang. Obama responded to Hu Jintao's remarks on all these, but refrained from commenting on South Asia. Though China's ambitions are not new and were first publicly outlined during Clinton's visit to China in mid-1998, Hu Jintao's remarks represented a push at the highest level for recognition of China's influence in the region of its perceived strategic interest.

The US-China Joint Statement suggests that in coming months India will face pressure on three issues, namely Kashmir, Afghanistan and the NPT and CTBT. Kashmir and Afghanistan are interlinked and developments relating to them will directly impact on India.

The recent rapid pace of developments centering on Kashmir suggests the subject has figured earlier in discussions between Washington and Beijing. Just days prior to the Hu-Obama Summit on September 22, Chinese Vice Foreign Minister He Zhengyue publicised China's willingness to mediate between India and Pakistan if requested and the offer was repeated twice soon after the Summit. Hurriyat 'leader' Mirwaiz Umar Farooq's assertion, made promptly after issue of the Joint Statement, that China has a role in settlement of the Kashmir issue, and disclosure that he will be travelling to Beijing

– the first time any Hurriyat member would go there – reinforces suspicion that Washington and Beijing have discussed the Kashmir issue possibly keeping Islamabad in the loop. Hurriyat leaders have, in any case, invariably been received at the US State Department during their visits to the US when they also separately meet personnel of the Pakistan Embassy. China's altered tougher stance on Kashmir is evident in its decision to issue loose leaf visas to residents of Jammu and Kashmir, thereby designating the status of the entire state as disputed. The opacity added to its policy very recently, by affixing a visa on the Passport in a select case, could be an insidious prelude to drawing definitive religious divisions in the state. China's close comprehensive ties with Pakistan have dictated its ambiguity on the Kashmir issue over the years, but Beijing now seems to be preparing for a proactive role.

The emerging situation in Afghanistan and apparent accommodation of China's interests by the US, coinciding with the altered US policy towards China, is again of direct and strategic relevance to India. Afghanistan continues to be of strategic interest for major powers, but the players are different now with conflicting interests and different stakes. Influence over Central Asia and the region's energy resources are the main allurements. The players this time are the US and the West, Russia, China, Pakistan and India. Their competition for energy resources is best described as: 'China needs them, Russia wants to control their distribution, and the Western powers want to ensure they are not monopolized by Moscow or Beijing'. But this is only part of the story. Short term interests could well see the emergence of a grouping motivated by immediate self-interest. This is likely to result in the US, West, China and Pakistan being arrayed opposite the forces of the Taliban and Al Qaeda. Over the longer term, however, their interests will collide. The US and West, backed by the NATO member-countries, will be unwilling to see Afghanistan and Central Asia slide under the dominant influence of either Russia or China. All the powers are preparing for such a future scenario and the definitive contours of a potentially new Sino-Pakistan strategic collusion in this strategically important region are becoming discernible. In time this could lead to NATO and the Shanghai Cooperation Organisation (SCO) forces opposing each other and the emergence of contention.

In the short term, reports filtering out of Afghanistan reveal that the US has begun choreographing a sequence of moves designed to draw China into accepting greater responsibility in Afghanistan. They appear to have reached some informal understanding on security issues in the effort to develop and rebuild Afghanistan. US forces deployed since February 2009 as part of ISAF in Wardak province, long known as a haven for the Taliban, began protecting Chinese workers engaged in construction of a two-lane highway. A platoon of US troops are bivouacked on a hillock overlooking the camp of the Chinese workers employed by the state-owned China Railway Shisiju Group Corporation, which has been awarded a US$ 50 million contract from Italian aid funds, to construct the thirty three mile highway past Momaki village. An engineer for the China Railway Shisiju Group Corporation said: 'if there's fighting we cannot work' on the road building project, which started in 2006. In an interesting coincidence, the US troops were deployed to protect Chinese construction workers engaged on the road construction project in the same month that US Secretary of State Hillary Clinton visited Beijing.

Another indicator of US-China cooperation in the security sector is the recent US$ 3.5 billion deal, concluded by China's Jiangxi Copper Group and the China Metallurgical Group, to develop the huge twenty eight square kilometer Aynak copper deposit in Logar province south of Kabul. The Aynak copper deposit is reputed to be the largest undeveloped field in the world and has been virtually untouched since the Soviet invasion in 1979. The deal, the biggest yet between China and Afghanistan, includes agreement to build schools, clinics, markets, mosques and a US$ 500 million 400mw coal-fired power plant. This area presently has no electricity and the coal-fired power plant proposed to be constructed will cater to the power requirements of the copper mine and the inhabitants of the area. It will have surplus electricity which will go to Kabul. The Chinese companies also plan to build a railway to link Afghanistan with China through Tajikstan and to Pakistan and open a rail route to the north from the mine. It will be the first long distance rail link in Afghanistan. An interesting sidelight is that the Aynak Valley is where the Al Qaeda planned and trained for the 2001 attacks on USA. Afghan officials support the project, which they claim will generate over 6000 jobs.

Security has been a serious concern for Chinese companies working in Afghanistan. Since 2004, at least eleven Chinese aid and commercial workers have been killed frightening away some Chinese companies. In June 2008, a Chinese engineer on the road project at Momaki was kidnapped and freed after a month by Afghan forces. The Chinese government, however, is unlikely to allow security considerations to come in the way of achieving national strategic objectives. A number of the projects being taken up by China are in disturbed areas infested by the Taliban, but China would expect assistance from Pakistan, which retains links with a wide spectrum of forces in Afghanistan, including the Taliban. This will supplement the tentative cooperation between US troops and Chinese commercial entities to safeguard Chinese interests.

By the end of 2008, Chinese companies had thirty three infrastructure projects valued at US$ 480 million. The Afghan Ministry of Mines has now announced it will seek bidders to explore for oil and natural gas in northern Afghanistan and exploit an 1.8 billion ton iron ore deposit in the Hajigak mountains west of Momaki along the road now under construction. A US geological survey estimated that Afghanistan's oil reserves were 1,596 million barrels and natural gas reserves were approximately 15,687 trillion cubic feet (Tcf). Afghanistan also has large iron ore deposits between Herat and the Panjsher Valley and gold reserves in the northern provinces of Badakhshan, Takhar and Ghazni. There are major copper fields in Jawkhar and Darband, all within about 30 km of south east Kabul. These resource-rich areas are situated in the relatively stable north and northwestern regions of Afghanistan. Afghanistan's Foreign Minister, who visited Beijing in June 2009, canvassed investment for these projects and Chinese companies are expected to bid for more contracts in Afghanistan.

As in the case of other countries where it has strategic interests, China is ensuring that its investments in Afghanistan have a high degree of permanence and it acquires influence in Afghanistan's political and governmental structure. This includes Chinese companies entering the fledgling telecommunications sector. The Chinese Telecommunications companies, ZTE and Huawei, partnered Afghanistan's Ministry of Communications and have set up digital telephone services in the country, providing almost 200,000 subscriber lines. ZTE and Huawei are both affiliated to the Chinese People's Liberation Army (PLA) and are, pertinently, major partners in Pakistan's telecommunications infrastructure.

Afghanistan is at a geo-strategically sensitive location. Apart from being sited atop immense reserves of oil, gas and precious and rare metals, it sits astride important trade routes that inter-link Central and South Asia. Afghanistan and Central Asia are today not under the dominance of a single major power and neither are any of the countries in this region under the influence of a specific power. It has accordingly become the scene of major power competition. The US, Western powers and countries under the NATO umbrella, are trying to strengthen their presence in the region. Their objectives include preventing Russia from resuming its preponderant influence over the region, preventing Russia and China from monopolizing the region's natural resources, and containing the growing influence of Russia and China in the region. Russia is keen on retrieving its economic and political dominance over the countries in Central Asia and getting a share of their natural resources, or at least having a say in their distribution. China has a multiplicity of interests. It is intent on insulating its sensitive north-western border from the spread of extremist Islamic ideas and putting a stop to the trans-border support that separatist Uyghur outfits receive from Central Asian countries. It sees expansion of its influence in the region as a buffer against problems arising from any future deterioration of relations with Russia and as a preventive against possible inimical plans by the US and West to step up support to Tibetans and Uyghur 'separatists' and encourage them to undertake adventures into Tibet and Xinjiang. The region's huge reserves of natural resources are an important factor. China sees their exploitation and overland transportation to China as enhancing its energy security. China views development of a transport network across the region as opening new economic opportunities and markets for its land-locked hinterland provinces. It is a matter of time before the China-dominated Shanghai Cooperation Organisation (SCO) is used to reinforce the efforts of Russia and China.

The railway line from western China through Tajikstan into Afghanistan and on to Pakistan is a major venture with immense strategic implications for China and the region. It will bring Afghanistan into the orbit of the largely Islamic Central Asian Republics. The railway line will ensure China's ability to transport cargo and passengers from western China to Gwadar in Pakistan. It will automatically upgrade China's military logistics capability, accelerating and facilitating movement of troops to the borders with Russia as well as into Afghanistan, if necessary, and to Pakistan. It will enhance China's influence in Tajikstan as the latter will get an alternate trade route instead of the solitary route through Russia as at present. Its investments in Afghanistan, and particularly the railway line, will give China a dominant influence in Central Asia and the Persian Gulf. China's involvement in Afghanistan's development will ensure it a place on the high table when Afghan issues are being discussed and settled by the Western powers. Pakistan will automatically acquire a powerful supporter. China's actions in Afghanistan will be coloured by Pakistan's concerns, including of acquiring 'strategic depth' against India.

India needs to adopt a more assertive foreign policy in this region to preserve its national security interests. It needs to draw the 'red line' for the agenda in bilateral discussions on Kashmir and isolate secessionist groups like the Hurriyat. On the wider region including Afghanistan, India could profitably contemplate closer coordination with the US in restoring stability to Afghanistan, but while confining itself to non-combat areas like logistics and training Afghan military and police personnel. It should enhance involvement in developmental projects. Such steps would ease pressure on the US, thereby contributing tangibly to the Indo-US relationship, and add profile to India's role in the international effort to bring stability to Afghanistan. India should simultaneously broad-base contact with the younger Afghans by offering large numbers of scholarships in different disciplines. Indian business and public sector enterprises should be encouraged to aggressively enter Afghanistan's economy. These measures should be supplemented by cultivating Afghan politicians across the political spectrum, and expanding operational 'reach' by acquiring a presence additional to the Farkhor Air Base in Tajikstan. India should simultaneously strive to quickly reach an understanding with Afghanistan by which it denies a third country's armed forces access or transit though Afghanistan.

This was published as an Issue Brief by the Centre for Air Power Studies on November 15, 2009.

22. China-US Summit: Wary Co-Existence

The recent Hu-Obama Presidential Summit in Washington was like two top ranked sumo wrestlers sizing each other up to assess how to edge the adversary out of the ring. Decisions on important global and strategic issues were, however, finally deferred till after 2012, when new leaderships would assume charge in China and the US. Hu Jintao and Obama, however, both strove to achieve their immediate objectives and were fairly successful.

An important objective of the visit for China was to boost Hu Jintao's domestic image as a statesman and leader who had stamped China's imprimatur on the world stage. China's official print and electronic media described the visit as a "historic masterstroke" and accorded it prominent front-page coverage emphasizing especially the ceremonial and protocol aspects. Special mention was made of the 'intimate' private dinner hosted by US President Obama for Hu Jintao on the night of his arrival in Washington, where matters were informally and candidly discussed. Hu Jintao's reception at the airport by US Vice President Joe Biden, ceremonial red-carpet welcome, honour guard and 21-gun salute, Vice Presidential luncheon and the state banquet were reported in detail. Comparisons were suggested with the landmark visit of Deng Xiaoping thirty two years ago. In a public relations exercise, the Chinese authorities publicized Hu Jintao's state visit in the US by showing a 60-minute promotional video on the screens in Times Square in New York on the night prior to his arrival. The promotional video was to play 300 times a day and feature Chinese-origin icons like baseball player Yao Ming, astronaut Yang Liwei and pianist Lang Lang. Reflecting the mood prevalent in China, the China-owned Hong Kong-based newspaper, Ta Kung Pao exulted that Chinese President

Hu Jintao's high-level reception by US President Obama was because of the resoluteness 'displayed by the Chinese government and people in building the nation; superiority of Chinese socialism; unity of the Chinese people; and improvement of Chinese society, which have been acknowledged and are respected by others'.

The state visit materialized after year-long tensions between the US and China as well as China and other countries in the Asia-Pacific. These were exacerbated by Beijing's unresolved maritime territorial claims with Japan, Vietnam and several other nations. It also coincided with the noticeably increased assertiveness in China's foreign policy. High on Beijing's agenda for the Summit, therefore, was securing acknowledgement of China's pivotal role in the Asia-Pacific region. In his speech at a luncheon hosted by US Friendship Groups in Washington on Jan 20, and attended by 500 CEOs, Chinese President Hu Jintao described the Asia-Pacific region as where the US and China have 'the most overlapping interests', adding that both are committed to promoting development and prosperity in the region. Hu Jintao stressed that Sino-US cooperation is 'crucial' to the regional situation and development of Sino-US relations. The 4000-word joint communiqué issued after the visit devoted three entire clauses to noting the importance of Sino-US cooperation in the Asia-Pacific region. The statement that 'China welcomes the US as an Asia-Pacific nation' implies China's acquiescence of continuing US presence in the region and its waters. In his speeches in the US, Hu Jintao had significantly omitted categorising the South China Sea as a 'core issue' for China while, for the first time, publicly describing Taiwan and Tibet as 'core issues' for China. Taiwan, described by China as a 'core issue', was anticipatedly mentioned in the joint communiqué. North Korea, an important issue for the US and an ally of China, was also mentioned at length in the joint communiqué with China, for the first time, expressing concern regarding the DPRK's 'claimed uranium enrichment programme'. The formulation was arrived at after many hours of negotiations between Chinese and US officials. The Iran nuclear issue, Sudan and Darfur were mentioned. At the joint press conference, Hu Jintao had asserted that 'Beijing and Washington shared expanding common interests and shoulder increasing common responsibilities in addressing global challenges'.

South Asia, including the Af-Pak region, was pertinently not mentioned in the joint communiqué despite its importance to the US and China because of India's sensitivities. India had criticised inclusion of the term 'South Asia' in the joint communiqués issued on two previous occasions in March and September 2009. This time the joint communiqué confined itself to mentioning only that China and the US had 'agreed to enhance communication and coordination to address pressing regional and global challenges'. That these 'pressing regional...challenges' referred to South Asia was, however, made clear by Hu Jintao in his speech to the US-China Business Council in Washington where he specifically referred to 'South Asia'. At other forums he made repeated references to 'hot-button regional issues', thereby clarifying that the US and China will continue to coordinate closely on matters concerning South Asia.

US President Obama, in turn, sought to use the visit to dispel the chill that had settled over Sino-US relations throughout the past year, and also to boost his domestic popularity by raising issues of concern to the US that his Administration had earlier soft-pedalled. In the process he effected a mid-course correction in his Administration's China policy. Obama mentioned these at the joint press conference. Human Rights was one such issue. He also urged continuation of talks between China and the Dalai Lama. Interestingly, in a display of China's stringent controls on the media and reminiscent of the treatment accorded some months ago to Premier Wen Jiabao's remarks to Fareed Zakaria on CNN, Hu Jintao's response at the joint press conference to a question on human rights, despite his having stressed that interpretations of human rights differ, was blanked out by China's official media except for the English-language 'China Daily', CCTV-International and the China News Service. The joint communiqué noted that promotion of human rights and democracy is an important part of US foreign policy. It simultaneously observed that China had 'stressed there should be no interference in any country's internal affairs'. Earlier, the joint communiqué noted the commitment of both countries to the promotion and protection of human rights 'even as they continue to have significant differences on these issues'.

Sino-US bilateral relations were smoothened during this visit with both countries, according to the joint communiqué, supporting the early entry into force of the CTBT, early negotiations on a Fissile Material Cutoff Treaty (FMCT) and cooperation on a range of other subjects. In the defence sector, the groundwork had been done by US Defence Secretary Robert Gates during his visit to Beijing from Jan 10-13, when he met his Chinese counterparts, including PLA Deputy Chief of General Staff, General Ma Xiaotian and Chinese President Hu Jintao. Gates' meeting with General Ma Xiaotian would have been important as he is a close associate of Hu Jintao and the putative President Xi Jinping and will bridge the transfer of power between the two. Gates discussed defence issues in detail and asserted that defence contacts should not be vulnerable to the vagaries of politics. He had suggested a new dialogue on nuclear weapons, space, cyber and missile defence but that elicited no positive response. The Chinese used the occasion of his visit to underscore China's technological advances in the manufacture of defence hardware and unveiled the J-20 Stealth fighter aircraft. In recent months China had announced the successful launch of the space vehicle Chang'e-2 and tested an Anti Ship Ballistic Missile (ASBM) capable of attacking aircraft carrier groups. Hu Jintao, in fact, personally confirmed the J-20's successful test flight to US Defence Secretary Gates during their meeting. The joint communiqué also noted US acceptance of a visit by PLA Chief General Chen Bingde in the first half of 2011 and agreement that the Defence Consultative Talks, Defence Policy Coordination Talks and Military Maritime Consultative Agreement will remain operative. A Chinese delegation was invited to visit NASA headquarters and facilities this year. It was decided that US Vice President Biden would visit China this year and that Chinese Vice President Xi Jinping would return the visit.

Economic issues were at the heart of the visit and used by both leaders to shore their respective positions. This was reflected in the joint communiqué, which asserted the importance of the Strategic and Economic Dialogue, and was dominated by clauses relating to economic issues. It noted that China had agreed to promote RMB exchange rate reform and enhance exchange rate flexibility as also strengthen IPR protection efforts. Obama had separately pointed out that the RMB remains undervalued and there needs to be further adjustment in the exchange rate. Hu Jintao did, however, mention at the press conference that the trade deficit could only be reduced if the US allowed hi-tech exports to China. The importance of the economic aspect of the relationship was additionally highlighted by Hu Jintao in his speeches, where he pointed out that bilateral trade presently exceeded US$ 350 billion, that US consumers were annually saving US$ 70 billion by purchasing Chinese-made goods and, that China currently held US debts valued at US$ 895 billion. US investments in China currently exceed US$ 60 billion while Chinese investments in USA now total US$ 4.4 billion. To emphasise China's economic might, agreements worth US$ 45 billion were signed during the visit, including an order for 200 Boeing aircraft valued at US$ 19 billion. Hu Jintao and Obama both highlighted that these would create 235,000 jobs in America.

Economic issues equally dominated Hu Jintao's visit to Chicago, where Mayor Richard Daley said Chicago's 'long-range goal was to be the most China-friendly city in the US'. The importance of economic relations with China was underscored by ensuring the presence in Chicago of a number of CEOs of Chinese companies. Wu Guangui, Chairman of China's biggest auto parts manufacturer Wanxing, showed Hu Jintao the dashboards for the Chevy Volt made at his US-based company employing 5,600 workers. Dalian Machine Tool Group, which acquired machine-tool maker 'Ingersoll' a decade ago, disclosed plans to build a new factory in the US employing 200 workers. Zhu Chunping, President of BFM Fire and Security Inc., which imports Chinese-made fire extinguishers, informed Hu Jintao that the company plans to build new plants in California and Ontario while the Tianjin Pipe Group Co disclosed plans to establish a US$ 1 billion factory on the Texas coast. Five months earlier, as part of preparations for Hu Jintao's visit, China's Commerce Minister had led a delegation to the US when agreements worth US $ 574 million were signed in Houston. Hu Jintao also delivered his first public speech in Chicago. His itinerary was obviously cast to highlight China's strengths and, more subtly, its soft power and included a visit to a secondary school where Chinese is taught. China has, incidentally, established over 60 Confucius Centres in the US and there are more than 500 schools in the US where Chinese is taught

An important agreement signed was one between General Electric and the Aviation Industry Corporation of China (AVIC) for setting up a hi-tech joint venture in Shanghai that will focus on avionics including the electronics for communications, navigation, cockpit displays and controls and a high performance computer system that operates as the avionics brain of the Boeing's new 787 'Dreamliner'. GE dismissed objections to the deal by other US defence manufacturers by saying that competition was inevitable and to stay ahead the US companies would have to develop more advanced technologies and equipment.

There were some discordant notes during the visit, which was carefully crafted and choreographed by the Chinese and US Administration. Three of the top four Congressional leaders including House Speaker Joe Boehner, Senate Majority leader

Harry Reid and Senate Minority leader Mitch McConnell stayed away from the state dinner hosted for the visiting Chinese President, though they cordially received Hu Jintao when he called at the Capitol to meet them. Congresswoman Ileana Ros-Lehtinen, Head of the House Foreign Affairs Committee, said she handed a letter to Hu Jintao concerning China's treatment of the Tibetan and Uyghur minorities and the Falungong spiritual movement. Tibetan, Uyghur and Falungong protestors also staged noisy demonstrations outside the White House and Capitol each day of the visit. On occasion they faced flag-waving nationalistic Chinese youth. There were critical foreign and domestic media comments too. Interestingly, at least one leading Russian newspaper and some from former Soviet bloc East European countries regretted that the leader of the 'world's largest democracy' was playing host to the leader of the 'world's largest dictatorship'. A few others suggested that US President Obama more forcefully raise the issues of Human Rights, democracy etc. The New York Times regretted that Li Xiaobo, the Chinese dissident and Nobel Prize winner remained incarcerated while another Nobel Prize winner hosted his 'jailor'. The mood of the Chinese, who had felt under pressure from the US over the past year, was reflected in their spontaneous reaction when US President Obama's favourite and Chinese-origin pianist, Lang Lang, played 'The Motherland' at the White House state dinner. 'My Motherland' is the theme of a 1956 Chinese movie set during the Korean War and features the defeat of the US on the battlefield! The Chinese invitees to the state dinner cheered loudly and Chinese President Hu Jintao, who normally betrays no emotion, warmly hugged the pianist after his performance. While Lang Lang, on his blog, said that playing the theme seemed to him 'like I was telling them about the power of China and the unity of the Chinese', Chinese 'netizens' promptly flooded cyber space with thousands of jubilant messages lauding Lang Lang for his 'insult' to the Americans. Chinese dissident Wei Jingsheng, exiled in the US since 1997, wrote to US Secretary of State Hillary Clinton expressing his 'shock' and explaining that 'My Motherland' was the best known Chinese Communist propaganda movie about the Korean War. American journalists subsequently lamented that the Obama Administration had bungled and created the opportunity for a 'great Chinese Communist Party propaganda victory'.

Chinese President Hu Jintao's 4-day state visit to the US, closely watched by nations around the world, was an important opportunity for China to demonstrate its economic might, portray itself as an important partner that the US needs, and project itself as a country almost comparable to the US in international influence. The joint communiqué confirmed close US-China cooperation on a range of international and other issues. China's official news agency Xinhua described the joint communiqué as the 'new guide to the development of China-US relations…'. It added that Hu and Obama had 'worked closely on major regional and international issues. These have all expanded the strategic content and global influence of China-US relations'.

Hu Jintao came to the US as the leader of a confident, powerful nation that had long term ambitions. Though during his visit he repeatedly emphasized that China is a developing country and 'China is not a military threat to any country…will never seek to dominate or pursue an expansionist policy', the visit did not succeed in dispelling mutual distrust. US President Obama also tried to deftly manage the visit to boost his own domestic popularity while simultaneously assertively re-setting his Administration's policy towards China. There was, however, sufficient indication that major global and strategic issues remain to be sorted out and that the next couple of years would be marked by caution, cooperation and competition.

This was published as an Issue Brief by the Centre for Air Power Studies on January 31, 2011.

23. Recent US Moves in Asia-Pacific Could Impact China-India Relations

China has been wary of Indo-US relations since they began warming. It suspects that the US is intent on forging a grouping comprising mainly Japan, Vietnam, Australia and India, to 'contain China'. Now with US' re-energised interest in the Asia-Pacific region, evidenced by Obama's recent visit to Australia and accompanying diplomatic activity, China sees the diplomatic gains it has made in the region are receding. To retard US diplomatic efforts, Beijing will try and pressure countries in the region including India.

Couched inside an article, which was seemingly temperate in tenor, in the authoritative, official Chinese Communist Party (CCP) newspaper 'People's Daily', on November 15, 2011, was a veiled warning to India's political and military leadership. Referring to reports of India deploying 100,000 troops in the northeast, it hinted at the forces that China could deploy in the event of future conflict. For the authoritative Party newspaper to hint at the use of missiles in the context of India-China relations is very unusual.

Unlike other articles, this observed that India's "*...action is completely not worthwhile. Currently, India has 40,000 troops in the disputed area, and if the further 100,000 is deployed, the total number of the troops will reach 140,000. In an era when precision-guided weapons are developing rapidly, everyone with common sense knows that concentrated troops could be eliminated easily*." It added that "security would not be guaranteed despite the expenditure of US$ 13 billion".

Interestingly, the article was first published by the '*Zhongguo Qingnian Bao*' (China Youth Daily), the official newspaper of China's

Communist Youth League (CYL) whose Chief, Lu Hao, is assessed to be on the career fast-track in the Chinese Communist Party (CCP).

China's military doctrine and articles in China's military literature amply clarify that China anticipates any future conflict will be on its periphery and of short duration. China's armed forces envisage opening the first phase in future conflicts with a massive cyber and electronic-jamming operations offensive to cripple the adversary's military, financial and public utilities' cyber infrastructure; electronic-based equipment; and command communications. This will be followed by precision-guided missile attacks on military targets as well as military command and population centres to overwhelm and destroy the military and political leaderships' will and resolve. Ground-based attacks will follow in the final phase.

The Nov 15, 'People's Daily' article implicitly underscores the use of missiles. In the eventuality of India-China hostilities a role would also have been envisaged for Huawei and ZTE, the two Chinese telecommunications companies which together virtually entirely control India's mobile and wireless telecommunications. Other articles in the official Chinese media have publicised the major military exercises recently conducted by the People's Liberation Army (PLA) in the remote fastness of the Tibetan Plateau opposite India.

Later, on November 24, the 'People's Daily' published another article captioned 'India's undue worry about China results from inferiority complex'. The article, apparently in reaction to former Minister Jaswant Singh's article 'Asia's Giants Colliding at Sea?', was publicized by China's official newsagency, 'Xinhua'. It claimed that "*India jitters at the sight of China gaining prestige in Asia, in particular, in South Asia and Southeast Asia, and takes China's ever-growing regional influence in recent years as a strategic encirclement to target and contain India*". It added "*But one thing is certain: Today's India, no matter how anxious it intends to lead the region and even the world, is far from potent and prosperous to act of its own accord – By currying favor with China's neighbor, in particular those who have brewed disputes with China, India would assume, it could instigate these smaller nations to engage in a gang fight against China and contain China's growing clout in the region*". Commenting on India's so-called 'failure' to adopt outward looking 'win-win' strategies similar to China's, the article seemed to reflect the opinion of at least a section of Chinese analysts when it said: "*Nowadays, it is no longer those who have only teeth and muscle that can finally loom on the horizon posing as winners, but those who are confident and courageous, and have a strong body with a sound mind, the latter more important for a great power*". "*Jealousy*", it added, "*can sometimes be put in the same breath of inferiority. India could trace its sense of being so self-abased to the brief border war with China in 1960s, when it was beaten by the Chinese army. And India has since eyed China with deep-seated distrust*". Asserting that this distrust had "put sand in the wheels of its own progress", it cited cross-border trade at Nathula as an example, describing it as "a picture of contrasts – ambitious tradesmen on the Chinese side vs. slackness of the Indian businessmen". It concluded that "*to grow up to be a real power and stand as a sound competitor, India needs to, first and foremost, break through its own psychological fence*".

China's growing suspicion about the nature of Indo-US relations have undoubtedly been heightened in recent weeks. Following the unveiling by the US of the 'AirSea Battle' concept, Beijing closely monitored US President Obama's visit to Australia, the East Asia Summit (EAS), and the accompanying unprecedented US diplomatic activity in the Asia-Pacific region.

US flirtation with Yangon would have especially irked Beijing. Myanmar, long known as a country close to Beijing, will for the first time in fifty years on December 1-2, 2011, receive a US Secretary of State. Hillary Clinton is scheduled to meet opposition leader Aung

San Suu Kyi during the visit. In another apparent snub to Beijing, Myanmar's new Defence Chief, Gen Min Aung Hlaing, travelled to Vietnam on November 14, on his first trip abroad instead of to China as his predecessors had done. These developments follow the sudden cancellation – since restored – by Yangon of a US$ 3.2 billion project for construction of a dam by a Chinese company.

In the Philippines, Hillary Clinton pointedly referred to the South China Sea as the 'West Philippine Sea', the name officially adopted by Manila. While there she reaffirmed USA's interest in the right to free navigation and neutrality of the sea lanes in the South China Sea as well as the peaceful settlement of disputes between China and the other claimant nations.

A White House briefing at the commencement of US President Obama's tour to Australia set the tone for his visit. The White House spokesman said, inter alia, that "a core message of this entire trip" is that as the wars in Iraq and Afghanistan end the US is "refocusing attention in a substantial way on the Asia Pacific region" and "that the United States is going to play a larger role and a long-term role in shaping the future of the region". He added "it's a part of the U.S. sending a signal that we're going to be present, that we're going to continue to play the role of underpinning security in this part of the region. Part of that context is a rising China. That's one part of the context for the future of this region".

In Australia, US President Obama declared that US marine troops will be based there. He asserted that USA intended retaining its influence in the Asia-Pacific, including the South Pacific, which was important to its growth and economic pre-eminence. He emphasised the US interests in Japan, Thailand, the Philippines, South Korea, Indonesia, Malaysia, Singapore, Vietnam, Cambodia and "in our welcome of India as it "looks east" and plays a larger role as an Asian power".

Addressing the Australian Parliament he referred additionally to US support for human rights, freedom and liberty. He said, "if this vast region and its people teach us anything, it's the yearning for liberty and progress will not be denied.... It's why the people took to the streets – from Delhi to Seoul, from Manila to Jakarta... It's why men of peace in saffron robes faced beatings and bullets, and why every day – from some of the world's largest cities to dusty rural towns, in small acts of courage the world may never see – a student posts a blog; a citizen signs a charter; an activist remains unbowed...". The references to human rights violations in China and to the Tibetan issue are almost explicit.

In another setback to China, maritime security and the South China Sea issue were commented on in varying degrees of specificity by sixteen of the eighteen leaders at the East Asia Summit, including Australia and India. Cambodia and Myanmar were the two exceptions. The speakers included ASEAN members Singapore, Philippines, Vietnam, Malaysia and Thailand, as well as Australia and India. All these countries referred directly to the South China Sea. Reports suggest there was consensus on a number of issues. The main principles spelt out by the speakers from Singapore, Philippines and Vietnam included the importance of protecting the freedom of navigation in the maritime domain in general and in the South China Sea in particular; the importance of adherence to the rule of law in approaching and settling disputes; and the applicability of the U.N. Convention on the Law of the Sea and the importance for all nations to abide by its terms. Nearly all speakers underlined the importance of a peaceful resolution and of the need for progress on a code of conduct, which was agreed to by ASEAN and China in 2002. Several stressed the importance of protecting legitimate commerce in the maritime domain and particularly in the South China Sea, and many called for a multilateral resolution of the conflicting territorial claims by the parties themselves. Indicative of Beijing's concern at India's stance, was that Chinese Premier Wen Jiabao raised the subject during his meeting with Prime Minister Manmohan Singh on the sidelines of the East Asia Summit.

A day prior to the Summit, the official 'Global Times', a subsidiary of the 'People's Daily', described efforts to include the South China Sea as bringing 'great pressure to China' and warned 'it is now expected that China will take some counter-measures'. It accused the US of 'encouraging China's neighboring countries to challenge China'.

China's ire was evident in the 'People's Daily' warning Australia against being ''caught in the crossfire". Song Xiaojun, a military commentator with China Central Television and former PLA Navy Communications officer, cautioned that "Chinese strategic missiles can reach Australia". Reports simultaneously surfaced that China is contemplating establishing a military base in Timor Leste, Indonesia's neighbour. Timor Leste, which is the recipient of Chinese fiscal development assistance, is yet to approve the proposal.

An intriguing sidelight was the disclosure by Xie Jingwen, Deputy Chief of the Tracking System for China's space program, of Australia being among China's global network of ground stations. The disclosure was first carried by HongKong's 'South China Morning Post' about two weeks before it was reproduced in 'The Australian' on November 16, seemingly timed to coincide with the commencement of US President Obama's two-day Australian tour. Later the same week, Canberra confirmed China's claim that the station was used to track the Shenzhou VIII, launched this month as part of China's plan to build a space station. China's Satellite Launch and Tracking Control General (CLTC), which uses the Mingenew station, is an arm of China's Commission of Science, Technology and Industry for National Defence (COSTIND). While China's space program has the use of four international facilities to help track its satellites, in Pakistan, Kenya, Chile and Namibia, the Mingenew station in Australia is the first such facility in a Western nation that is a close ally of the US. The Mingenew station, which is 400 kms north of Perth, is part of the PrioraNet global network of strategically located ground stations that sell services to space agencies on a commercial basis.

The issue gained prominence because of the accusation by Des Ball, an Australian expert on space-based espionage, that the Chinese are using the facility to locate Australian and US warships in the region. He claimed that the "ground station would help China's space-based listening devices to more precisely locate the electronic emissions from aircraft carriers, destroyers and other navy ships" and particularly carrier battle groups operating in the western Pacific and Indian Oceans.

China views the recent US diplomatic activity in the region as an effort to 'contain China' and forge an 'anti-China alliance'. The official 'Global Times' reflected this when it quoted Major General Peng Guangqian of China's Academy of Military Sciences as saying that the US was trying to use Australia to contain China in a "pincer" movement. He added that it would be a historical setback if the US was trying to provoke a "21st-century new cold war".

Pertinently, India has received other warnings in the context of the dispute in the South China Sea. Official media articles critical of the US-ROK military exercises in 2010, bracketted Japan, India and Vietnam as countries that were drawing closer to the US to 'contain' China. Earlier articles had observed that history had imposed limits on the extent to which China's relationship with Japan and India could develop. Some suggested that China would have to ultimately use military means to settle outstanding border disputes and while doing so would choose one of two bigger nations, namely India or Japan and, that in such a case, India will likely be the first choice. On July 22, 2011, an Indian Navy amphibious warship, 'INS Airavat', received a broadcast on an open radio channel while off the Vietnamese coast from someone identified merely as the "Chinese Navy". The broadcast said the ship was entering "Chinese waters," and instructed it to leave. More recently, a few weeks ago, reacting to a commercial contract for off-shore oil exploration signed between India's ONGC and Vietnam, China warned India against proceeding with off-shore oil exploration plans. Another warning was subsequently addressed to all foreign companies operating in the area.

China's criticism of the US has, however, been comparatively restrained, partially because the Chinese leadership does not want the issue to enter into the US Presidential debate. Chinese analysts have indicated that Beijing's priority continues to be to maintain stable Sino-US relations. Shen Dingli, a Professor at the Centre of American Studies in Shanghai's Fudan University appeared to aptly sum up Beijing's perspective when he said: "At the moment, we lose, but in ten years, the U.S. will lose". At the same time, Beijing is not likely to resile from its stance on the South China Sea issue. It has already announced plans last week for exercises by the PLA Navy in the western Pacific and separately offered to fund and participate in a regional maritime force to preserve safety of the sea lanes.

In this backdrop, China can be expected to try and dilute perceived US 'anti-China' efforts by exerting pressure on some countries in the region and especially India. China's demand last week, that Government of India prevent Indian Buddhists from organizing an international religious conference in Delhi where the Dalai Lama is scheduled to speak, is an instance. The recent 'People's Daily' articles and other Chinese official media articles reinforce Chinese actions and, therefore, assume significance. India should be prepared for a period of increased tension in India-China relations and guard against yielding ground despite growing Chinese pressure.

This was published as an Issue Brief by the Centre for Air Power Studies on November 28, 2011.

24. China's Yuan Preparing to Challenge US Dollar?

China's efforts over the past couple of years to have its currency, the RMB (Renminbi or Yuan), included in the IMF's Special Drawing Rights (SDR) slowly inched forward on March 31, 2011 at the G-20 Monetary Reform Seminar held in Nanjing. The proposal will undoubtedly be finally vetoed by the US, which needs to sell bonds worth at least a trillion dollars each year for many years to come to keep its economy afloat. In the interregnum Beijing, which has emerged as the world's largest exporter, has opted to broaden the acceptability of the RMB among its major trading partners through currency swap agreements.

A quick analysis of official Chinese media reports indicates that China's leadership has been determined, at least since the international economic crisis highlighted China's economic strengths, to explore ways of strengthening China's currency in order to optimize Beijing's international influence. Investing in countries of its interest and increasing the use of its currency are steps intended to help China move in this direction.

In this context, Chinese Vice Foreign Minister Cui Tiankai was quoted by the Beijing-owned Hongkong-based newspaper, 'Ta Kung Pao', as saying on March 5, that during his visit to Europe in November 2010, Chinese President Hu Jintao travelled to Portugal and France at a time when they were in economic difficulty and signed a US$ 20 billion industrial purchase deal. Cui Tiankai claimed this had given a setback to USA's strategic objective of 'besieging China in the Asia-Pacific region'. The newspaper added that both the European countries are focussed on using the G-20 forum as a platform to gradually break through and change governance by the

US, 'which benefits itself at the expense of others, and the country's overbearing attitude as well'. Earlier in January 2011, China's Vice Premier Li Keqiang had revealed his country's intention of buying about Euros 6 billion of Spanish public debt. Other reports disclosed that China had purchased Portuguese and Greek debts amounting to Euros 6 billion as part of efforts to forge closer relations with Europe.

Ahead of the G-20 summit in April 2010, China had proposed the introduction of a new stable international reserve currency, through substantial increase of the IMF's Special Drawing Rights (SDR), for its considerable international reserve holdings which are mainly in US dollars. This year again, prior to the G-20 seminar in Nanjing, Xu Hongcai, Deputy Department Director at the 'China Centre', a major Chinese government think-tank, issued a report which candidly stated that 'nations around the world have no way of restricting dollar issuance by the Federal Reserve. The current international monetary system lacks both stability and fairness'. Xu Hongcai asserted that the world had fallen in to a 'dollar trap' and it would be prudent to reduce dollar holdings in official currency reserves. Beijing's efforts appear to have found some resonance, though they will be staunchly opposed by the US. The G-20 seminar has now agreed to study whether to include the Chinese Yuan within the basket of currencies that make up the IMF's Special Drawing Rights (SDR). French President Nicolas Sarkozy suggested on March 31, 2011, that given the importance of emerging economies such as China to global growth, their currencies should be added to the SDR basket. "Without rules and supervision, the world runs the risk of being condemned to increasingly serious and severe crises," said President Sarkozy. The US Treasury Secretary and French Finance Minister were, however, very guarded in welcoming the suggestion and insisted that China would first have to fulfill certain conditions. Yu Yongding, a former Chinese central bank adviser who also spoke at the conference, said applying such conditions was a contentious issue. The matter will be discussed at the G-20 Summit in November 2011 in Cannes.

China's efforts to challenge the 'global financial hegemony' of the US dollar has also been the subject of recent articles in authoritative official Chinese publications. The articles simultaneously reflect the negative mood about the US within Chinese leadership circles and their deep rooted suspicion of US intentions. Two articles are especially pertinent.

'Zhongguo Qingnian Bao', the official newspaper of China's Central Communist Youth League (CYL), which claims a membership of nearly 75 million and counts a number of former members among China's current top leadership echelons, recently published a lengthy article by Qiao Liang. The 7,009-word article published on March 8, 2011, focusses entirely on the financial aspect of US' global domination. It appeared to buttress the arguments advanced in another signed article, published earlier on December 10, 2010 in the authoritative Chinese Communist Party (CCP) theoretical magazine '*Qiu Shi*' (Seeking Truth), but sounded a strong note of caution. The lengthy *Qiu Shi* article had recommended counter-measures, in the economic and strategic spheres, to neutralize US efforts to dominate China and prevent it from realizing its aspirations. Recent initiatives and statements by senior Chinese leaders now suggest that the views expressed in the '*Qiu Shi*' article probably reflect the prevailing trend of opinion among China's leaders.

This *Qiu Shi* article discussed, inter alia, the manner in which China should deal with the issue of its huge US Treasury Bill holdings — currently estimated at US$ 1.16 trillion — and how it should try and undermine the US' position as a 'financial super power' attained by virtue of the US dollar being designated the world's reserve currency. It asserted that China's 'most powerful weapon today' is 'our economic power, especially our foreign exchange reserves. The key is to use it well. If we use it well, it is a weapon; otherwise it may become a burden'. It described the US government's action of increasing the number of dollars in circulation, thereby devaluing the value of the dollar, as harmful to countries with high foreign exchange reserves who possess US dollars. Arguing that the US itself loses nothing by increasing the number of dollars in circulation, it said the only way that countries holding US dollars can restrain the US from printing more currency is by not purchasing US dollars. To achieve this it would be necessary for these countries to either arrive at a consensus not to buy any more US dollars, or for one country to take the lead and not purchase US dollars.

It observed that to reach a consensus China, Japan, the U.K., India, and Saudi Arabia need to align their thinking. 'Japan is constrained by the Japan-U.S. Security Treaty and will not break away from the U.S., so the probability of Japan cooperating is very low. Great Britain has always followed the U.S', but Prime Minister Cameron has adopted 'a new strategy toward China that increases the possibilities for cooperation, making it a more likely player than Japan'. 'India has stayed closely allied with the U.S. in recent years, and Obama promised to support India for a permanent membership in the UNSC. Thus, the probability for India to cooperate with China is also not great. India's purchasing power of foreign exchange reserves is very limited anyway, so it cannot influence the overall situation much. Saudi Arabia does not have much political interest in the U.S.; its purchase of foreign exchange reserves is purely commercial. So they are more likely just to follow the market'. The article concluded that the idea of reaching a consensus was, therefore, unrealistic and China should accordingly muster the courage to take the lead. It could either sell its holdings of US dollar reserves or decide not to purchase any dollars for a certain period of time. It said the first option might lead to devaluation of the US dollar leading to a severe loss for countries like China, which have large US dollar holdings. China would have to examine whether it can sustain such a loss.

The second option is for China to use its foreign exchange reserves, presently stated to be US$2.8 trillion, to buy the Euro, British Sterling, Japanese Yen, Indian Rupee, Russian Ruble and Brazilian currency. Describing this as a cost effective move, it said such an initiative will 'help promote good relations and economic and trade relations with these countries and enhance China's economic influence in these countries'. China's action will have a demonstration effect and other countries are 'very likely to follow'. It added that since excess dollars once printed cannot be sold leading to accelerated depreciation of the dollar, the adverse impact on America's wealth will be 'enormous'. Stressing that the crucial issue is whether China has the 'necessary courage and determination' to withstand US pressure, it said that such a move will show just how much the US needs China and the 'US will start to fear us'.

Emphasising that the US dollar's position as the world's reserve currency is what makes the US a financial superpower, the article recommended that China explore ways of confronting the US and challenging the US dollar. It enumerated ways in which the Renminbi (RMB) could also become the world's reserve currency thus putting pressure on the US dollar.

The more recent article in the *'Zhongguo Qingnian Bao'* by Qiao Liang has been described by him as an effort to examine economic and financial issues from the perspective of military affairs and strategy. Currently a Major General in the People's Liberation Army Air Force (PLAAF) and Professor at the Air Force Command College, Qiao Liang rose to prominence with the publication in February 1999 of the quasi-official book, 'Unrestricted Warfare'. A Senior Colonel in the PLAAF at the time, Qiao Liang co-authored the book with another PLA Senior Colonel, Wang Xiaogui. The book examines the advantages of a weaker nation waging asymmetric warfare against a stronger adversary. It states that, 'the first principle of such warfare is that there are no rules and there are no limitations'. Since then, Qiao Liang has continued exploring different aspects of asymmetric warfare.

Qiao Liang's article claims to detail the USA's rise as an economic power and attributes this primarily to the world's currencies being pegged to the US dollar and, till August 15, 1971, the US dollar being pegged to gold. Protecting the status of the US dollar, he says, protects the 'global hegemonic status' of the US. The other 'pillar' of US hegemony is its powerful S&T innovativeness. Qiao Liang claimed that in October 1973, the US Treasury Secretary William Simon successfully persuaded the Saudi Minister of Petroleum to agree that all global trading in oil would be in US dollars. This move ensured the emergence of a 'new financial colonial empire never before seen in the history of empires' because regardless of how high the price of oil rose, the US would not be adversely affected as it would lead to an increased global demand for US dollars which the US could easily print. As evidence, he pointed out that USA's GDP in the two hundred years prior to 1990 never exceeded US$ 7 trillion, but in the past twenty years it had burgeoned to US$ 14 trillion. He added that the US had taken into account the reality that 'hot money' requires a safe place for investment. To ensure that the US remains a safe destination for such funds and because the global internet has accelerated the flow of funds, the Pentagon is presently engaged in establishing a 'prompt global strike system'. The objective, the author explains, is to strike militarily at countries that become attractive destinations for such funds thereby prompting the funds to be pulled out and re-invested elsewhere. At the time the war broke out in Kosovo, the article claimed, 'hot money' valued at almost US$ 700 billion was floating around in Europe. After the commencement of the war nearly US$ 200 billion found its way to the US leading to an 'unprecedented ninety months of prosperity'.

Another US$ 200 billion went to Hongkong. The 'mistaken' bombing by the US of the Chinese Embassy in Belgrade, Qiao Liang asserts, ensured that China was no longer viewed by investors as a safe investment destination resulting in these funds also being diverted to the US from Hongkong. Reiterating that the US is an 'empire founded on currency' and the US has to maintain the 'hegemony' of the dollar, Qiao Liang concludes with the warning that 'it now seems that the United States has no efficacious tools to achieve this other than military methods'. Qiao Liang's article appears to caution China's financial strategists to guard against the possibility of attracting hostile US action.

Meanwhile, China has been examining the options available to it to secure the value of its huge US dollar holdings, estimated by the US Treasury in its annual report in December 2010, at US$ 1.16 trillion. The latter has additionally been a topic of public concern. A report in the Guangzhou Ribao (March 7) said that: 'China's holdings of US Treasury Bonds have become a topic of concern for all citizens.... Unfortunately we still have not seen any information released by the relevant Chinese authorities on changes in China's holdings of US Treasury Bonds. State foreign exchange reserves are the common wealth of the masses, and the masses have a right to know'. The US Treasury's report separately noted that China's dollar holdings had dropped from the US$ 1.164 trillion in November 2010. The Chinese authorities have simultaneously been trying to diversify investments of their foreign currency reserves. Accordingly, Beijing began using its foreign currency reserves to purchase Euros. At the same time any sudden reduction in holdings by these countries would weaken the dollar and dilute the value of their assets.

As a major step towards making China's currency acceptable in international trade, Beijing has concluded sizeable currency swap agreements with a number of countries that are its trading partners. These include Argentina, Belarus, Brazil, Hong Kong, Indonesia,

Malaysia and South Korea. The swap agreements enables these countries to pay for Chinese exports in Yuan rather than dollars. During the recently concluded National People's Congress (NPC) session too, Chinese Premier Wen Jiabao spoke of expanding the use of RMB in cross-border trade and investment and of plans to press ahead with making the RMB convertible under the capital account.

This was published as an Issue Brief by the Centre for Air Power Studies on April 15, 2011.

25. The Dalai Lama And India-China Relations

Mention of 'Buddhism' today conjures up images of ochre-robed Tibetan monks and Tenzin Gyatso, the present Dalai Lama. The rise in international profile of the Tibetan cause over the past three decades has, in its wake, generated a minor revival of the 'Mahayana', or Tibetan, version of Buddhism. This is due primarily to the current XIVth Dalai Lama, who despite having been dealt a weak hand, played it with considerable deftness all these years. He disarmingly advocated the cause of Tibet and its people in international forums and foreign capitals to garner adequate support to help build pressure on China to enter into a dialogue with his envoys. In the process, the Dalai Lama effectively became the 'face' of Buddhism for the international community. Award of the Nobel Peace Prize in 1989 further enhanced his stature.

Material and other support from the US and West helped the Dalai Lama and his cause considerably. The bedrock of the movement that the Dalai Lama built to support the Tibetan cause was, however, the sanctuary afforded to him by India and consequent proximity to his erstwhile homeland of Tibet. It was this proximity which secured access to him for the Tibetans inside Tibet and guaranteed constant nurturing of the movement. This proximity ensured that the Dalai Lama's message filtered through into China and kept alive the faith, hope and aspirations of Tibetans inside China and the global Tibetan diaspora. Together these enabled the Dalai Lama to successfully build and maintain domestic and international pressure on the communist Chinese leadership. India's stance on the Tibet issue was valuable to the Dalai Lama's cause while retaining for India an undeclared element of potential pressure on China.

The Dalai Lama's endeavours benefitted him within the Tibetan religious orders too. As he gained in international stature, the XIVth Dalai Lama acquired a pre-eminent position among the Tibetan Buddhist religious sects and emerged as the unrivalled leader of the Tibetans. This helped consolidate the Tibetan community in exile and facilitated his campaign for Tibet. It provided the Tibetans with a charismatic and venerated leader and prevented the emergence of any significant schisms within the Tibetan Buddhist communities. In India, his leadership ensured that the Tibetans lived peacefully with the local populace and were equipped to earn a livelihood.

The Tibetan movement and institution of the Dalai Lama are today, however, at an uncertain and critical stage. The changing geopolitical situation and China's rise as an economic and military power have coincided with the XIVth Dalai Lama's advancing age. China's increased influence in global affairs now threatens to impact adversely on the movement that the Dalai Lama has assiduously built since his escape to India in 1959 and this could have far-reaching consequences for India-China relations.

Recognising the opportunity China has, after decades of patient maneuvering, initiated the 'end game' to finally resolve the Tibet issue and eliminate opposition by a Dalai Lama to its occupation of Tibet. Systematic efforts to undermine the current Dalai Lama's pre-eminent position and prestige within the Tibetan Buddhist hierarchy, reduce his influence among Tibetans inside China, and restrict his international support base, have been expanded by China and given impetus. The objective is to undermine the Dalai Lama's efforts of the past thirty years and dilute the awareness and material and diplomatic support with which he exerted pressure on Beijing and put China on the back-foot. It was to deflect this sustained international pressure that the communist leadership in Beijing had reluctantly commenced negotiations with him. It had then decided to try and lure the Dalai Lama home to China and, failing that, wear him down through protracted negotiations intended to whittle down his demands.

China's policy was to wait out the Dalai Lama. Chinese Tibetologists calculated that Dalai Lama's on average do not live beyond 55 years – they were very wrong in this case – and assessed that the Tibetan problem would resolve itself soon thereafter. China's assessment continues to be that opposition would fade once the present Dalai Lama passes from the scene as the Tibetans would be leaderless. Beijing anticipates that, as in the case of the Panchen Lama, it would have the decisive say regarding the next Dalai Lama. It sought to prepare a legal basis for this through a regulation issued by the State Administration for Religious Affairs in 2007. The Chinese communist leadership also decided, though as part of efforts to assuage popular discontent in the wake of economic reforms, to loosen controls on religious worship and in 2006 cautiously began describing Buddhism as a non-aggressive and old Chinese religion. Official endorsement of Buddhism, it was calculated, would later afford legitimacy to Beijing's claim to recognize the next Dalai Lama.

Beijing's tough new policy on Tibet became evident early this year on the occasion of the fiftieth anniversaries of the uprising in Lhasa and Dalai Lama's flight from Tibet on 10 March. These marked the launch of an intensified campaign against the Dalai Lama intended to show that his popularity was on the wane. The Chinese communist leadership, for which Tibet remains a high priority national security issue, crafted a multi-pronged propaganda and diplomatic offensive. China's wealth, at this time when the international economic crisis has shaken the world's developed economies, helped reinforce the campaign.

Under cover of a media black-out, large numbers of armed security personnel were deployed throughout the Tibet Autonomous Region and in Tibetan-dominated areas to suppress protests and demonstrations against Chinese communist rule. Only a minor rash of scattered protests resultantly occurred in March in smaller towns and Lhasa remained largely peaceful. The Dalai Lama's influence was evident, though, in this rash of protests and especially those that occurred at major monasteries like Drepung, Sera and Tashilhunpo. Chinese authorities for the first time used the state-controlled media to turn the majority Han population against the Tibetan minority.

On the diplomatic and propaganda front, the Chinese Communist Party leadership for the first time sent a delegation of Tibetan Buddhists, led by a 'living Buddha' of the Kagyu sect, to the US to 'explain' the issue to representatives of the US Administration and Congress. Convening of the G-20 at the end of March indirectly benefited Beijing and gave it an opportunity to publicly flex its muscles on the issue. Beijing made a meeting between Chinese President Hu Jintao and French President Sarkozy on the sidelines of the G-20 dependent on France clarifying its position on the Tibet issue. Sarkozy had angered Beijing by earlier receiving the Dalai Lama at the Elysee Palace. France capitulated and assured that its official position regarding Tibet remained unchanged and it would not 'support Tibet independence in any form'. Earlier in October 2008, Britain, in a written statement by its Foreign Secretary, revised its ninety year-old position on Tibet claiming that the concept of suzerainty was no longer valid. This could adversely impact on the India-China border negotiations. More recently the US signalled its heightened sensitivity to China's concerns when in February this year Hillary Clinton, during her first visit to Beijing as US Secretary of State, omitted any reference to the Tibet or Human Rights issues in meetings with Chinese leaders. Confirmation of the altered US policy became available when US President Obama dispatched two envoys to Dharamsala to explain to the Dalai Lama that he would not be received at the White House – for the first time since 1991– during his visit in October because he did not want to upset the Chinese before his trip the following month. These successive Chinese diplomatic successes have impacted on the Dalai Lama's campaign.

As part of the 'end game', China decided to expand and internationalise the campaign against the Dalai Lama so as to legitimize its claim to a leadership role in the Buddhist movement. In doing so it has drawn the international Buddhist movement into the competition. Here it is a deadly serious struggle for leadership between China's communist leadership and the highest ranking personage of Tibetan Buddhism, the Dalai Lama. The outcome will not only affect the Dalai Lama's future and that of the Tibetan refugee diaspora, but usurp India's cultural space and sharply undermine India's traditional leadership in this realm.

Beijing's initial move was to convene the first World Buddhist Forum in China in 2006. Buddhist religious leaders from 35 countries attended and the Chinese-nominated Panchen Lama was given international profile. After three years, the second World Buddhist Forum was held in Wuxi, Jiangsu on March 28, 2009 and was attended by over twelve hundred religious personages, including heads of different Buddhist sects, from over 50 countries. The Dalai Lama was again excluded, but this time labelled a 'disruptive element'. Representatives of Shugden Diety worshippers, opposed to the Dalai Lama were invited. The China-appointed 11th Panchen Lama's stature as second-highest ranking Tibetan Buddhist Lama was again sought to be reinforced by his valedictory address to the Forum.

This Forum was a major victory for an additional reason, namely that its closing session was held in Taiwan. By agreeing to this, Taiwan became a joint organizer of the event indirectly supporting China's claim to leadership of any international Buddhist movement. In addition to sharing a common view on the border issue, including the disputed borders with India, the two entities now share a common viewpoint on Buddhism, especially Tibetan Buddhism and China's role.

A crucially important aspect of this struggle between the Dalai Lama and China centers on the next reincarnation of the Dalai Lama, where he will be 'discovered' and his nationality. The Dalai Lama, acutely aware that his successor would take years to become a full-fledged monk and mature as a leader, will want to ensure that the momentum he has been able to build is not lost. He would be keen to facilitate his successor's efforts to retain the pressure on China's leadership. He would also want his successor to be acknowledged by the heads of all Tibetan Buddhist sects as their leader and that of the Tibetan people and not just of the Gelugpa sect. Where the XIVth Dalai Lama's next reincarnation would be found is integral to this.

From the Tibetans' strategic geopolitical perspective, the Dalai Lama's reincarnation should ideally be of Tibetan stock and be accessible to the Tibetans inside China. The manner in which the Chinese dealt with the Panchen Lama's reincarnation, selected by the Dalai Lama in 1995, is a constant reminder of how the Chinese would act in a similar situation in the future. The Dalai Lama's reincarnation would, therefore, have to be born outside China. Arunachal Pradesh, described by the Chinese as 'southern Tibet' and which has in history periodically been under Tibetan suzerainty, including at times sovereignty could, from the Tibetan point of view, be an ideal place for the reincarnation to be born. If he is of Tibetan stock it would afford the reincarnate Dalai Lama 'ethnic' and 'geographic' legitimacy in the eyes of the Tibetan people. He could, furthermore, conveniently locate himself in the monastery at Tawang, which was got built by the Vth Dalai Lama. The symbolism would be immense for the Tibetan people who would recall that the VIth Dalai Lama, who was later defrocked for his errant libertine ways, was born in Tawang.

A reincarnate Dalai Lama born in Tawang, though handicapped in his efforts to acquire international acceptance and support by circumstances of age and time, would nevertheless be easily accessible to Tibetans inside China. He would be able to convey his message to them and be in a position to keep alive their aspirations and faith while staying outside China's clutches. This interregnum till the reincarnate comes into his own, will, however, severely test the efficacy and durability of the mechanism that the present Dalai Lama puts in place to assist his successor. It will simultaneously test the loyalty of the individuals entrusted with the task of teaching and training the young reincarnate Dalai Lama and their acceptability to the Tibetan refugee population. The latter will be an important determinant in continuance of the Tibetan movement as it exists presently.

The Chinese leadership would be acutely aware of the possibility of such a development and have been carefully assessing the Dalai Lama's visit to Arunachal Pradesh. Fresh efforts have already been initiated to discredit the Dalai Lama by calling him a 'liar' and publicizing that a niece of his is a member of the Chinese Communist Party. Chinese academics who traveled to India in October '09 and other interlocutors have all expressed the view that the Dalai Lama went to Arunachal Pradesh at the Indian Government's instance. A punitive response was hinted. China will promptly further increase pressure on India on the border issue once it senses that the Dalai Lama's reincarnation could be 'discovered' in India and especially Arunachal Pradesh. It will try to exploit the latent discontent and factional disputes within the Tibetan Buddhist religious sects. The over 4000 kilometers long Himalayan belt, which stretches along the length of India's northern border with Tibet and whose inhabitants are mainly followers of Tibetan Buddhism, is a vulnerable region.

There are over 180 monasteries in this belt, each exercising considerable influence within their traditional jurisdiction. The entire belt does not, however, comprise only of adherents of the Gelugpa sect. For example, in the eastern stretches around and including Sikkim, the Karma Kagyu sect is predominant. This is led by the Gyalwa Karmapa, a position currently mired in controversy and with three prominent claimants for the position of the XVIIth Gyalwa Karmapa. There are lingering suspicions about the leading contender, Ugyen

Thinley Dorje, who managed to 'escape' from Tsurphu Monastery near Lhasa and clandestinely arrive in India. He has been staying at Dharamsala and because of his visible physical proximity to the Dalai Lama is viewed by many as a potential successor. This is a cause for some discomfiture to many Tibetan religious personages, including persons in the Dalai Lama's entourage. The other potential problem and one that the Chinese have attempted to stir is that of the Shugden Diety worshippers. This group favours worship of the Shugden Diety which the Dalai Lama has opposed since 1996.

The initial post-Dalai Lama phase will be one of some uncertainty for India. It will put to test India's ability to face up to enhanced Chinese pressure without withdrawing support to the Tibetan people or institution of the Dalai Lama. Such resilience will ensure for India a potentially powerful lever in managing relations with China. Failure to do so would severely weaken India vis-à-vis China and adversely impact on the border negotiations. India will also lose its cultural space and traditional dominance in international Buddhism, which will irreparably dent its 'soft power'. Minor concerns will be the monitoring of the almost one and a half lakh Tibetan refugees settled in India who will be adjusting to a new leadership, and settling any internecine factional squabbles which might erupt within the various sects as also disputes between senior Tibetan leaders. Such a future scenario would also throw up fresh opportunities for India.

This was published as an Issue Brief by the Centre for Air Power Studies on December 1, 2009.

26. China Re-Engages with Dalai Lama: Hollow Gesture

Beijing decided to recommence negotiations with the Dalai Lama after a fifteen month hiatus just as the Tibetans were getting ready to celebrate 'Losar' and the Chinese prepare to usher in the new 'Year of the Tiger'– both on February 14. The ninth round of talks, from Jan 27-31, 2010, were held as the situation becomes more complex and the US and the West begin to apply pressure on China on a variety of issues, including Human Rights and Tibet. While the US, UK and Canada expressed 'strong support' for the resumption of negotiations, China responded by publicising the Chinese Communist Party (CCP) leadership's views on Tibet through a series of official media reports on a couple of high level meetings. An official Chinese spokesman urged the Dalai Lama to 'cherish this opportunity and respond positively to the request of the central government'. These suggested that the Dalai Lama's representatives were left little room for manoeuvre. It is clear that there has been negligible forward movement during these talks.

A 5-member delegation led by the Dalai Lama's special envoy, Lodi Gyari, left New Delhi for China on January 26, 2010. Prior to its departure the delegation, which included Kelsang Gyaltsen, Bhuchung Tsering, Tenzin Phuntsok and Tenzin Atisha, was briefed in Dharamsala on January 22 by the Kalon Tripa Samdong Rimpoche and the Dalai Lama. It is pertinent that despite Chinese requests to replace some members, the composition of the Dalai Lama's delegation remained unchanged.

The Chinese carefully arranged the backdrop for negotiations in the months preceding the talks. Buoyed by self-confidence stemming from its perception of a heightened international stature and adhering to its policy of assertiveness, Beijing opted for an unyielding posture towards the Dalai Lama and the Tibet problem. Initial steps included conviction of a Tibetan monk for alleged illegal possession of arms. In late December, a Tibetan film producer, Dhondup Wangchen and his friend were sentenced to six years' imprisonment. They were charged with causing 'instability' because their film, 'Leaving Fear Behind', featured interviews with Tibetans who spoke of their love for the exiled Tibetan spiritual leader. The Chinese authorities had, since the March 2008 riots, adopted a pro-active propaganda policy. The Standing Committee of the Tibet Autonomous Region (TAR) People's Congress took the initiative in foreign propaganda. It dispatched seven groups comprising 47 persons to the US, UK, France, Japan, Canada and other countries to clarify the 'true' picture in Tibet. Official reports claimed that these missions had 'broken the Dalai clique's monopoly on public opinion in some countries', 'deeply exposed the rebellious political nature, religious hypocrisy, and deceptive practices of the Dalai, made a strong counterstroke against the Dalai clique's slander and attack, and expanded the international influence of Tibet'. This propaganda was reinforced by China's tough posture towards those countries whose leaders received the Dalai Lama. Separately, the central government's propaganda apparatus had since November begun publicizing the benefits accruing to the people of Tibet from the developmental projects launched in TAR. The American movie 'Avatara' was also suddenly withdrawn from twenty cinema houses across China, ostensibly on the ground that people had been offended by the portrayal of a stronger country and people dominating the weak. There is speculation that the withdrawal could have been prompted by the uncomfortable similarity between the theme of the movie and plight of the Tibetans and Uyghurs inside China.

There has been no easing of controls internally and armed personnel continue to patrol cities in the Tibet Autonomous Region (TAR) and Tibetan majority areas elsewhere in the neighbouring provinces. A report in China's official media, commenting on the People's Liberation Army (PLA)'s annual troop rotation in Tibet, revealed that authorities could now send troops directly to various locations inside Tibet from the Chinese mainland facilitating control. The drive to ensure compliance with the policy to register the qualifications of monks, nuns and 'living Buddhas' has been intensified in recent months. Websites operated by NGOs and cadres with more liberal viewpoints, associated with the late Party General Secretary Hu Yaobang and Vice Premier Xi Zhongxun, father of Chinese Vice President Xi Jinping, were also shut down in the past few months as the conservative viewpoint on handling minorities began to gain ascendance.

The enlarged meeting of the Politburo of the CCP Central Committee (CC), convened in Beijing on January 8 to discuss Tibet, is significant. This was the first such meeting held in nine years. It was also the first time the Politburo met to discuss Tibet since the riots in March 2008. The importance of the meeting is easily gauged from the fact that Hu Jintao, who combines the posts of CCP CC General Secretary, Chairman of the Central Military Commission and China's President, presided over the meeting and Premier Wen Jiabao, Vice President Xi Jinping, widely tipped to be Hu Jintao's successor, and Li Keqiang, tipped to take over as the next Premier, attended. The policies adopted at this meeting have, therefore, been endorsed by the successor leadership. This includes the new appointments in TAR.

At this meeting Hu Jintao launched a rare personal attack on the 74-year old Dalai Lama. He has normally avoided such direct attacks. In his speech at the Politburo meeting, Hu Jintao accused the exiled Tibetan leader of engaging in 'Tibetan independence' activities and 'sabotaging' social stability in the Tibetan region. He warned that his government would take 'substantial measures' to ensure 'normal order' of Tibetan Buddhism in Tibet. In an unusually candid admission of the existing discontent in Tibet and influence exerted by the Dalai Lama, Hu Jintao said that Tibet faced 'special contradictions between people of all ethnic groups and separatist forces led by the Dalai clique'. Acknowledging the seriousness of the problem, he said 'these contradictions had made leapfrog development and lasting stability major themes of the work on Tibet'. Hu Jintao exhorted the TAR Government to prevent and strike at 'penetration and sabotage' by 'Tibetan independence' separatists to 'safeguard social stability, the socialist legal system, national unity and ethnic solidarity'.

This Politburo meeting was followed by convening of the TAR People's Congress from January 10-15, 2010, where Beijing unveiled policies heralding tougher and more stringent controls over Tibet and Tibetans. Most obvious was the appointment of Padma Choling as Governor of TAR. This was promptly noticed by the Dalai Lama's establishment in Dharamsala. 58-year old Padma Choling, who served seventeen years in the People's Liberation Army (PLA) from 1969-86 in the Tibet and Qinghai provinces and was TAR Deputy Governor since 2003, is reputed to be tough. He served as Secretary of the Party cell in the important TAR Party General Office when Hu Jintao was TAR Party Secretary from 1988-92 and has easy access to the Chinese President. He has been responsible for law and order in TAR since the 2000s and earned a reputation as a hard-line enforcer of Beijing's tough policy against the 'three evil forces', namely separatism, terrorism and religious extremism. In a six minute press interview on the day of his appointment, publicized by the official news agency 'Xinhua', Padma Choling declared that 'stability is of overwhelming importance'. He added 'we will firmly oppose all attempts at secession, safeguard national unification and security, and maintain unity among different ethnic groups in Tibet'. Padma Choling replaced 62-year old Qiangba Phuncog, who has been appointed head of the TAR Regional People's Congress. Qiangba Phuncog was TAR Governor during the March 2008 riots and has apparently been blamed for ineffective handling of the riots.

Padma Choling's appointment will reinforce the policy being pursued by Zhang Qingli, the all powerful TAR Party Secretary. Zhang Qingli also has a PLA background and is a hardliner. Just after the March 2008 riots in the Tibetan region, he was severely critical of the Dalai Lama and had described him as 'a wolf in monk's clothes' and 'a devil with a human face, but the heart of a beast'.

These meetings were followed by a high-level Tibet Planning Conference held in Beijing from January 18-20, 2010, which was also attended by Chinese President Hu Jintao. The meeting, the fifth ever held and attended by 362 persons including delegates from all Tibetan areas in China, approved a massive development package for TAR as well as Tibetan areas in the adjoining provinces of Sichuan, Yunnan, Gansu and Qinghai. These areas were among those where rioting occurred in March 2008. The decision confirms that the Chinese leadership continues to be of the view that development and improvement in peoples' living standards will negate the Dalai Lama's influence and co-opt the Tibetans into accepting Chinese rule.

Hu Jintao described the slogan for the conference as 'Chinese characteristics, Tibetan flavour' (zhongguo tese, xizang tedian). Xinhua highlighted that Beijing had invested in excess of US$ 45.6 billion since 2001 in TAR and that it's GDP in 2009 is estimated at US$ 6.4 billion. Hu Jintao promised TAR an influx of investment, technology and experts and fixed the target for growth of its GDP at 12 percent. Schemes for TAR envisaged in the Twelfth Five Year Plan (2011-2015) focus on infrastructure, tourism, mining and manufacturing. Shares of the few construction, mining and transport companies that operate in the TAR and are listed on the Shanghai Stock Exchange promptly registered a sharp rise.

Projects include construction of Nagqu airfield situated at 4,436 metres above sea level at a cost of US$ 263.5 million. A circular subsequently issued by the Civil Aviation Administration of China (CAAC) on January 25 disclosed that 59 airports are being 'reconstructed' in the Region. It added that while only Lhasa, Qamdo and Nyingchi are currently linked with nineteen cities in the mainland and Kathmandu, the new airport in Nyingri Prefecture will become operational later this year. Separately, the People's Liberation Army Air Force (PLAAF) was credited with building the airports at Bangda, Ali and Kanding, described as among the highest in the world.

Beijing's concerns and stance it would adopt during the talks with the Dalai Lama's representatives was evident in articles in the authoritative Party newspaper 'People's Daily', its Tibetan version and its subsidiary the 'Global Times'. Just weeks before commencement of the talks, the People's Daily on Jan 22 criticised the Dalai Lama for describing himself as a 'son of India' and sought to portray that he had ignored the interests of the Tibetans and China, his motherland. It accused him of forgetting that 'Chinese Buddhism (had) played a very important role in the formation and development of Tibetan Buddhism and the Sakyamuni statue in the Jokhang Temple was taken to Tibet by Princess Wenchang of the Tang Dynasty….'. The China-India border dispute was brought into the spotlight by a People's Daily article. The day the Dalai Lama's representatives arrived in Changsha (Hunan Province), a People's Daily (Jan 27) article raised the issue of Arunachal Pradesh and questioned the Dalai Lama's loyalty to Tibetans. It asked 'will a guy who betrayed southern Tibet to India really care about the well-being of the Tibet people'. At the previous round of talks the Chinese had severely castigated the Dalai Lama for stating that Arunachal Pradesh was part of India. Later on Jan 30 the English-language 'Global Times', in an uncompromising editorial, cautioned that 'at the age of 75, time is not on the side of the Dalai Lama'. It claimed that China's 'progress had impressed the world' and that the Dalai Lama for 'his own sake needs to make the most of the opportunity provided by the current round of talks with the central government.' Progress, it asserted, is possible only when he gives up 'Tibetan independence', eschews separatist activities and acknowledges that Tibet is an inalienable part of China. The editorial attributed the West's support to the 'Dalai clique' to 'mystification' of the issue and said 'more westerners have come to realise that supporting the Dalai Lama will be in vain and do them no good'. In conclusion the editorial warned that 'any unrealistic request from the Dalai Lama could only further delay his desire to end the 51-year old exile and return home'.

The Chinese side comprised virtually the same set of officials from the CCP CC's United Front Work Department (UFWD) as at the eighth round of talks. The Tibetans met UFWD Minster Du Qinglin for talks on Jan 30 and talks the subsequent day were led by Zhu Weiqun, Executive Vice Minister of UFWD accompanied by Sita, UFWD Vice Minster and TAR Executive Vice Chairman Nyima Tsering, who replaced Padma Choling.

The itinerary for the current round included a visit by the Tibetan delegation to Changsha (Hunan province) and then to Beijing for detailed discussions. The selection of Changsha, which is closely associated with Mao Zedong and regarded as a revolutionary communist base, is symbolic. Implicit is the message that communist China is not going to change its system of government. The Dalai Lama's proposal for 'greater autonomy' would, therefore, need to be revised to bring it in line with the existing Chinese constitution. The Tibet Planning Conference also effected a major policy change by framing plans for the 6.5 million Tibetans living in Tibetan areas outside TAR. While this indirectly acknowledged that Tibetan majority areas outside TAR continue to lag behind the rest of the country, it provides an additional reason to turn down the Dalai Lama's proposal for 'Greater Tibet'. The latter has been consistently opposed by the Chinese on the ground that it covers almost one-fourth of China's land area. The Tibetans, however, feel the Conference resolutions incorporate many of the points raised by them.

During these talks with the Dalai Lama's representatives the

Chinese have unambiguously delivered the messages, transmitted earlier by the official media. The reference to 'southern Tibet' clearly signals that the Dalai Lama has been again castigated for stating that Arunachal Pradesh is part of India. During the border negotiations with India, the Chinese have cited the sentiments of the Tibetan people as justification for their claim on Tawang and the Dalai Lama's statement, that Tawang is part of India, undercuts that argument. In the context of reincarnation, the Chinese have reminded the Tibetans that Beijing has accorded recognition to the Dalai Lama since the Qing dynasty and that he remains subject to Chinese law. The demands that the Dalai Lama should give up activities related to 'Tibetan independence', drop the demand for greater autonomy, and endorse that Tibet is an inalienable part of China, have been reiterated. Notwithstanding the Tibetan assertion that the Dalai Lama has no personal demands, the Chinese would have sought to play on his sentiments and assure that he was free to return to China and spend his remaining days in peace, subject to his fulfilling these conditions. It has been made apparent that there will be no change in the Chinese position and that Beijing is waiting for the Dalai Lama's departure from the scene. The demands presented by the Tibetans, which included 'greater autonomy' and preservation of Tibetan culture and religion in the 'Cholka Sum' (Greater Tibet), have been rejected. The door for another round of talks has, however, been left open.

This was published as an Issue Brief by the Centre for Air Power Studies on February 1, 2010.

27. New Chinese Strategy Targeting Tibetan Buddhists has Implications for Nepal and India

Nestled in the lee of snow capped mountains in the sub-Himalayas, for nearly half a century landlocked Nepal stayed on the outer fringes of the often turbulent geo-political maneuvering in South Asia. During this period it deftly balanced the triangular relationship between Kathmandu, Delhi and Beijing, which remained generally undisturbed. The situation, however, altered from the middle of the current decade with the unchecked rise to political prominence of the Maoist movement, emergence of Prachanda as a factor in Nepal's power structure, and with an economically resurgent China beginning to assert efforts to achieve its strategic objectives in Nepal. Domestic instability prompted by the advent of King Gyanendra accentuated these tensions.

Nepal has been important to China's South Asia policy. After China took over Tibet in 1951, it viewed Nepal, along with Ladakh, Sikkim, Bhutan and Arunachal Pradesh, as a 'new buffer' between India and China. Its efforts in Nepal were, however, till recently circumscribed by culture and geography. China's strategic objectives in Nepal have nevertheless been clear. These are to neutralize and eliminate Indian influence, secure China's borders by ensuring that the Tibetan refugee population is effectively curbed, and recover what it considers as one of its 'lost' territories seized by 'imperialists'.

A series of recent events reveal that China's geo-strategic policy continues to have Nepal firmly in its cross-hairs and is determined to bring it definitively under its influence. The latest move emanating from Beijing is in the form of a proposal with potentially far reaching implications, particularly for India. Intended to achieve multiple objectives, it retains the focus on Nepal while seeking to: neutralize Tibetan activism; undermine the Dalai Lama's influence, including in Nepal; consolidate China's political and economic influence in Nepal; and help China achieve its long-term strategic goal of bringing Nepal irrevocably under its influence. Success in the last two means that China will have crossed the Himalayas and established its influence up to the lower foothills bordering India. Most important though is that the proposal actually aims to penetrate the crucial mind-space of Buddhists subscribing to the Vajrayana Tradition (or Tibetan Buddhism) who mainly inhabit the entire vulnerable Indo-Himalayan border belt. This includes the area stretching uninterruptedly from Ladakh to Arunachal Pradesh.

The footprints of the People's Liberation Army (PLA) are visible in this new proposal, which comes in the immediate wake of the visit of the PLA Chief to Kathmandu in March 2011 when, ignoring the protestations of Nepal's Ministry of Defence, he signed a US$ 19.8 million defence agreement directly with Nepal's Army. Now, the Beijing-based and supported Asia Pacific Exchange and Cooperation Foundation (APECF) has proposed a US$ 3 billion Area Development Plan for Buddha's birthplace, Lumbini, ostensibly 'with no strings attached'. China's communist regime, which in 2006 for the first time officially described Buddhism as a 'peaceful' and 'ancient Chinese religion' and has held two World Buddhist Forums, has apparently decided to expand efforts to co-opt and seek legitimacy from Buddhists residing abroad and especially in areas bordering the Tibet Autonomous Region (TAR). Apparently coincidentally, the move has materialized as the issue of the 76-year old XIVth Dalai Lama's reincarnation has begun to acquire prominence.

Composition of the board of the Asia Pacific Exchange and Cooperation Foundation (APECF) hints strongly at Chinese Communist Party and PLA links. Nepal's Maoist leader Prachanda, is Vice Chairman of the Asia Pacific Exchange and Cooperation

Foundation and has attended two events in Malaysia and Singapore in October 2010 and March 2011 respectively. He has claimed a major role in getting China's support for this project.

Political interaction between Nepal and China, incidentally, accelerated during the period Prachanda was Prime Minister. He broke with tradition and travelled to Beijing on his first visit abroad. He went twice more. An estimated 38 Chinese delegations visited Nepal in 2008-09 while 12 high-level Nepalese economic, technology and defence delegations travelled to China. China cultivated a spectrum of political parties including the Communist Party of Nepal-Maoist (CPN-M), the Nepal Communist Party (United Marxist-Leninist) and the Madhesi People's Rights Forum. In April 2009, a NCP-UML delegation led by Jhala Nath Khanal visited Beijing and was informed that China wants "a new kind of relationship" with Nepal. Correctives to this pronounced pro-China tilt were sought to be applied by GP Koirala once he was installed as Prime Minister.

Xiao Wunan, a senior Researcher at the prestigious Tsinghua University and senior Chinese Communist Party cadre, is Executive Vice President of the APECF. He is concurrently a Deputy Director of an office of China's National Development and Reform Commission in Western China. He was formerly Vice President of the Editorial Board of the journal 'Study on Maoism'. More significantly, he is Vice President of the World Buddhist Peace Foundation, which has helped organize the two Beijing-sponsored World Buddhist Forums held so far. The Executive Director of the APECF is Eric Tay, who graduated in 1993 from China's Air Force Institute of Engineering. He owns companies in Beijing and Shenzhen which invest in the lucrative commodities and energy resources sectors.

This proposal, which is a combination of 'soft power' backed by cheque-book diplomacy, reinforces the road and rail projects linking Lhasa with Kathmandu which are already under discussion. The APECF proposal promises a huge cash infusion to a country with a GDP of barely US$ 15 billion and unemployment hovering at almost 47 percent. The APECF Area Development Plans for Lumbini envisage construction of temples, an airport, a highway, hotels, convention centres and a Buddhist University. Expectations are that Lumbini, which presently attracts 500,000 tourists annually and is just two hours drive from India's Gorakhpur, will become a trans-border tourist attraction and spawn numerous ancillary service enterprises generating a steady revenue stream. Plans will be to link Lumbini to the Buddhist sites in India like Gaya, and possibly by air to Delhi, so as to benefit from 'Buddhist tourism'. It will be used to demonstrate Beijing's 'benevolent' attitude towards Buddhism to international visitors and will also provide useful propaganda to shore China's description of Buddhism as an 'ancient Chinese religion'. Xiao Wunan, Vice President of China's World Buddhist Peace Foundation, has articulated the objective of the proposal and said he hopes the Lumbini project will bring together all three Buddhist Traditions, namely 'Mahayana, Tibetan Buddhism and Theravada'. The proposed university in Lumbini will rival that planned at Nalanda. More importantly, it can be anticipated that it will offer hundreds of scholarships for free monastic education to monks from all over. The target clientele will be the monks practicing Tibetan Buddhism in India, especially in the areas along the Indo-Himalayan border belt which includes Ladakh, Nepal, Bhutan, Sikkim and Arunachal Pradesh. If the faculty of the university at Lumbini includes religious tutors from China they will certainly impart 'political education'.

Unstated is that the construction projects in Lumbini will be awarded to Chinese companies and probably PLA-affiliated sub-contractors, or engineering personnel, will be employed. The suggestion of PLA involvement in the APECF points to this. This would imply long term Chinese presence and, going by the experience of many countries in Africa, the mushrooming of illegal Chinese settlements along Nepal's borders with India.

This proposal, which follows the three day (March 23-25, 2011) visit to Kathmandu by PLA Chief General Chen Bingde, noticeably underlines the PLA's role in the formulation of China's policy on Nepal. It comes in the backdrop of persistent efforts by Beijing to expand influence in Nepal. The trend accelerated with the advent of Maoists, and especially Prachanda's government, in Nepalese politics. China has initiated efforts to create belts of influence by unilaterally disbursing old-age pensions in Nepal's poorer northern border areas and establishing a string of 35 Chinese Study Centres along Nepal's borders with India. Once completed, extension of the Lhasa-Xigaze railway to Kathmandu will exponentially expand China's influence. It will facilitate transportation of huge volumes of goods and supplies to Nepal, thereby bringing Nepal closer to dependence on China. India's special trade and transit treaty with Nepal will additionally permit Chinese goods to flow into India on extremely concessional terms.

Chinese General Chen Bingde's visit, the first to Nepal by a Chinese Army Chief in a decade, prompted calls from certain sections of the media for the Chinese visitor to be conferred the rank of Honorary General in the Nepal Army, an honour thus far reserved solely for the Chief of the Indian Army. The visit did achieve some major successes. It was the first time that China's PLA signed a military aid agreement directly with the Nepal Army, ignoring the request of Nepal's Ministry of Defence that the agreement should be signed with it. It was also the first time that a Chinese PLA Chief asserted on Nepalese soil that China would not tolerate a third country coming in the way of friendship between Nepal and China.

The last statement, which is code for interference by India, reinforces the cautionary remarks made by a senior Party leader in 2008 and again in 2009. In November 2008, Liu Hongcai, Vice Minister of the Chinese Communist Party's (CCP) International Liaison Department, which is responsible for the CCP's relations with foreign countries, stated that 'China will not tolerate any meddling from any other country in the internal affairs of Nepal—our traditional and ancient neighbour'. Three months later he declared 'we oppose any move to interfere in the internal affairs of Nepal by any force'.

The composition of the 15-member Chinese military delegation to Nepal was interesting. It included: Qiu Guohong, China's Ambassador to Nepal; Wang Jianping, Commander of the Chinese People's Armed Police Force (PAPF); Yang Jinshan, Commander of the PLA's Tibet Military District; Qian Lihua, Director-General of the Foreign Affairs Office of China's Ministry of National Defense; Zhang Yanling, Director of the Health Department of the General Logistics Department of the PLA; and Wang Jin, Deputy Director of the First Department (Operations) of the PLA's General Staff Department (GSD). Inclusion of the Commanders of the PAPF and Tibet Military District reflects the importance accorded to issues relating to activities of Tibetan exiles, border security and cementing of military ties. This was reflected in the talks General Chen Bingde had separately with Nepal's President Dr Ram Baran Yadav, Prime Minister Jhala Nath Khanal and Defence Minister Bishnu Poudel.

General Chen Bingde prefaced all discussions by emphasizing that good Sino-Nepal relations are essential for regional peace and stability. The issue of the almost 20,000 Tibetans resident in Nepal was a central topic. To President Rambaran Yadav and Prime Minister Jhalanath Khanal, he expressed concern that the European Union (EU) might 'instigate' the Tibetans and extracted assurances that Nepali territory would not be permitted to be used against China. He had extensive talks with his Nepalese counterpart, General Chhatra Man Singh Gurung, which were reportedly more candid. The Chinese General voiced China's resentment with the EU, US and India for 'instigating the Tibetans' or interfering excessively in Nepal's internal affairs.

Incidentally, the Chinese PLA Chief's visit, materialising soon after Kathmandu declined to allow Tibetans settled in Nepal to vote for a new 'prime minister', or 'Kalon Tripa', of the Tibetan 'government-in-exile' earlier in March, indicated the warmth in relations. Last year the Nepalese government had disallowed voting in internal elections of the Tibetan organisation, Chu Shi Gang Druk. China's appreciation was reflected in the highest-ever military aid extended by China to Nepal and totalling US$19.8 million. It includes medical equipment for the Military Hospital in Kathmandu, engineering equipment including heavy construction vehicles, and logistics for rescue operations.

The latest US$ 3 billion overture to Kathmandu has been accompanied by an apparent decision by Beijing to shed its earlier aversion to non-formal contacts with prominent Tibetans and Tibetan entities. This subtle, but significant, shift was noticed during Governor of Sichuan, Jiang Jufeng's 3-day visit to India this April. Jiang Jufeng met privately with Dolkar Lhamo Kirti, President of the Tibetan Women's Association (TWA) and Samten Choedon, Vice President, in the Maurya Sheraton Hotel, Delhi. They discussed the protests in Kirti Monastery where 300 monks have been in jail since March 16. Accepting their petition, Jiang Jufeng assured the matter would be examined.

This is the first time a visiting senior Chinese official privately met exiled Tibetans in India and that too from the Tibetan Women's Association (TWA), which has in the past been subjected to vehement criticism by the Chinese authorities. It could be a tactic to divide the exiled Tibetan community, or an attempt by both sides to find new methods at accommodation. The latter possibility is suggested by the Tibetan community's failure to stage the routinely organised protests during the visit of former hard-line Tibet Party Secretary, Zhang Qingli, to Australia, New Zealand and Fiji this May.

Government of India needs to urgently neutralise China's efforts. The window, for formulating and implementing a counter strategy, is unlikely to remain open beyond around five years. At the outset, India needs to clearly and emphatically demarcate to Kathmandu the 'red lines' that India considers are inviolable if the relationship is to remain mutually beneficial. Specific to the US$ 3 billion plan proposed for Lumbini, India must emphasise its pre-eminent position as the birth place of the 'Buddha Dharma' and country that has unstintingly granted safe refuge to the heads and followers of all Buddhist Traditions. Some other steps could include promoting international and domestic Buddhist tourism by encouraging daily flights between Delhi and Gaya; undertaking the planned urban development of Gaya, Varanasi and Nalanda with modern amenities for tourists; and accelerating completion of the university at Nalanda. It should also be appropriately propagated that monks, especially of the Vajrayana Tradition, avoid studying in seminaries where tutors are 'approved' by communist China. Present, of course, is the possibility that China's development plans could face opposition from the Tharu tribe inhabiting the area, which constitutes 6.67 percent of Nepal's population and of which the Lord Buddha was said to be a member.

This was published as an Issue Brief by the Centre for Air Power Studies on July 4, 2011.

28. China uses 60th TAR Anniversary to Undermine Dalai Lama

Mystery continues to shroud the high mountain fastness of Tibet where, to this day, persons who revere the Dalai Lama are engaged in a serious tussle with cadres of the Chinese Communist Party (CCP) for the loyalty of Tibetans. Some weeks ago, China celebrated the 60th anniversary of the 'peaceful liberation' of Tibet by Chinese troops. The celebrations, which were held on July 18 instead of the date of the actual anniversary on May 23, coincided with a month-long ban on foreigners traveling to the Tibet Autonomous Region (TAR) imposed by the authorities till July 25. Publicity in China's official media seemed to be low key for the event, where the importance of social stability and combating the 'Dalai Lama separatists' were consistently emphasized.

Signifying the importance of the event China's Vice President, Xi Jinping, arrived in Lhasa on July 18, 2011, at the head of a 59-member delegation. The Chief of the People's Liberation Army (PLA), Chen Bingde was, quite pointedly, part of the entourage as was General Wang Jianping, Commander of the People's Armed Police Force (PAPF). The delegation included Vice Premier Hui Liangyu; Vice Chairman and General Secretary of the Standing Committee of the National People's Congress (NPC) Li Jianguo; Vice Chairman of the National Committee of the Chinese People's Political Consultative Conference (CPPCC) and Head of the United Front Work Department of the Chinese Communist Party (CCP) Central Committee Du Qinglin; Vice Chairman of the National Committee of the CPPCC Pagbalha Geleg Namgyai; and the Vice Chairman of the Standing Committee of the 10th NPC, Raidi. Hard-line TAR Party Secretary Zhang Qingli accompanied Xi Jinping throughout his stay in Tibet.

Coinciding with the anniversary, China's State Council announced in Beijing on July 20, 2011, that the central government will invest 138.4 billion yuan (US$21.38 billion) in TAR over the next five years to support 226 major construction projects involving a total investment of 330.5 billion yuan. The projects envisage construction of facilities for TAR's public services and infrastructure such as railways, highways, airports and hydropower plants.

The visit by Xi Jinping, who is virtually certain to succeed Hu Jintao as President of China at the 18th Party Congress scheduled for October 2012, also had symbolic value. His father, Xi Zhongxun, a contemporary of Mao Zedong and a veteran Party cadre, was reputed to be an individual with a somewhat liberal bent of mind. Xi Zhongxun, was an interlocutor for the Dalai Lama's Special Envoy Lodi Gyari in the 1980s and apparently carried a photo of the Dalai Lama. Prior to that he had some association with the 10th Panchen Lama, Tibet's second most important religious leader. While this is unlikely to influence Xi Jinping, who was present throughout the Tibet Work Forum held in January 2010, it could have some meaning for the Tibetans.

On July 18, Xi Jinping's delegation visited Tibet University and along with 850 other invitees participated in "Sing a Folk Song to the Party Again", held at the People's Hall of Tibet. At a public reception in Lhasa the following day, Xi Jinping presented Party and Government leaders of the Tibet Autonomous Region (TAR) a huge gold plaque inscribed by Chinese President Hu Jintao. Speaking to over 20,000 people gathered in the square in front of the Potala Palace, former residence of the Dalai Lama, Xi Jinping asserted that "as long as we stick to the CCP's leadership, the socialist system, the system of regional ethnic autonomy and a development path with Chinese and local Tibetan features, Tibet will enjoy greater prosperity and progress and embrace a brighter future,". He added that 'social stability provides the basis' for 'leapfrog development and long-term peace'.

On July 20, Xi Jinping told a carefully selected audience of more than 100 monks, as well as 'representatives from religious circles', at Jokhang temple in Lhasa to 'stay clear' of separatist forces. This temple's monks were involved in the severe riots that erupted across Tibet on March 14, 2008. The riots prompted authorities to launch a year-long 'political education' campaign in all the 505 monasteries in Tibet. Calling Tibet an inalienable part of China since ancient times, Xi Jinping lauded members of 'religious circles' for helping to maintain social stability, national integrity and ethnic unity. Xinhua quoted him as saying that 'the Party and the government will not forget your positive contributions.' He urged them to be patriotic, 'stay in line with the Party and the government' and work for Tibet's development.

The central leadership's heightened concern about the situation in Tibet and influence of the Dalai Lama was reflected in all the remarks by Xi Jinping during his stay in Tibet. He emphasized the need to 'fight against separatist activities by the Dalai Lama group, rely on cadres and people of all ethnic groups, seek long-term policies and take measures that address the root cause, and completely destroy any attempt to undermine stability in Tibet and national unity.' He described Tibet 'as an important security screen for the country' and referred to it as 'a major base of strategic resources reserves'. Interestingly, Xi Jinping appeared to take a cue from Hu Jintao and avoided using the pejorative term 'Dalai clique' while referring to the Dalai Lama and his supporters.

The message was sought to be reinforced by Lhagba, Party secretary of Lhasa's Bagarxol village who, speaking at the ceremony, claimed 'we treasure our life now and nobody is allowed to sabotage it'. Du Yongbin, a researcher with the Beijing-based China Tibetology Research Center, underlined Beijing's concerns by candidly acknowledging that Tibet faces many challenges. He observed: 'Politically, there are separatist forces undermining Tibet's security;

culturally, there is the conflict between ongoing modernization and preserving traditions.'

The second leg of the tour took Xi Jinping to the village of Bagyi in the Nyingchi prefecture in southeastern Tibet across Arunachal Pradesh. The choice of Nyingchi is interesting. It is the site of an underground missile base and a recently built modern airport, the third in Tibet. China claims that Arunachal Pradesh is part of Nyingchi prefecture. Nyingchi is also the area where China has plans to construct a mega dam on the 'Great Bend' of the Brahmaputra River.

China's official media publicized that Xi Jinping, who last visited Nyingchi thirteen years ago as Deputy Secretary of the Party Committee of Fujian Province, while visiting the homes of rural families of Nyingchi observed that many villagers had become rich. Xi Jinping reminded the people that their prosperity was a result of the Party's efforts and that the 'Han and different ethnic minorities are inter-dependent on each other'. He urged local officials to maintain long-term social stability and appreciated the contributions of personnel of the People's Liberation Army (PLA), the People's Armed Police Force and the police forces in Nyingchi.

Little publicized in the official Chinese media, but a move with potentially far reaching implications, were the invitations to select high ranking Tibetan monks residing abroad to attend the celebrations. The list appeared to have been meticulously crafted to accentuate divisions within the exiled Tibetan community and isolate the Dalai Lama.

This dovetails neatly into other efforts noticed to have been initiated by Beijing to win over Tibetan Buddhist monks. These include the apparent shedding of its earlier aversion to non-formal contacts with prominent Tibetans and Tibetan entities. This subtle, but significant, shift was noticed during Governor of Sichuan, Jiang Jufeng's 3-day visit to India in April, 2011. Jiang Jufeng, met privately with Tibetan activists and received Dolkar Lhamo Kirti, President of the Tibetan Women's Association (TWA) and Samten Choedon, Vice President, in the Maurya Sheraton Hotel, Delhi. They discussed the protests in Kirti Monastery where 300 monks have been in jail since March 16. Accepting their petition, Jiang Jufeng assured the matter would be examined. This was the first time a visiting senior Chinese official privately met exiled Tibetans in India and that too from the Tibetan Women's Association (TWA), which has in the past been subjected to vehement criticism by the Chinese authorities.

The Paris-based Khensur Lungri Namgyel Rinpoche, the 101st and former Ganden Tripa and head of the Gelugpa sect to which the Dalai Lama belongs, visited China in the first week of July specifically to meet the Chinese-nominated Panchen Lama, Gyancain Norbu. He did not, however, attend the 60th anniversary celebrations. The former Gaden Tripa would have been invited to bestow some legitimacy on the Chinese appointee, who is not recognised by the Dalai Lama, and thereby also embarrass the Dalai Lama. As if to emphasise his differences with the Dalai Lama, the former Gaden Tripa took along Yongyal Rimpoche and Lama Thubten Phurbu, two outspoken US-based Shugden worshipping monks. Both are former residents of the Sera Mey Monastery's Pomra Khangtsen (House) in Bylakuppe, Karnataka. Two living Buddhas, Kondhor Jewon Tulku, and Khanang Jam-yang Ten-pen-yima, who currently live in Switzerland met officials from the CCP's United Front Work Department. Their visit coincided with a conclave of Shugden Diety worshippers held in Chengdu, capital of Sichuan Province, in July 2011. The former Gaden Tripa worships the Shugden Diety, which has been prohibited by the Dalai Lama, but which group has been overtly backed by the Chinese authorities since 2007. Deepening the schism, the Chinese-appointed Panchen Lama also worships the Shugden Diety.

A variety of other high ranking monks resident abroad travelled to China for the 60th anniversary celebrations of the 'peaceful liberation' of Tibet. Among them were Gangchen Lama, a well known critic of the Dalai Lama and worshipper of the Shugden Diety. The Milan-based monk travels often to China and has been permitted to renovate a couple of monasteries in Tibet. Akong Tulku, a former close associate of Tai Situ Rimpoche and who retains close links with the Chinese authorities, was another invitee. Akong Tulku has his headquarters at Samyeling Monastery in Scotland and has ongoing projects in Tibet. He has been critical of the Dalai Lama's establishment. There was another representative from the UK, namely Karma Hardy, who till recently used to head the Tibet Foundation, UK. Invitees included representatives of other traditions like Jamyang of Sweden of the Kargyu Drikung tradition and Thinlay Rinchen, an Australia-based high ranking monk of the Sakya tradition. Kondor Tulku Jigme Palden, possibly of the Taklung Kagyu tradition, and Tsultrim Taser were two high ranking monks visiting from Switzerland. Of them, Kondor Tulku Jigme Palden was conferred an honour by the Chinese.

There was, predictably, a bid to use the anniversary celebrations to garner legitimacy for Gyaincain Norbu, the Chinese-nominated Panchen Lama and get him acceptance among Tibetans. Gyaincain Norbu was scheduled to visit the Labrang Tashi Khyil Monastery in Tibet's Amdo region from July 20 to 30, but this had to be aborted due to 'opposition' from local Tibetans. Labrang Tashi Khyil is the main Tibetan Buddhist monastery in the area and was the scene of major demonstrations against Chinese rule during the protests in 2008. Gyaincain Norbu is now likely to visit the monastery some time in August, 2011 for an extended stay that could stretch to a few months and possibly include visits to other monasteries. The Norzin Potrang Palace in the monastery has been readied for Gyaincain Norbu and CCTV cameras and armed police personnel deployed around it. It is currently the residence of the head of Labrang Monastery, Jamyang Jabpa, who is also Deputy Director of the National People's Congress (NPC) in Gansu Province.

The decision of the Chinese authorities to base Gyaincain Norbu here, at least for some period, instead of in Beijing would be intended to keep him in the midst of Tibetans so that he could expand his political role and influence. It is an attempt to acquire control over Tibetan Buddhist culture in the Amdo region, where Tibetan identity is strong and has found popular expression periodically. There is neither any precedence for installing a Panchen Lama at Labrang. The Panchen Lama's traditional seat is the Tashilhunpo Monastery near Lhasa and his second seat is at Kumbum Monastery in Qinghai province. The move to shift Gyaincain Norbu in the midst of Tibetans would be an important element in the plans of Chinese authorities to boost his influence while conveying the impression to the outside world that Tibetan Buddhist traditions are being protected. Gyaincain Norbu has indicated his political and ideological leanings in his remarks that Buddhism's responsibility is "to foster patriotism and national unity." He has already been appointed Vice-President of the official Chinese Buddhist Association and appointed to the Chinese People's Political Consultative Conference (CPPCC).

China perceives the present time as opportune to undermine the position and influence of the Dalai Lama. It has accordingly stepped up efforts to sow division in the Tibetan religious ecclesiastical hierarchy and divide the exiled Tibetan community. It is simultancously attempting to undermine the influence of the Dalai Lama and isolate him. Beijing perceives the present situation as ideal to weaken the Dalai Lama's movement and compel the XIVth Dalai Lama's successors to find new methods at accommodation. Invitations to the World Buddhist Forums, TAR anniversaries etc are all calibrated to weaken the unity of Tibetan Buddhist monks.

This was published as an Issue Brief by the Centre for Air Power Studies on August 16, 2011.

29. Implications of the Karmapa Rivalries

Successions are often a messy business. When power, patronage and pelf are added, the scrabble for spoils is sharply accentuated. Even the incense-laden, cloistered confines of abbeys and monasteries in remote mountain redoubts are not immune from this affliction.

The Karma Kargyu, or Black Hat, which is a sub-sect of Tibetan Buddhism's second oldest sect and one which first propagated the Oral Tradition and practice of reincarnation, is currently in the grip of bitter succession rivalries. This rivalry is not restricted only to capturing the throne of the Gyalwa Karmapa, head of one of the four sub-sects of the Kargyu Tradition, but, more importantly, for the considerable influence, patronage and wealth that the position offers. The large number of Buddhists, particularly in Asia where the number of adherents is growing, ensures that high ranking Buddhist personages will continue to command a lot of influence.

The history of Buddhist sects in Tibet is, interestingly, replete with vivid accounts of often bitter infighting and intrigue. For nearly eight hundred years till the Gelugpa, or Yellow, sect finally gained the upper hand, the various sects struggled for territory as well as primacy and influence over Tibet. In the process, they interacted and sided with the Chinese Emperors and Mongol Khans. The latter were actually Buddhists and followers initially of the Sakya sect. It was, in fact, after the Mongol ruler Altan Khan invited Sonam Gyatso, the highly regarded abbot of the Drepung Monastery of the Gelugpa, or Yellow, sect to teach him and thereafter became a follower of the Yellow sect, that an imperial decree was promulgated granting the spiritual and temporal leadership of Tibet to this high ranking lama. It was also Altan Khan who bestowed the title of 'Dalai Lama', or

Ocean of Wisdom, on Sonam Gyatso of the Gelugpa sect in 1579. Interestingly, at the time these magnanimous gestures were made by the Mongol Khan a high ranking Karmapa monk was resident in his court! These developments preceded the dissipation of power of the then most powerful Tibetan Buddhist sect, namely the Sakya, and enabled the Gelugpa sect to edge ahead of the Nyingma, Sakya and others.

Ranjung Rigpi Dorjee, the XVIth Gyalwa Karmapa, fled from his monastery in Tsurphu in Tibet in 1959 after the Chinese communist regime took over Tibet. He managed to bring out considerable wealth belonging to the sect with him. Once in exile he established the first monastery of the Karma Kargyu sect at Woodstock in the US. He later travelled to Sikkim where he was welcomed by the then Chogyal and allotted land at Rumtek to build a monastery. The monastery that he built at Rumtek between 1962-65 became his designated spiritual seat in exile. The Gyalwa Karmapa presides over the Karma Kargyu, or Black Hat, sect with presently approximately 160 financially well endowed Dharma Chakra Centres spread across the world. The Karma Kargyu is a wealthy sect and it is also the dominant sect in sensitive areas along India's borders surrounding, and including, Sikkim and Bhutan. It has numerous monasteries owing allegiance to it in the vulnerable Indo-Himalayan belt. It is this that makes the internecine rivalry and its outcome a matter of direct concern for India.

After the demise of the XVIth Gyalwa Karmapa a council of four Regents was entrusted with the task of 'discovering' the reincarnation. It was only after a lapse of ten years, during which two of the Regents died, that Tai Situ Rimpoche suddenly found the relevant clues and, after numerous visits to China, 'discovered' Ughyen Thinley Dorjee as the reincarnation of the XVIth Gyalwa Karmapa in 1992. Thereafter, Ughyen Thinley Dorjee escaped from Tsurphu monastery in Tibet in 1999. The circumstances surrounding the escape raise serious doubts. According to accounts revealed by Ughyen Thinley Dorjee's close aides, the monk shimmied down from his residence on the second floor of Tsurphu monastery without arousing the guards on patrol either inside the monastery or its perimeter and got in to a waiting jeep in which he travelled most of the distance to the border. He covered some of the distance on foot and horseback before arriving on the border with Nepal. From there he took a waiting helicopter to India. The account is vague as to how he slipped past the guards at the monastery and how he avoided the PLA guards deployed at the bridges along the route. Considering that security in Tibet had become stringent after the March 1988 riots, it is difficult to imagine that PLA guards would allow a jeep to cross a protected bridge without checks. That there was prior planning for the escape is evident also from the advance visits of Ughyen Thinley Dorjee's sister and another accomplice to Bodh Gaya. She finally escaped with Ughyen Thinley Dorjee while six of his other siblings and parents remain behind in Tibet. Another area of doubt concerns Ughyen Thinley Dorjee's age. On arrival in India he was given a thorough medical examination at the PGI in Chandigarh where it was suggested that he was almost six years older than his declared age of 14 years.

Meanwhile, the other Regent, Shamar Rimpoche, who had serious differences with Tai Situ Rimpoche, propped up Thaye Thinley Dorjee as another candidate. Both these claimants were born in Tibet. There are two other claimants to the position of the XVIIth Gyalwa Karmapa, but it is Ughyen Thinley Dorjee and Thaye Thinley Dorjee who are the better known. Tai Situ Rimpoche, the Regent who 'discovered' and supported Ughyen Thinley Dorjee was also successful in securing the recognition of the Dalai Lama and Beijing for his candidate. This puts Ughyen Thinley Dorjee in the unique position of presently being the only claimant aspiring to head a Tibetan Buddhist sect who is formally recognized by both these entities. As long as the heads of the other major Tibetan Buddhist sects and the Dalai Lama are alive, the Gyalwa Karmapa will remain only the head of one of the sects. Thereafter, however, he could be one of the very few highest ranking lamas of Tibetan Buddhism who is formally recognised and will wield considerable influence over Buddhists. It is this that gives a sharp edge to the claims of the contending candidates for recognition as the true reincarnation of the Gyalwa Karmapa and what could probably make the office of the Gyalwa Karmapa considerably more important and vulnerable to pressure and manipulation by Beijing. This vulnerability, especially in case the incumbent's leanings are unclear, would be a matter of serious discomfort to India.

Though the ongoing court battles over possession of the Rumtek monastery have delayed the formal enthronement of the Gyalwa Karmapa, among all the claimants Ughyen Thinley Dorjee has emerged as the front-runner as he is the more widely known. Formal enthronement at Rumtek monastery is mandatory for recognition as the Gyalwa Karmapa because the monastery is the spiritual seat of the Karmapa and the Black Hat, which is the religious symbol of office and said to be made of the black silken hair of angels, is kept there. Other riches belonging to the Gyalwa Karmapa and the sect are also kept in safe custody of the court in a strong room in the Rumtek monastery. Ughyen Thinley Dorjee and his supporters and followers have, therefore, repeatedly staged protests and made demands that he be allowed to visit Sikkim and the Rumtek monastery.

Thanks to the deft management of circumstances, Ughyen Thinley Dorjee has benefited from his physical proximity to the Dalai Lama. For convenience of receiving teaching and guidance from the Dalai Lama, the then 14-year old Ughyen Thinley Dorjee was lodged in the Gyutoe monastery in the same compound as the Dalai Lama's establishment. This had the advantage of affording Ughyen Thinley Dorjee an opportunity to attend the Dalai Lama's occasional public audiences and prayers and, because of the absence of the heads of the other sects and virtue of his position, be seated next to the

Dalai Lama. In public perception this made Ughyen Thinley Dorjee second in rank to the Dalai Lama. This proximity simultaneously encouraged followers coming for an audience with the Dalai Lama to meet Ughyen Thinley Dorjee too, and the number of his adherents increased. Ughyen Thinley Dorjee's supporters, some of whom are in the Dalai Lama's establishment, have also vigorously propagated his cause in India and abroad.

Another advantage for Ughyen Thinley Dorjee is the effective machinery that his aides seem to have created to popularize his claims. An example is the manner in which in the midst of recent revelations that some of his aides had engaged in large-scale illegal financial transactions including the 'benami' purchase of land at different locations, numerous articles in the media incorrectly referred to him as the XVIIth Gyalwa Karmapa. His sympathizers and followers also quickly organized public protests in a bid to divert attention from the financial irregularities and pressurize the government into waiving legal provisions. The Dalai Lama publicly expressed support for Ughyen Thinley Dorjee, though he did say that the money should have been handed over to a trust and that the financial irregularities must be enquired into. From the media revelations there appears to be little doubt that large sums of cash of different currencies, estimated to exceed one and a half million US dollars, were kept in Ughyen Thinley Dorjee's office. His close aides have also, it is alleged, been engaged in 'benami' land deals in various locations. The matter is serious and deserves a thorough probe, particularly to ascertain the locations where land was proposed to be purchased and whether the money was used for purposes other than purchase of land.

In the interregnum, while Ughyen Thinley Dorjee has been receiving religious instruction at the Gyutoe monastery and the succession issue among the various claimants remains unresolved, Beijing has chosen to remain silent regarding the rival claims. This contrasts with its actions of roughly five years ago at the time the Dalai

Lama was dealing with the problem of the Shugden worshippers. Beijing has also, quite significantly, refrained from any criticism of Ughyen Thinley Dorjee during the decade he has been in India and the latter too has eschewed any statement that could be deemed as critical of the regime in China or supportive of India. In contrast, Beijing loses no opportunity to severely and repeatedly castigate the Dalai Lama. Beijing is apparently waiting for the situation to evolve. Beijing did, however, react very recently to officially deny Indian media reports that Ughyen Thinley Dorjee was a Chinese agent—an allegation for which no substantive evidence has emerged as yet.

The departure of the Dalai Lama from the scene will introduce an additional complication. There is likely to be enhanced restiveness among the almost six million Tibetans inside China and the one and a half million-strong Tibetan diaspora in exile would be leaderless. In this backdrop the role of any council to manage the transition, that the Dalai Lama may constitute while he is alive, will be crucial. This council will have to retain the Tibetan peoples' confidence and provide them leadership till such time as the next reincarnate Dalai Lama is able to assume the mantle. It will simultaneously need to continue the activities started by the present Dalai Lama and maintain the relationships forged with various governments, parliamentarians and organisations. This phase where the council would have to play a vital role could last for anywhere up to fifteen years, which is the time a reincarnate of the present Dalai Lama would require to get ready to take on his responsibilities. The role and character of the inheritor to the throne of the Gyalwa Karmapa at such a time will, therefore, be crucial. These developments together will impact on India's border negotiations with China and its ability to maintain stability and calm along the vulnerable Indo-Himalayan border belt which is dominated by followers of Tibetan Buddhism.

Reports of the financial irregularities involving close aides of Ughyen Thinley Dorjee have surfaced at an inconvenient time.

The matter would need to be handled with caution and prudence, particularly as Ughyen Thinley Dorjee has already been in India for over a decade. While investigations must be thorough and compliance with laws enforced, the Tibetan community in exile in India would simultaneously require re-assurance that there will be no witch-hunt and no need for panic. It would also need to be ensured in the larger national interest that aspersions are not cast on the Dalai Lama and his institution.

This was published as an Issue Brief by the Centre for Air Power Studies on February 14, 2011.

30. China Uses Buddhism for Strategic Objectives

The Foreign Affairs establishments of major nations usually include, among their practitioners of '*realpolitik*', a select band of Sinologists, Kremlinologists, multi-lateral experts and the like. China's foreign affairs establishment appears to have a group of professionals specializing in *kasaya* (the garment worn by Buddhist monks and nuns) politics, or '*kasayapolitik*'! These experts are to be found mainly in the Chinese Communist Party (CCP) Central Committee (CC)'s United Front Work Department (UFWD)--which has responsibility for the Party's interaction and relationship with China's ethnic minorities, non-communist party entities as well as Taiwan--and China's Ministry of Foreign Affairs. A China-based Tibetan source claims that at least two members of the UFWD, who are autonomous in their functioning, are posted in the Chinese Embassy in New Delhi.

The CCP indicated official approval of Buddhism slightly over five years ago by describing it as an "ancient Chinese religion", and since then the Chinese communist authorities have sought to use it to achieve strategic and domestic objectives. A major step intended to appeal to the large number of Buddhists in China as well as portray to the neighbouring, predominantly Buddhist, countries that China's communist regime is tolerant of Buddhism, has been the decision to convene the World Buddhist Forums. It, additionally, projects China's 'soft power'.

Kok Kwong, Chairman of the Hongkong Buddhist Association, was one of eight persons who proposed that a World Buddhist Forum be held. Earlier, in 2004, Kok Kwong had urged Hongkong's Buddhists to be 'content with the Government' and not join anti-China protests.

Others who 'initiated' the proposal included Yi Cheng, Chairman of the Buddhist Association of China till 2010, and Master Hsing Yun of Buddha's Light Association of Taiwan. The latter's support to China's venture has cost him the support of some Buddhist organizations in Taiwan.

China held the first World Buddhist Forum in Putuo Mountain in 2006, when the current Chinese Vice President Xi Jinping, tipped to take over as President from Hu Jintao in 2012 and at that time Party Secretary of Zhejiang province, mobilised resources for the convention. Beijing utilized this Forum, to which a large number of foreign monks, nuns and scholars were invited, to project the Chinese-appointed Panchen Lama, Gyancain Norbu. The second World Buddhist Forum, which was held at Wuxi in 2009, had expanded objectives and held its concluding ceremony in Taiwan. This Forum continued the pattern of projecting to the Buddhist populace in China's neighbourhood the approval of the Chinese communist authorities to Buddhism. In addition to the China-appointed Panchen Lama Gyancain Norbu again attending the Forum, on this occasion Beijing emphasised that the Dalai Lama had not been invited to the Forum as he was a 'disruptive element'. A third World Buddhist Forum is now planned to be held in Hongkong tentatively from April 25-30, 2012. It is likely that Gyancain Norbu will attend. Interestingly, two of the prominent foreign Buddhist personages who proposed the World Buddhist Forums are based in Taiwan and Hongkong, both territories claimed by China.

In the midst of these initiatives, China accelerated preparations for a post-Dalai Lama phase and in 2007, promulgated regulations asserting that Beijing alone could accord final approval to the 'living Buddhas' and high lamas, including the Dalai Lama and Panchen Lama. It simultaneously stepped up active interaction with other 'traditions' (or schools) of Tibetan Buddhism and high-ranking lamas, preferably those critical of the Dalai Lama. The Chinese authorities supported worshippers of the Shugden Diety, banned by the Dalai Lama and began disbursing extra subsidies to their monasteries. The sixtieth anniversary celebrations of the 'peaceful' liberation of the Tibet Autonomous Region (TAR) was used to invite Buddhist religious personages, including those based abroad, critical of the Dalai Lama.

The Dalai Lama has, meanwhile, been closely watching developments. After a three-day (22-24 Sept 2011) conclave with senior Tibetan Buddhist leaders in Dharamsala primarily to discuss the issue of his reincarnation, he issued an unusually tough 4,041-word statement at a special press conference on September 24. The statement criticized the Chinese authorities for manipulating Tibetan religious beliefs and practices for political ends. He described as "outrageous and disgraceful" the regulations promulgated by the Chinese in 2007, and said they were intended to enable Beijing to assert control over the Tulkus. He contradicted Beijing's claims that it had accorded approval for recognition of high lamas, including the Dalai and Panchen Lamas, since the twelfth century and declared that only two of his predecessors were selected by drawing lots from the 'Golden Urn.' Asserting that "they are waiting for my death and will recognize a Fifteenth Dalai Lama of their choice," the Dalai Lama cautioned Tibetans to "bear in mind that, apart from the reincarnation recognized through such legitimate methods, no recognition or acceptance should be given to a candidate chosen for political ends by anyone, including those in the People's Republic of China." Hinting that the struggle was not over, he assured "the main purpose of the appearance of a reincarnation is to continue the predecessor's unfinished work…"

The Dalai Lama used the occasion to also preempt the Chinese and demonstrate his spiritual authority. He accorded official recognition to the *Jonang,* after hundreds of years, as a fifth and legitimate 'tradition' of Tibetan Buddhism. It is an interesting coincidence that the largest number of *Jonang* monasteries are located in Ngaba, Sichuan province, very close to Kirti Monastery, which has emerged as a veritable centre of anti-Chinese protests.

Beijing similarly began cultivating the Karma Kagyu 'tradition' of Tibetan Buddhism which, as one of the oldest 'traditions', exercises considerable influence in large areas of Tibet and the mountainous Indo-Himalayan border belt. A large number of the Buddhists in Ladakh are followers of this 'tradition' as are the majority of those resident in Sikkim and Bhutan.

The Karma Kagyu is presently riven with dissension with at least four claimants to the position of the XVIIth Gyalwa Karmapa, who heads the 'tradition'. Ughyen Thinley Dorje, who has been recognized as the XVIIth Gyalwa Karmapa by the Dalai Lama and Beijing, escaped from Tsurphu monastery near Lhasa into India in 2000, and resides in Dharamsala. While suspicions about the manner of his escape continue to linger, an interesting new disclosure was recently made by a Hongkong-based source. The source, who claims first-hand knowledge of the incident, states that the day after Ughyen Thinley Dorje's escape, a prominent Hongkong-based businessman and interlocutor with Beijing, TC Wu, received an urgent summons to reach Beijing the same day for a meeting with the State Council. While there, TC Wu, acting on instructions, placed a call to a confidante in Hongkong to ascertain whether Ughyen Thinley Dorje had escaped to India. After checking from reliable sources, including the Dalai Lama's legal counsel Michael Van Waalt, the confidante called the given telephone number of the State Council in Beijing and confirmed that Ughyen Thinley Dorje had escaped and was in India.

In this backdrop, the visit this February to Hongkong by Thaye Thinley Dorje, a major rival to the position of XVIIth Gyalwa Karmapa, as also the large convention organized by the Hongkong Buddhist Association in mid-October to felicitate 900 years of the Karma Kagyu 'tradition', assume significance. Neither could have been organized in Hongkong without Beijing's approval.

Earlier in mid-September, all the English and Chinese language newspapers in Hong Kong commenced publicising an upcoming 'Hong Kong & Macau Karmapa 900 Years Celebration' at the HK Convention and Exhibition Centre from October 7-9, 2011, with an extra day in Macau. Several thousand people attended, including some officials from Beijing. Interestingly, the guest of honor was the 9th Khenchen Thrangu Rimpoche, the Regent of Rumtek Monastery who sided against Sharmar Rinpoche and recognizes Ughyen Thinley Dorje. The latter was invited but did not attend. A number of senior Tibetan lamas traveled to Hong Kong from India and other international capitals to attend the event.

Such a large convention attended by high-ranking Tibetan Buddhist lamas could not have been organized in Hongkong without the approval of Beijing and the UFWD. It strongly suggests that the UFWD has made inroads into the Karma Kagyu 'tradition' and is attempting to woo Thaye Thinley Dorje. The presence of the 9th Khenchen Thrangu Rimpoche, the Regent of Rumtek Monastery who is opposed to Shamar Rimpoche, suggests he could be the subject of Beijing's blandishments. The UFWD's objective would be to either prevent Ughyen Thinley Dorje from ascending the throne in Rumtek Monastery near Gangtok in Sikkim, or to exercise control over the influential Karma Kagyu 'tradition' of Tibetan Buddhism. At the least its objective would be to ensure a schism among followers of the Karma Kagyu 'tradition'.

Certain administrative measures have also been taken by the authorities in recent months to tackle the restive TAR and Tibetan areas. In addition to investing large sums of capital in developmental projects and announcing (Tibet Daily, Nov 23, 2011) pensions for monks, a couple of high-level personnel changes have been effected. More are likely to follow. Lobsang Gyaltsen, ranked tenth in the TAR Party heirarchy, handed over the post of Director of the TAR United

Front Work Department to Chodak, another Tibetan cadre with long experience of dealing with senior personages among the Shugden Diety worshippers. Lobsang Gyaltsen continues in TAR possibly awaiting an elevation. Another ethnic Tibetan cadre, replaced a Han cadre as Party Secretary of Lhasa Municipality in November 2011.

Zhang Qingli, a reputed hardliner credited with the statement in March 2008 that "the Dalai Lama is a wolf in monk's robes, a devil with a human face but the heart of a beast" and who was TAR Party Secretary since 2005, was transferred out in August 2011. He was replaced by Chen Quanguo, who could be planning to strengthen the emphasis on development work. Chen Quanguo was born in 1955 and has a Master's Degree in Economics. Interestingly, a remark by Zhang Jinan, the Vice Minister of the CCP CC's powerful Organisation Department who had specially flown in from Beijing and convened a large meeting of TAR officials in Lhasa on 25 August 2011, to introduce Chen Quanguo, hinted that personnel of the Region's security establishment possibly had reservations about the change-over. While introducing Chen Quanguo, the CCP CC Organisation Department Vice Minister, Zhang Jinan, pointedly disclosed that Chen Quanguo had once served in the PLA. Notably, the official CCP biography of Chen Quanguo made no mention of such service!

Zhang Qingli's transfer is most likely a prelude to his promotion. Born in 1951, Zhang Qingli is in the right age bracket and a CCP Central Committee member. Added to that is his unique work experience of having managed tough assignments in Tibet since 2005 and for three years prior to that in Xinjiang. He is presently acting Party Secretary of Hebei, which has a large number of Christians, since November 2011. Favouring Zhang Qingli is the fact that he is a nephew of General Zhang Wannian, a former Vice Chairman of the Central Military Commission, and a 'princeling'. Also, he has worked with Hu Jintao and for seven years with Security Czar and

PBSC member Zhou Yongkang. His work in Tibet has been praised by Xi Jinping. He is a potential candidate for elevation to the CCP CC Politburo where he can be expected to have an important input in affairs relating to Tibet, Xinjiang and China's minorities.

In the interregnum, tension in the TAR and Tibetan regions inside China continues to be high. Monks and nuns mainly spearhead resistance to the Chinese. The twelve unprecedented instances of self-immolation, by formerly ordained monks and nuns reported so far in Tibetan areas of China, have heightened tension. All those who committed self-immolation are under thirty years of age with the majority being under twenty. Beijing has not yet fashioned a response to these incidents or to the Dalai Lama's September statement on his reincarnation. There has also been no indication of a move to resume the dialogue between Beijing and the Dalai Lama's envoys, though these have remained suspended now for the longest period.

Instead, and probably prompted more by developments in Indo-US relations and the Asia Pacific region, Beijing tried to further circumscribe the Dalai Lama's activities in India. In the process it intruded on India's sovereignty and values. More such pressure can be expected. The major leadership changes anticipated at the Eighteenth Party Congress scheduled in October 2012, could have slowed down Beijing's response, but any change in Beijing's policy towards Tibet even after the new leadership takes over is unlikely.

This was published as an Issue Brief by the Centre for Air Power Studies on December 28, 2011.

31. China's Attempt At Playing Buddhist Politics Fails And Reveals Schisms In Party's United Front

A combination of factors provided a severe setback to the Chinese Communist Party (CCP)'s efforts in late April 2012, to play politics with Buddhism and use it to further China's strategic agenda.

Important among them are the CCP's apparent unwillingness to address the issue of the growing incidence of self-immolations among Tibetan Buddhists; inability to calm restiveness in Tibet and Tibetan-populated areas in China; and policy of consistently excluding the Dalai Lama including absence of contact with him or his emissaries. One prominent factor, cited by reports filtering out of Beijing, is the factional in-fighting within the CCP's United Front Work Department (UFWD), which handles all matters relating to China's non-communist entities and ethnic minorities, including Tibet and the Dalai Lama.

Beijing had planned, for the first time, to demonstrate its influence in Nepal and among that country's Buddhists by organising an international convention in Buddha's birth-place of Lumbini between April 27-30, 2012. To maximize impact, it decided to concurrently convene its third World Buddhist Forum in the Hongkong Special Administrative Region (HKSAR) to project its influence within the global Buddhist community and among Buddhists in China, as well as enhance the legitimacy of 22-year old Gyaincain Norbu, the Chinese-appointed 11th Panchen Lama.

China's interest in Lumbini first became public in June 2011, when a Chinese government-sponsored NGO with dubious credentials namely, the Asia Pacific Exchange and Cooperation Foundation (APECF), proposed a US$ $3 billion development plan for Lumbini to the Nepalese government. The plan was on the verge of being approved without consultation with Lumbini's inhabitants who, once alerted, got agitated. There were serious protests from elsewhere too. The composition of APECF's board is revealing and hints strongly at its links with the CCP and the People's Liberation Army (PLA).

Xiao Wunan, a senior CCP cadre who is Deputy Director of an office of China's National Development and Reform Commission in Western China, is Executive Vice President of the Foundation. He is also Vice President of the World Buddhist Peace Foundation, which originally proposed and later helped organise the Beijing-sponsored World Buddhist Forums, and was formerly Vice President of the editorial board of the journal 'Study on Maoism'. Xiao Wunan views the proposed university in the Lumbini project as bringing together all three Buddhist Traditions, namely Mahayana, Tibetan Buddhism and Theravada and rivalling the university planned at Nalanda. The Executive Director of the Foundation is Eric Tay, who graduated in 1993 from China's Air Force Institute of Engineering. He owns companies in Beijing and Shenzhen which invest in commodities and energy resources. The appointment of Nepal's pro-Beijing Maoist leader Prachanda, as Vice Chairman of the APECF, emphasises China's interest in Nepal. Prachanda claims a major role in getting China's support for this project.

Following protests and to soothe ruffled Indian feathers, the Nepalese government dropped plans to approve the APECF's proposal, but indication of its unwillingness to reject China's proposal was the constitution of the Greater Lumbini National Development Directive Committee (GLNDDC) under the Chairmanship of Pushpa Kamal Dahal, better known by his nom de guerre 'Prachanda'. The GLNDDC, whose members include Dr Manglasiddhi Manandhar of CPN-UML, Dr Minendra Rijal of Nepali Congress and Nepal's

Culture Minister, Gopal Kiranti — who had ordered removal of the Namboodri Brahmin priests from the Pashupati Nath Temple where they have been traditionally employed through the centuries — took the initiative to organize the three day 'international' event in the Buddha's birthplace of Lumbini, which was scheduled to open on April 28, 2012. UN Secretary General Ban Ki Moon's visit was to be the highlight and accord the event international 'recognition'. He was to be accompanied by UNESCO Director General Irina Bokova and both were to co-chair an international conference on Lumbini with UCPN-Maoist Chairman Pushpa Kamal Dahal. An International Peace Conference was scheduled to be held in Lumbini on April 30. China's agenda was evident in the exclusion of the Dalai Lama from this essentially Buddhist event and comment of a GLNDDC member, that the Dalai Lama could visit after "the leadership of China will find ways to deal with His Holiness the Dalai Lama, which will be respectful of the Chinese people"! Ban Ki Moon's decision to visit Lumbini predictably attracted widespread media criticism in Nepal. The UN Secretary General's initial acceptance of the invitation to attend this event and, incidentally also send a message of greetings to the third World Buddhist Forum held in Hong Kong, is intriguing.

While it hints strongly at China's influence, a key role was played by Xiao Wunan, who has worked hard to revive the Lumbini proposal ever since it was scuttled last year. Xiao Wunan used his wide network of contacts and friends in South Korea, developed over the years through his various Buddhist exchange projects with Korean monasteries and academic Buddhist Studies scholars. Xiao Wunan traveled especially to South Korea in September 2011, to meet his contacts and work out a strategy to contact Ban Ki Moon. Later, in October, one of the APECF Co-Chairmen and a retired Australian Ambassador to South Korea from 2001-2005 with business interests in mining ventures in China, Colin Heseltine, was requested to set up a meeting in Australia with a traveling Ban Ki Moon specifically to discuss re-floating of the Lumbini project and to obtain the UN Secretary General's endorsement. That Ban Ki Moon and his mother are both devout Buddhists would have helped. Prime Minister Baburam Bhattarai followed up Xiao Wunan's efforts with an official invitation to Ban Ki Moon on March 16.

There are indications that at some stage Xiao Wunan worked with the UN.The UN official with whom the Lumbini Memorandum was signed last July was Hu Yuandong, who till July 2011 had worked for 20 years in China for the Investment & Technology Promotion Office (ITPO) under the UNIDO (UN Industrial Development Organization). Within two weeks of UNIDO voiding the Lumbini Memorandum, Hu Yuandong seems to be untraceable. Hu Yuandong was, incidentally, a PRC diplomat serving outside China from 1983 to 1989.

Despite Xiao Wunan and the CCP Central Committee (CC) UFWD's efforts, however, the events planned in Lumbini failed to attract the necessary publicity and the conferences failed to materialise. Reports additionally suggest that differences exist within the CCP's United Front Work Department (UFWD), with one group siding with the military and security establishment which favours a firmer governmental grip over Nepal rather than pushing ahead with this 'soft power'.

Beijing's other major initiative in *kasayapolitik*, or Buddhist politics, this April was to host the third World Buddhist Forum from April 25-27, 2012, in the Hong Kong Special Administrative Region (HKSAR). The objective of the third World Buddhist Forum continued to be to obtain legitimacy and support of the domestic and global Buddhist community and enhance tacit recognition of the Chinese selected Panchen Lama, thereby seeking to confirm Beijing's role in approving the selection of high-ranking monks including the Dalai Lama. The latter assumes significance following the Dalai Lama's assertion last September that Beijing has no legitimacy in such selections. The forums are additionally intended to project China's global leadership of Buddhists.

While China's official media publicized that over a thousand religious personages, monks and leading scholars from 50 countries attended, the failure of prominent religious leaders to attend the event considerably muted its impact.

A large number of Buddhist religious personages, monks and scholars, including from India, were invited to the Forum. Many had attended earlier Forums. Beijing's special targets have been Tibetan Buddhists and the effort is to influence them, sow division in the Tibetan refugee community and undermine the Dalai Lama. China is simultaneously intent on spreading its influence among the Tibetan Buddhists who mainly inhabit the Indo-Himalayan belt.

Zhu Weiqun, Executive Vice Director the CCP CC's UFWD who attended the Forum, read out a message from CCP CC Politburo Standing Committee (PBSC) member Jia Qinglin on the opening day. Later, Wang Zuo'an, Director of the State Administration for Religious Affairs (SARA), told the gathering that the Chinese government is "firmly committed to the policy of freedom of religious beliefs, values the positive role played by all religions, including Buddhism, and dedicates itself to promoting harmonious relations among religions". In his first public appearance outside mainland China, the Chinese Communist Party appointed 11th Panchen Lama, Gyaincain Norbu, delivered a keynote speech on the Buddha Dharma. The Forum decided that Lingshan of Wu Xi, a city in the east China's Jiangsu Province, will be the permanent venue of the World Buddhist Forum.

Among the greetings messages received by the Forum, was one from UN Secretary General Ban Ki-Moon. He said the proposals raised by the forum would be "helpful for the work of the UN in the fields of peace, development and human rights"!

Virtually no prominent religious personages attended the Forum. Absent were the supreme religious patriarchs, prominent religious personages and delegates from Myanmar, Vietnam, Cambodia, Laos,

South Korea, Sri Lanka, Nepal, Bhutan, Mongolia, Russia and Japan despite the close government level relations between China and these countries.

The highest ranking attendees were the Junior Khamba Lama and Chief Abbot of the Dashicholing Monastery of Mongolia, Ch. Dambajav, and the Mahasangharaja of Dhammayutta Sangha of Cambodia, Ven Bour Kry. Others included the Secretary General of the World Fellowship of Buddhists, Thailand, Phallop Thaiarry who has business interests in China and is CEO for South East Asia of the Avis car rental agency; Rector of the Mahachulalongkonrajavidyalaya University (MCU) and Chairman, International Conference of UN Day of Vesak, Thailand, Ven Prof Dr Phra Dharmakosajarn; President Buddhist Association of Taiwan, Ven Ming Kuang; Buddhist Aid Foundation, Bangladesh, Bhikku Sunandapriya; and Vice Chancellor of the Buddhist and Pali University, Colombo, Sri Lanka, Ven Prof Ittademaliye Indasara Thero.

Approximately a dozen persons from India attended. They included Ven Dhammaviryo, reportedly of doubtful antecedents and a critic of the Dalai Lama; Dr KTS Sarao, Head of the Department of Buddhist Studies, Delhi University; and Ven Sanghasena Mahthera, a Theravada monk of the Mahabodhi International Meditation Centre in Leh (Ladakh) and Head of the India chapter of the Buddha Light International Association (BLIA), Taiwan. Quite surprising is the congratulatory message sent by Dr. Ravindra Panth, Director of the Nava Nalanda Mahavihara (Deemed University), India!

Among those attending were, predictably, avowed critics of the Dalai Lama namely, Akong Tulku of Samyeling Monastery and the Rokpa Trust, Scotland and Gangchen Lama, Founder of the LG World Peace Foundation, Italy and worshipper of the Shugden Diety which is actively supported by the Chinese authorities. Interestingly, many of those who attended the 60th anniversary celebrations of the 'peaceful' liberation of Tibet last year were not present.

Importantly, the third World Buddhist Forum revealed the factionalism inside the CCP's United Front establishment. It was prompted by the Xiao Wunan-led APECF's bid, for the first time, to take charge. The APECF established a Hong Kong-registered company, 'Link-wise', to handle all communications and funds for this and future World Buddhist Forums. The two earlier World Buddhist Forums held by China in 2006 and 2009 were organized by the CCP CC's UFWD with assistance from the local provincial authorities. The creation of APECF, however, introduced a rival organization and the latest move prompted pronounced differences in approach. Reports suggest that Wang Zuo'an, Director of the State Administration for Religious Affairs (SARA), declined to release funding for the third World Buddhist Forum unless the money already disbursed so far to APECF was first accounted for. Consequently, the Hong Kong Buddhist Association, which hosted the Forum, received only approximately US$ 1.75 million and that too barely a month or two earlier. It had to raise the rest of the funds on its own. Indicative of the extent of the rift was that Xiao Wunan, though one of the original promoters of the Word Buddhist Forums, pointedly did not attend the third World Buddhist Forum.

The differences within the UFWD could be reflective of the infighting underway at the highest echelons of the CCP. Jia Qinglin, fourth ranked PBSC member and Chairman of the Chinese People's Political Consultative Conference (CPPCC), owes a lot to Jiang Zemin whose intervention protected him when he was tainted by a scandal during his term as Party Secretary in Fujian in the mid-1990s. 1947-born Zhu Weiqun, Executive Vice Director of the UFWD, joined the CCP in 1970 during the Cultural Revolution and seems to be an upward mobile cadre. He did a stint in the General Office in 1991-99 and has since then spent a long time in the UFWD. He is a member of the 17th CC. Wang Zuo'an, the youngest official in the UFWD was born in 1958 and joined the CCP in 1985. He succeeded

Ye Xiaowen as Director of SARA when Ye was promoted as Minister in 2009 and transferred to be Party Secretary of the Central Institute for Socialism. Ye was known to have a hard-line non-compromising approach towards the Vatican, on the Tibet issue and the Falungong. Though reputed to be personally affable, Wang Zuo'an is credited with having the same ideological approach, namely that religious freedom is an innate right which it is only the Party's prerogative to bestow or determine. Xiao Wunan, who according to rumours circulating in Beijing is associated with Xi Jinping, does not fit into the mould.

This was published as an Issue Brief by the Centre for Air Power Studies on May 14, 2012.

32. Tibet: Colossus of Asia's Environment

Tibet occupies a unique geo-strategic space and damage to the environment, climate and waters of Tibet will compel South and South East Asia to confront a potential existential threat.

The 2.5 million square kilometers of the sparsely populated high altitude Tibetan Plateau is an area of incalculable geo-strategic importance. Its ecology, environment, climate, glaciers and rivers impact the region around it. Attempts to tinker with these will affect at least ten countries and a billion people. In this backdrop, plans to launch massive development programmes in Tibet arouse concern. Ominous are the feasibility studies and construction underway to divert the waters of Tibet to China's parched north. Adversely affected will be Pakistan, India's vast Indo-Gangetic belt, Bangladesh, Myanmar, Thailand, Laos, Cambodia and Vietnam. The flows of China's two longest rivers namely the Yangtze and the Huang Ho will also be diminished.

The glaciers and annual snowfalls in the Himalayas and Tibetan Plateau feed rivers providing for the needs of at least 47 percent of mankind. Four of the world's ten major rivers, the Brahmaputra (or Yarlung Tsangpo in Tibetan), the Yangtze, the Mekong and Huang Ho have their headwaters on the Tibetan Plateau. Other major rivers originating in Tibet are: the Salween, Irrawaddi, Arun, Karnali, Sutlej and the Indus. About 90 percent of their runoff flows downstream to China, India, Bangladesh, Nepal, Pakistan, Thailand, Myanmar, Laos, Cambodia and Vietnam. The Indus-Sutlej river system and Brahmaputra are also fed by these glaciers and climatic and environmental changes in Tibet will directly impact forty crore people residing in the Indo-Gangetic plains.

Rising temperatures in the Tibetan Plateau threaten the glaciers. Official data confirms that temperatures are rising and that the past winter was the fifteenth warmer-than-average winter in Qinghai since 1986. The average temperature from December to February was minus 7.4 degrees Celsius, almost 2 degrees Celsius higher than the average of the past decade, according to the Provincial Climate Center. A researcher of the Institute of Geographic Sciences and Natural Resources Research of the Chinese Academy of Sciences, noted that 'annual precipitation has decreased by 13.99 millimeters every 10 years'. Significantly, except for its western-most section, the headwaters area has been generally getting warmer and drier in recent decades. Reduced precipitation means less snowfall, or less ice and less water in the rivers. Indirect admission of reduced precipitation was contained in an official Chinese news agency, Xinhua report of July 12, 2010. It disclosed that drought conditions have existed since last October in the areas along the Yarlung Tsangpo (Brahmaputra) where the main farmlands are located. It is estimated that the warming of Tibet will be at twice the average global rate in the twenty first century and this warming will directly affect the extent of glaciers covering the surface and their rate of retreat. Retreat of the glaciers will mean a reduced flow of water into the rivers.

The Himalayas have the world's third largest glacier reserve of 1 trillion cubic meters in an area of 11,000 square kilometers. Data released by the China Meteorological Administration reveals that 82 percent of glacial surfaces on the plateau have retreated and the glacier area has decreased by 4.5 percent in the past 20 years. Some estimates claim that in the past 50 years, 82 percent of the Tibetan plateau's glacier ice has melted. The plateau has lost 10 percent of its permafrost layer in the past decade. More than 15,000 glaciers in the Himalayas show evidence of shrinkage. Some 2,000 Himalayan glaciers have disappeared since 1900. The Asia Society in July 2010 released photographs of Mt Everest taken in 1921 and at the same spot in 2010, which show that the ice mass is 'disappearing' fast. The main Rongbuk Glacier has shrunk and withered.

Human and construction activity is a major cause of warming. In the past fifteen years the Chinese authorities have focussed on the development of Tibet. This includes operations to exploit the estimated US$ 106.5 billion of mineral deposits, construction projects and building of modern all-weather road and rail networks with the ensuant increase in vehicular traffic and emissions. Construction of the Qinghai-Lhasa railway contributed to warming of the Tibetan Plateau. Rail and road construction activity has damaged the permafrost layer, which protects the underground lakes, in Tibet. Professor Wu Chenghu of the Chinese Academy of Sciences has warned that by 2050 the Tibet Railway could be confronted with major problems due to warming of the Tibetan Plateau. Another official Chinese team reported that some sources of the Yangtze are drying up and the area is turning to desert. Tibet's wetlands and grasslands have already shrunk affecting livestock herders. China's plans envision the construction of 59 airports in and around the Tibet Autonomous Region (TAR). That means there will be dozens of aircraft flying into Tibet, which will release large quantities of nitrogen oxides etc in addition to carbon dioxide into the atmosphere. Carbon dioxide is known to stay aloft keeping heat captured for decades. After the terrorist strike of 9/11 in the US in 2001, when all aircraft throughout the country were grounded for three days, scientists confirmed that the difference in day-time and night-time temperatures had expanded by an entire one degree centigrade. Studies show that temperatures in the vicinity of airports are almost one degree celsius higher than elsewhere. Airports are also proven sources of ground water pollution with hydrocarbons in solution permeating hundreds of metres. Aviation fuel was found to migrate over 700 metres within five months through fissure systems in sandstones. Official Chinese reports publicise that each airport expects to handle at least a million visitors a year. The adverse impact of these millions of visitors on the temperatures and resources of Tibet will be immense. Concerns are accentuated with China's announcement in June 2010 that it will invest US$ 100 billion in twenty three new infrastructure projects in the western regions including Tibet. Investments will be in railways, roads, airports, coal mines, nuclear power stations and power grids, all of which will accelerate warming and impose further stress on Tibet's water sources.

The warming of the Tibetan Plateau and accelerated glacial melt will impact adversely on food production. For each degree celsius rise in temperature above the norm during the growing season, farmers can expect a 10% decline in wheat, rice, and corn yields. Since 1970, the earth's average surface temperature has increased by 0.6 degrees celsius, or roughly 1 degree fahrenheit. And the Intergovernmental Panel on Climate Change (IPCC) projects that the temperature will rise by up to 6 degrees celsius during this century!

Most estimates indicate that global cereal production will barely keep pace with the growth in population by 2025. By then the world's population is expected to touch eight billion. Estimates are that China and India are headed towards becoming net importers of grain. While some optimistic assessments project that both countries will be able to maintain adequate levels of cereal production, in India's case there is the important caveat that this is dependent on good monsoons. Any decline in the flow of the river waters originating in the Tibet region will adversely affect India's food production.

Since 'liberation' China's leaders have accorded importance to food security, but efforts have been hampered by perennial water scarcity. China's surface and near-surface water availability is approximately one-fourth the global average and water resources are distributed unevenly. The north and northwest, where approximately 400 million people, or 30 percent of the population, reside has more than half the country's arable land but only 7 percent of its surface water. Under

Mao Zedong's directions large scale exploitation of ground water began in the 1960s but this is unsustainable. Underground aquifers are estimated to completely disappear in 30- 40 years. While China is attempting to encourage conservation and curb wastage of water, measures like commercially realistic pricing of water are not feasible as it will mean decreased agriculture output and hurt the marginal farmer. It will also undercut the policy of promoting grain production.

In this backdrop China's leadership has been exploring the feasibility of diverting southern river waters to the north and northwest. The late Chairman Mao Zedong, possibly encouraged by the 1200-mile Grand Canal completed in 610 AD, first proposed the idea of the diversion in 1952. His intention was to ease the growing water shortages in the cities of Beijing and Tianjin and the northern provinces of Hebei, Henan and Shandong. One of the possibilities was to divert waters from the Great Bend of the Yarlung Tsangpo, north of the McMahon Line, by building a mega structure. The scheme received fresh impetus with the appointment of Hu Jintao and Wen Jiabao, both hydraulic engineers, as China's President and Premier. It was formally approved by the State Council on August 23, 2002. The project is the brainchild of a senior PLA engineer, Guo Kai, who worked closely with experts from the Chinese Ministry of Water Resources and the Chinese Academy of Sciences. In November 2005, the Great Western Route project got a boost with the publication of a book entitled *Save China Through Water From Tibet*, written by Li Ling. Indication of high level military support was evident in the foreword of the book, which was written by Zhao Nanqi, Chief of the PLA's General Logistics Department.

Briefly, the three-part US$ 65 billion South-North Water Diversion Scheme envisages transportation across the country of 44 billion cubic metres of water from south to north. The Eastern Route will take water from the lower Yangtze in Jiangsu Province to Tianjin following roughly the route of the Grand Canal and onward to the

Shandong Peninsula. The Central Route starts near the Three Gorges Dam in Sichuan and terminates at Beijing.

The Western Route directly affects India and is the most difficult. This will take water from the Yarlung Tsangpo (or Brahmaputra), Dadu, Tongtian and Jinsha rivers (all flowing into the Yangtze) across high mountains and the Qinghai-Tibet Plateau into the Yellow River which, in turn, would carry the water to north China. Work on this segment began this year and is scheduled for completion in 2050. There is talk of a mega construction at the Great Bend just north of where the Brahmaputra enters India. This is the point where the river can be tapped for the maximum hydro-electricity estimated at 40,000 MW. Plans provide for a hydropower plant (38,000 MW) at Motuo and Daduqia, both near the border with India. The alternate route to building the massive dam at Motuo is Daduqia, which does away with the need for big dams by taking advantage of the 2400 meters drop in altitude. The proximity of this location to India is the deterrent. Though Chinese President Hu Jintao officially denied plans to divert the Brahmaputra while meeting Indian Prime Minister Manmohan Singh in Delhi in 2006, there is evidence, including satellite photographs, that construction of dams at various points along the river has started.

According to available information, China has completed ten dams on the Yarlung Tsangpo, or Brahmaputra, three are under construction, seven are under active consideration and eight more are proposed. Five large dams are also proposed to be constructed on the Bumchu (Arun river) and one large dam on the Loro Chu (Subansiri river).

The scheme to either dam, or divert, these rivers emanating from Tibet, which account for 30 percent of China's entire fresh water supply, will have adverse consequences for the lower riparian nations and possibly China too. China, which has over 90,000 dams, has unrivalled expertise in the construction of huge dams. Nevertheless, constructing dams in the fragile Himalayas and on rivers that provide livelihood and sustenance to millions of people of lower riparian countries is a threatening prospect. The dams will disturb the fragile ecology of the Himalayas and inundate vast areas of the reservoirs submerging a huge variety of vegetation which could emit poisonous methane gasses into the atmosphere. In addition, dams constructed in the Himalayan region will lead to erosion and landslides. They will contribute to silting of rivers impeding inland water transportation, reduce the rivers' water flows impacting adversely on agriculture, submerge estuaries and create sandbanks and, finally possibly alter the course of the river. The dams will affect the hydro potential of the lower riparian nations.

Members of the Mekong River Commission held in April 2010, to which China is not a signatory, expressed serious concern at the potentially decreasing water flows. Even Thailand, which is usually careful to avoid offending China, endorsed calls for greater cooperation from China. While the reduced flow in the Mekong, which originates in Tibet, can not all be attributed to the warming in Tibet or glacial melt, that is a major factor as are the eight dams China has planned along the river in southwestern Yunnan province. The Mekong Basin is home to approximately 60 million people and is one of the most productive inland fisheries in the world and agriculture, along with fishing and forestry, employs 85 percent of the people.

The warming of the Tibetan region, south-north diversion of river waters and construction of dams on the upper reaches of the major rivers flowing down to South and South-East Asia constitute an existential threat to the lower riparian states. In addition to reduced food production and water, the consequences could include unstoppable mass illegal migration.

International law is ambiguous on the subject of the rights of lower riparian states and no treaties exist. Given China's domestic imperatives and determination of its leadership, any move towards international arbitration would be unsuccessful. The lower riparian nations are left with little option other than to raise this issue, which actually has global dimensions, with Beijing. It would be beneficial for each country to individually highlight its concerns. A hint of China's willingness to acknowledge these concerns was evident in the intervention of the Chinese Vice Minister at the Mekong River Commission talks. Another indicator is the access afforded to US academics from the Washington State University to research the Yarlung Tsangpo diversion project. China has also earmarked US$ 66 billion for an environment protection project in the Tibet-Qinghai area. A mechanism could be proposed whereby scientists, climatologists and experts from China and the affected nations together try and tackle China's water related concerns as well as the issue of warming of the Tibetan Plateau in a manner that also safeguards the interests of the lower riparian nations.

India particularly and the other lower riparian states need to simultaneously fast-track their own projects for harnessing, augmenting and conserving domestic water resources and boosting agriculture production. Expert studies need to be quickly initiated to monitor water flows at the points of entry into India of glacier-fed rivers and study data to ascertain the actual extent of damage that could potentially be caused.

List of dams being built or proposed,
the Tibet Autonomous Region (TAR)

Name	Size (MW)	Name	Size (MW)	Name	Size (MW)
Bayi	3.1	Jiacha	320	Sangdangla	560
Jaingzi	1.0	Jiexu	n/a	Shali	392
Mania	20	Langzhen	600	Sothang	840
Najin	7.5	Langda	n/a	Sumdzom	320
Nimaxian	1.26	Motuo	38,000	Yiwong	640

Pulan	n/a	Palong	2,760		
Qiangwang	3.2	Zhongda	n/a		
Shequanhe	6.4	Axiangbila	480		
Tanghe	6.4	Daduqia	43,800		
Woka	20	Drakke	632		
Xueka	40	Kanggona	312		
Yanghu	90	Laxiang	408		
Zanda	n/a	Lhari	340		
Zhikong	100	Nyewo	300		
Laohuzui	102	Pome	580		
Pangdou	120	Qudang	420		
Zangmu	510	Sangba	480		

This was published as an Issue Brief by the Centre for Air Power Studies on July 30, 2010.

Index